THE UNKNOWN COUNTRY: DEATH IN AUSTRALIA, BRITAIN AND THE USA

Also by Kathy Charmaz
THE SOCIAL REALITY OF DEATH, AGING, SELF AND COMMUNITY (*co-edited with Jaber F. Gubrium*)
GOOD DAYS, BAD DAYS: The Self in Chronic Illness and Time

Also by Glennys Howarth
LAST RITES
CONTEMPORARY ISSUES IN THE SOCIOLOGY OF DEATH, DYING AND DISPOSAL (*co-edited with Peter C. Jupp*)
THE CHANGING FACE OF DEATH: Historical Accounts of Death and Disposal (*co-edited with Peter C. Jupp*)

Also by Allan Kellehear
DYING OF CANCER: The Final Year of Life
EXPERIENCES NEAR DEATH: Beyond Medicine and Religion

The Unknown Country: Death in Australia, Britain and the USA

Edited by

Kathy Charmaz
Sonoma State University
USA

Glennys Howarth
University of Sussex
England

and

Allan Kellehear
La Trobe University
Australia

First published in Great Britain 1997 by
MACMILLAN PRESS LTD
Houndmills, Basingstoke, Hampshire RG21 6XS and London
Companies and representatives throughout the world

A catalogue record for this book is available from the British Library.

ISBN 0–333–67041–8

First published in the United States of America 1997 by
ST. MARTIN'S PRESS, INC.,
Scholarly and Reference Division,
175 Fifth Avenue, New York, N.Y. 10010

ISBN 0–312–16545–5

Library of Congress Cataloging-in-Publication Data
The unknown country : death in Australia, Britain, and the USA / edited by Kathy Charmaz, Glennys Howarth, Allan Kellehear.
p. cm.
Includes bibliographical references and index.
ISBN 0–312–16545–5 (cloth)
1. Death—Social aspects—Cross-cultural studies. 2. Death–
–Social aspects—Australia. 3. Death—Social aspects—Great Britain. 4. Death—Social aspects—United States. I. Charmaz, Kathy, 1939– . II. Howarth, Glennys. III. Kellehear, Allan, 1955– .
HQ1073.U55 1997
306.9—DC20 96–34794
CIP

This book is printed on paper suitable for recycling and made from fully managed and sustained forest sources.

10 9 8 7 6 5 4 3 2 1
06 05 04 03 02 01 00 99 98 97

Printed and bound in Great Britain by
Antony Rowe Ltd, Chippenham, Wiltshire

Contents

Preface

Death is less the 'undiscovered country' than it is the unknown one. We know death comes for us. But that universal circumstance covers a great diversity of meanings and it is often difficult to know what these diverse meanings might be for different people. But it is not all chaos and diversity, with no discernible patterns of meaning. On the other hand, the idea that attitudes and experiences of death can be characterized in some collective notion of 'Western attitudes' deserves some qualification, even critical scrutiny.

There has also been a preponderance of literature which has viewed death primarily from a medical perspective, discussing death in terms of euthanasia, palliative care, medical disclosure or the definitions of death itself. And here, too, we witness much of this style of discussion glossing over the many ways in which particular cultures, traditions and histories have shaped our national experience, knowledge, awareness and responses to mortality.

In this volume our aim is to understand the experience of death, that great 'unknown country', by beginning an analysis of the experiences of death within the specific cultures in which it appears. How do countries such as Australia, Britain or the United States shape the personal experiences of death for their citizens? What are the similarities and the differences in the way each of these cultures construct their particular understandings of death?

We provide this analysis by asking six or seven social science writers to discuss their view of some of the major national meanings of death in their respective countries. So much of our national understandings of death have been stereotyped, and the unique concerns of each country have often been overshadowed or lost in the globalized medical discussion of death. Australia's experience of death is assumed to be merely derivative of its British origins as a colony. America's experience of death is assumed to be well-characterized by its expressive and grandiose style, while the British are frequently assumed to be the quintessentially reserved people of the Western world.

In the first chapter, Kellehear and Anderson explore the Australian way of death, arguing that its key images serve as myths which marginalize other voices and experiences of death in that country. They compare the deaths of Australian Bushmen, the 'Digger'-Soldier death, and the deaths of Australian suburbia with those of Australian aboriginals to show that the Australian way of death, like the Australian way of life, is patriarchal, gentrified and medicalised. These images are repeatedly reflected and echoed in the next five chapters as each of the Australian authors take up their individual studies of the experience of death in Australia.

Fitzpatrick and Martin, take up the themes of how the experience of a social marginal and patriarchal society has shaped Australian experiences of death in art and writing respectively. The dominance of that masculinist idea of death continues its influence in the Australian experience of disasters, and this is explored in the chapter by Raphael. D'Alton takes up the idea of the impact of the Digger-Soldier experience for Australian images of death, while Fraser examines Australia's long-standing concern about suicide.

Chapter 7 begins the British discussion of death in that country, and Glennys Howarth begins this section with the question: is there a British way of death? The chapter continues the book's concern with *difference* and highlights cultural construction and change in death mores. It also questions whether it is possible, or indeed helpful, to attempt to trace a 'British', or for that matter, a peculiarly 'English' way of death.

Adams looks at class- and gender-specific variations in In-Memoriam notices, tracing changes in the developing social roles of women in Britain during the twentieth century. Bernard Smale examines the social construction of the funeral in Britain and suggests that the recent interest in innovation in death rituals may release the funeral directors' control over this important ceremony. Tony Walter continues the theme of diversity by challenging the idea that the 'stiff upper-lip' approach to grieving is British, insisting that this style of response is actually English. Jupp looks at why British peoples appear overwhelmingly to prefer cremation to burial, and Small looks at the peculiarities of British responses to AIDS.

Chapter 13 introduces the first of the American chapters devoted to reflections and observations about death in that country. Leming and Dickinson provide an overview of American attitudes to death and dying. They examine the American approach to explaining death to children, death attitudes and fears, ways of dying and grieving, and the contemporary American funeral. They provide a broad-based introduction to the American experience of death so that against this tapestry of culture and attitude, the following authors may situate their additional arguments and observations about American death.

Michael Kearl argues that there is a strong immortalist ethos present in American culture. He examines the main local reasons why, among all the major Western countries of the world, it is Americans who are consistently in the business of denying death. And Kathy Charmaz continues this examination of local historical and cultural reasons behind the particular ways in which Americans grieve.

Bendiksen, Levy and Amick take our gaze into the American health system. Bendiksen examines the differences that exist between hospices, institutional ethics committees, advance directives and other ethical consultations surrounding the issue of death and dying. Levy and Amick examine the experiences of both active street addicts and prevention staff in managing constant exposure to HIV infection and the threat of becoming fatally ill. They explore the social strategies that staff and clients use to manage the constant spectre of death.

Finally, in a highly relevant conclusion for most Western nations, Donald Irish provides us with case studies of how persons from diverse cultures or ethnic traditions vary their response to death and dying just as they do in life itself. This is a critical point for all three of the countries examined in this book because all three have long traditions of foreign migration.

In 1974, the French historian Phillipe Ariès wrote *Western Attitudes to Death* and thereby unwittingly continued a long-standing tendency to speak about Western responses to death as if the differences in these countries were minor or unimportant. Since death is universal, academic discussion of that topic is frequently given to over-generalization. In providing nation-specific discussions about death, we hope to open up new comparative and local understandings about this event that will find an important role in the policy and care provisions surrounding death and dying in the three countries discussed. Furthermore, the examination of death in this way may lead to other countries developing a more critical gaze for their own particular cultural experiences of death. By acknowledging the global influences but identifying that which is local, we perhaps lessen the strangeness of death, thereby preventing it from becoming a totally 'unknown', if still foreign, country.

KATHY CHARMAZ, USA
GLENNYS HOWARTH, UK
ALLAN KELLEHEAR, Australia

Notes on the Contributors

Sheila Adams is currently researching into the funeral and the role of crematoria in the management of death. She is author of 'A gendered history of the social management of death and dying in Foleshill, Coventry, during the inter-war years', in D. Clark (ed.) *The Sociology of Death* (Blackwell, 1993).

Daniel J. Amick is Associate Professor of Sociology at the University of Illinois, Chicago, USA. His research interests are in social psychology, human sexuality and the sociology of AIDS. He and a colleague are authors of a textbook on multivariate statistical analysis that is widely used at universities in the USA.

Ian Anderson is Chief Executive Officer of the Victorian Aboriginal Health Service. In 1993 he was one of seven indigenous presenters in the Australian Broadcasting Corporation's (ABC) Boyer Lectures. Apart from his training as a medical practitioner, Ian has also been a postgraduate in the School of Sociology and Anthropology at La Trobe University, Melbourne, Australia. He is the author of *Koorie Health in Koorie Hands* (1988).

Robert A. Bendiksen is Professor of Sociology at the University of Wisconsin, La Crosse, USA. He is co-editor of *Death and Identity* and *Teaching Sociological Practice: A Resource Book* and associate editor of *Clinical Perspectives on Illness and Loss.* He has published numerous articles on children and dying, AIDS, health-care resources, and hospices. He is a certified clinical sociologist and has recently been both a visiting scholar and research fellow in bioethics.

Kathy Charmaz is Professor and Chair of the Sociology Department at Sonoma State University, California, USA. She is the author of *The Social Reality of Death* and *Good Days, Bad Days: The Self in Chronic Illness and Time. Good Days, Bad Days* was awarded the 1992 Distinguished Scholarship Award by the Pacific Sociological Association and the 1992 Charles Horton Cooley Award of the Society for the Study of Symbolic Interaction.

George E. Dickinson is Professor and Chair of the Department of Sociology and Anthropology at the College of Charleston in Charleston, South Carolina, USA. He is coauthor with Michael Leming of *Understanding Dying, Death and Bereavement* and has written many articles in this and related fields. For over twenty years he has taught classes on death and dying, and conducted research on the attitudes of medical personnel toward terminally ill patients.

Phillip D'Alton is Lecturer in Sociology at the University of Wollongong, Australia. His research interests include communications, Asian cultures and Eastern ideologies, peace and war and the environment. He is author of *Men in Combat: Myth or Reality* and co-editor of *Four Dimensional Social Space.* Accepted as a disciple of Shaolin Temple, Hennan Province, China, in 1990, he also runs a martial arts school which teaches Shaolin Temple Boxing, White Crane Kung Fu and meditation.

Lesley Fitzpatrick has recently combined consultancy work in the health sector with a part-time Associate Lectureship in Sociology at Deakin University in Geelong, Australia. Prior to this, she was Director of the Barwon Region Health Education Centre which provided professional development and support services for primary-care workers. She currently provides undergraduate and continuing education to general practitioners in rural Queensland.

Mary Fraser works at La Trobe University, Bendigo, Australia, where she is an Associate Lecturer in Sociology and a Careers Counsellor. Her areas of interest are the sociology of health, occupations and death. She is currently researching health and employment issues and their effects on people in a rural and regional environment.

Glennys Howarth was formerly the T.H. Marshall Fellow in the Department of Sociology at the London School of Economics. She is currently Lecturer in Sociology at the University of Sussex and is the author of *Last Rites* and editor (with Peter Jupp) of *Contemporary Issues in the Sociology of Death, Dying and Disposal* and *The Changing Face of Death.* She is also foundation editor (with Peter Jupp) of the journal *Mortality,* the first major international journal of death, dying and bereavement outside the United States.

Donald P. Irish is Professor Emeritus at Hamline University, USA, where he also served as Chair. He is co-editor of *Ethnic Variations in Dying, Death and Grief: Diversity in Universality* and of *Death Education: Preparation for Living.* He continues to write about diversity and has recently focused on children and death. He has been on the board of directors of both the Minnesota Coalition on Terminal Care and the Minnesota Memorial and Funeral Society and served as President of both organizations.

Peter C. Jupp is a United Reformed Church minister. He works for the Institute of Community Studies as Director of the National Funerals College. He was Convenor of the British Sociological Association's Sociology of Religion Study Group, 1991–94. His doctoral thesis investigated the development of cremation in England. He is editor (with Glennys Howarth) of *Contemporary Issues in the Sociology of Death, Dying and Disposal* and *The Changing Face of Death*; *Postmodernity, Sociology and Religion* with Kieran Flanagan; and *Death: Interpretations and Practice,* with Anthony Rogers. With Glennys Howarth he is editor of the journal *Mortality.*

Michael C. Kearl is Professor of Sociology in the Department of Sociology and Anthropology at Trinity University, San Antonio, Texas, USA. He is the author of *Endings: A Sociology of Death and Dying* and has written broadly on death's cultural impacts, including the political uses of the dead in civil religion, the rise of gerontophobia, and moral relativism and the medicalization of death.

Allan Kellehear is Head of Research Development at Turning Point Alcohol and Drug Centre, and Honorary Visiting Professor at La Trobe University (Bundoora campus) in

Melbourne, Australia. He is the author of *Dying of Cancer: The Final Year of Life*; *The Unobtrusive Researcher: A Guide to Methods* and *Experiences Near Death: Beyond Medicine and Religion.* He is also co-editor (with Derek Colquhoun) of the two-volume *Health Research In Practice.*

Michael R. Leming is Professor of Sociology at St Olaf's College, Northfield, Minnesota, USA. He is co-author (with George E. Dickinson) of *Understanding Dying, Death, and Bereavement* and *Understanding Families: Diversity, Continuity and Change.* He is also co-editor of *Annual Editions: Dying, Death and Bereavement.* Professor Leming founded the St Olaf Social Research Centre and served on the board of directors of the Minnesota Coalition on Terminal Care.

Judith A. Levy is Associate Professor of Health Policy and Administration at the University of Illinois School of Public Health, USA. Her research interests include the sociology of chronic illness, AIDS, drug abuse, and ageing and the life course. She currently serves as Principal Investigator for a five-year research demonstration project funded by the National Institute on Drug Abuse. This project examines the efficacy of the delivery of community-based, social support to stop drug abuse and reduce HIV transmission among active street addicts.

Sue Martin is Lecturer in the School of English at La Trobe University, Melbourne, Australia. She has also taught at Monash and Melbourne Universities and was Visiting Fulbright Fellow at Amherst College in Massachusetts, 1989–90. She has published on nineteenth-century Australian, American, Canadian and English fiction, particularly women's fiction, and on contemporary cultural studies. Her book on nineteenth-century Australian understandings of domestic and external space is forthcoming from Oxford University Press.

Beverley Raphael is currently Director, Centre for Mental Health for New South Wales and was previously Professor and Head of Psychiatry at the University of Queensland. She has had extensive research and clinical experience in the area of bereavement, trauma and disasters. A Fellow of the

Australian Academy of the Social Sciences, she is author of *The Anatomy of Bereavement* and *When Disaster Strikes* and co-author of *International Handbook of Traumatic Stress Syndromes* and *A Handbook of Preventative Psychiatry.*

Bernard Smale is a Lecturer in Sociology at Croydon and Carshalton College, Surrey, UK. His doctoral thesis, 'Death Work', was a sociology of funeral directing. His current research interests are in the sociology of folklore, the loneliness of agnosticism, the central importance of musical sound, and the view from the wheelchair.

Neil Small is Senior Research Fellow at Trent Palliative Care Centre and the University of Sheffield. He is the author of *Politics and Planning in the National Health Service* (Open University Press, 1989) and *AIDS: the challenge. Understanding, education and care* (Avebury, 1993). His current research involves a study of the post-Second World War history of the hospices.

Tony Walter was a freelance writer for many years before becoming Lecturer in Sociology at the University of Reading, UK, in 1994. He has written extensively on the modern way of death, including three books: *Funerals – and how to improve them; The Revival of Death*; and *The Eclipse of Eternity – a sociology of the afterlife.* He is currently researching the increase in belief in reincarnation; media representations of death; and bereavement. He is a founder member of the National Funerals College.

1 Death in the Country of Matilda

Allan Kellehear and Ian Anderson

There is an Australian way of death. At least there is an officially endorsed set of cultural images of death. These images deliberately, or in *de facto* ways, silence the genuinely pluralist experience of death in Australia. There are three powerful, national self-images of 'being Australian'. These are the Bushman, the Soldier, and *Homo suburbia* – the suburban dweller. Those three national self-images are principally a triad of great myths about Australian identity. But by referring to those images as 'myths' we do not mean to suggest that they are untrue. Rather, myths function to *select and privilege* certain experiences while marginalizing or ignoring other experiences.

In this chapter our aim is to briefly sketch these national self-images and connect them to their particular experiences of death. We will show that these particular images partially record the history of Australia's social mobility and also its part in the broad processes of globalization. The hallmarks of these processes are patriarchy, gentrification and medicalization.

In the second half of the chapter we will see how these dominating images act to silence, muffle or marginalize other experiences of death which do not fit well with them. As politically and historically celebrated images of national identity, each of these images act as cultural pointers for which deaths count as important. We use the Aboriginal experience of death to illustrate how one important experience of death has been victim to these processes.

WHITE EXPERIENCES OF DEATH – BUSHMAN, SOLDIER, *HOMO SUBURBIA*

Experiences of death for many Australians can be explained by describing the three major national self-images that are embraced by them at different historical periods. Each of these identities are folk-images of themselves, images which allowed them to see themselves as uniquely different but intimately related to their cousins in Britain. At the time of Federation most of the country could boast that they were of British descent. In this way, the historian Lake (1992: 312) argues that it was not an ethnic or linguistic model of nationalism that was promoted or sought in Australia but rather a gendered, masculinist one. This can be seen in the promotion and acceptance of the early image of Australians as Bushmen through to the more recent idea of the Australian as a suburban dweller.

Death and the Australian Bushman

The Australian Bushman was an image which suggested to Australians and others that Australians were free-spirited, mobile, independent, loyal to 'mates', and fearless of the perils of the open country. Rarely showing much emotion, they thought little of authority, or attempting to farm an unforgiving piece of dirt or herding cattle across semi-arid country in the grip of drought. The contemporary film character of Crocodile Dundee created by Paul Hogan, or the equally comic film portrayal of the bush ranger Ned Kelly by Yahoo Serious, are direct descendants of this mythical, socially marginal Australian icon.

This particular image was the mythical or ideological canvas used to explain the experience of death in the fledgling Australian colonies of the eighteenth and nineteenth centuries. The long distances from Britain or from other Australian towns produced frequent deaths. Deaths during the trip from England came from scurvy, dysentery or accidents whilst yet other deaths came from accidental falls from horses or buggies. Death from starvation, being lost in the wilderness, or from Aboriginal attacks were also regularly occurring. As Welborn (1982: 26) remarks: 'One observer of bush life at this time said that short of running a piece of metal through a man there was probably nothing more like warfare than life in outback Australia. Men of the north greeted the sight of a corpse in the bush with an indifference born of familiarity.'

The isolation which characterized the life of the early Bushman settler was also thought responsible for the high suicide-rate – a rate at one time higher than those in England (Welborn 1982: 17). At other times suicide was a way for escaped convicts or robbers to avoid capture (see Collins 1798: 153, 344) and possible execution by the colonial authority of the day.

The Bushman settler also had his fair share of wild weather, from severe droughts to rain, ice and dust storms. Many died on the land from flood, bushfire, malnutrition and even lightening strikes (Collins 1798: 278). These early experiences of death were made sense of through acceptance of an image of the poor white Bushman battling these kinds of problems.

Here Australians saw themselves doing battle, in fact warring, with the wild forces of an untamed land. The unpredictability of the weather or of an indigenous people (widely seen as part of the strange fauna of the country) were sources of death. So too were the predictable responses of colonial authority, and the unforgiving vast distances of the country which swallowed the luckless casual wanderer as greedily as it did the experienced explorer. Isolation killed Bushmen as surely as did the trip from England for many people.

In these early days death was an exterior event, an event that came from outside of a man. In a telling account of a death in 1888 Gilbert (in Davison *et al.* 1987: 333) describes how a man came to understand the death of his brother who dies from aortic aneurysm. Despite express medical opinion to the contrary this man continued to believe that his brother actually died from mishealed broken ribs inflicted during a shipping mishap years earlier.

Death and the Australian Soldier

On the eve of the twentieth century Australia entered a war with Britain against Boer farmers in South Africa. Welborn (1982: 17) reports Henry Lawson's 1899 reaction to Australia's entry in this conflict: 'Lawson decided that the hopeless, flat monotony of the country and its history must be the reasons why Australians suddenly became madly eager to cross the sea and shoot men whose quarrel was nothing to do with them.'

After the Boer conflict came Australia's entry into the First World War, a largely European affair. And after that Great War, Australia entered the Second World War in Europe, Asia and the Pacific theatres. Finally, when the major wars had ended Australia contributed to various actions during the paranoid anti-communist years of the 'Cold War' period – the Korean and Vietnam Wars. The costs were immense. In the first World War alone, Australia lost 60,000 lives, 'a large number in a nation of only four million' (Lake 1992: 313).

The national grieving that went with that loss, plus the national processes of mythologizing their contribution to Australia's idea of 'the birth of a nation', created enduring social and physical reminders of that war and others since then.

Annual Anzac Day marches in every significant town and city; Armistice Day silences across the nation at 11 a.m. on 11 November; and the proliferation of grand war museums and so many memorials has inspired more than one observer to argue that these events and places are the basis of an Australian form of civil religion (Freeland 1985).

There are also countless popular and documentary films about all these wars, with *Gallipoli*, *Blood Oath* or *Cowra Breakout* being only the more memorable examples. RSL (Returned Servicemen League) clubs are scattered in every small town and suburb where there is a modicum of population. Finally, government benefits privileged the servicemen either with disability pensions, rehabilitation allowances, resettlement schemes, housing schemes, retraining or preference in employment.

In any case the servicemen were first-class citizens compared to those who 'stayed at home'. Wherever one looks in Australia the reminders of Australia's war effort and losses are emblazoned in their holidays, clubs or social policies: 'The Great War transformed the bushman as a cultural hero into the new national hero, the Digger or Anzac' (Lake 1992: 313).

There are several reasons why Australians entered so many wars against so many nations which did not directly threaten it. First, Lake (1992) argues that Australia felt that nations, 'like men' had to be tested, to show that they could elevate themselves above the private domestic (feminine) sphere of self-interest. Secondly, Australians really did think they were Britons merely residing in another land. The threats and affronts to Britain were genuinely seen as offences to Australia. This may partly explain our enthusiasm for frays in Europe and Africa.

Finally, Australians had what Lake describes as 'severe anxieties' about Asians, especially the Chinese and Japanese. Their huge populations and Australia's vast emptiness encouraged a prolonged Australian preoccupation with defence that has only recently shown signs of abating.

Whatever the reasons, the same characteristics of the Australian Bushman were grafted on to the Australian Soldier so that the same cockiness, independence, fearlessness and doggedness of the former was associated with the latter. The war was no longer against aborigines and the other dangers of nature, the 'Huns' of Europe or the 'Yellow Peril' to the north of Australia. Death still came from exterior sources, but now it came from a bullet or from enemy executions or torture. These experiences of death dominated the popular imagination during these times of war and still later in the countless films and annual memorial events since.

Death and *Homo Suburbia*

Australia has one of the highest rates of home-ownership in the world. The idea of owning one's home is regularly described as the 'Great Australian Dream'. And this dream is a suburban one. About two-thirds of Australians own their own home (Kemeny 1986). Although home-ownership has been emphasized and encouraged in Australia since at least the 1920s, it was really only the post-Second World War period of mass immigration and prosperity which gave Australia record levels of home-ownership.

Maher (1986) discusses several possible reasons for the national taste for a house in the suburbs. Among these are the role of Australian cities as trading rather than industrial centres; the abundance of space commensurate with a recently developed transport system to service urban sprawl; the desire of immigrants for this space and the privacy that came with it; and finally government social policies which encouraged home-ownership.

But the above reasons provide us an understanding of the necessary but perhaps not sufficient reasons for such high rates of home-ownership. There is little doubt that space was attractive to new immigrants, that land was available for the taking provided that one had the money, and in the prosperity of the 1950s people also had the money. But the ideology of home-ownership was also crucial in motivating these 'New Australians'. How was one to understand being an Australian when the Bushman and Soldier images were no longer relevant to the fledgling but growing middle classes, the people whose children would become known as 'Baby-boomers'?

Once again, government tapped into the nationalist sentiments of old and 'New' Australians alike by exploiting masculinist images of war and territory. In the context of the Cold War of the 1950s, successive governments became concerned about the 'threat of communism'. A number of politicians expressed concern over the allegiances of the working classes in Australia's industrial system seen through the belligerent prism of the trade union movement (see Kemeny 1986: 256). Consequently, it was thought to be wise social policy to encourage workers to gain a stake in the system as a bulwark against the idea of rejecting it. Now buying one's own home was part of the fight against communism. You were not only a good worker but a patriotic one as well.

Popular magazines and political statements of the day also emphasized the masculinist idea of home as haven, the one territory were man was ruler of his kingdom. Here the man comes away from the place of work to recuperate and procreate. The suburban home became the ideal for all Australians, because the idea of the nuclear family that was wealthy enough to afford its own home was the Australian dream of social and personal success. Reiger (1991: 34) demonstrates the ideology of the times, quoting a builder's advertising blurb: 'To own your own home is the hallmark of *Good* citizenship. It marks you as one possessing the virtues of a *Real Man . . . The Joy of Home Ownership* is natural. It is the parental instinct of man, animal or bird life. It forms the very basis of the *Happily Married State.*'

The dream of *Homo suburbia*, then, is quintessentially the bourgeois dream of much of Western industrial society –

privacy , comfort, control, predictability, safety and financial and marital security. The deaths that 'count', that are the focus of *Homo suburbia*'s anxieties, are those that break with those qualities. Furthermore, it is deaths that come from within the home or that threaten it from within that are important. Death no longer comes from outside a man but within him.

Babies that die suddenly and inexplicably (Sudden Infant Death Syndrome – SIDS) shock *Homo suburbia*, making Red Nose Day in Australia a memorable, comic and the most public of medical appeals. HIV/AIDS also attracts much media and popular concern partly because it raises a threatening combination of death and sexual images and partly because it affects so many younger people in the Australian community. Both SIDS and AIDS have the threatening quality of a silent enemy that threatens to tear families apart, first by revealing the unexpected, and secondly from death itself.

Suicides also gain major attention, particularly youth suicide, and here the problems relate to the pressures on contemporary youth and their ability or otherwise in handling that stress – from unemployment, lack of supports, or school examination and study demands. Death from car accidents is also a preoccupation in Australian society, with the Traffic Accident Commission releasing a rolling set of public advertising compaigns aimed principally at young drivers – major casualties in the annual road carnage. Again, what threatens the welfare of children questions the haven-like images which are so important to *Homo suburbia*.

Finally, the two top killers in Australia are the two top killers in most of the Western world – cardiovascular disease and cancer. Death is interior again, its name medicalized, its origins thought to be in diet or other personal habits or the very processes of ageing itself. The deaths which threaten the life-style of Homo Suburbia, and that are a product of that life-style, are the deaths which are considered 'the Australian way of death' today.

Recurrent Themes in Australian Death Iconography

The social position of the Bushman and the Soldier was largely poor and marginal and many of the deaths were characteristic of the epidemiology of that life-style. Unskilled and with little training for the wild landscape of rural Australia or war, most of these men succumbed to accidents and infectious diseases. Others died from recklessness and naive enthusiasm for the fight – against the 'primitive' Aborigine, against colonial authority, or the 'Turk' at Gallipoli. These experiences and cultural figures have been fuel to a lasting lower-class self-image which has lasted even to now in parts of Australia's popular culture.

Recently however, there have been widespread misgivings about that image, particularly in contemporary media portrayals of a working-class Paul Hogan or of Barry Humphries. Some Australians are embarrassed by this working-class portrayal of themselves, an image they see as anachronistic. Infectious diseases do not characterize the mortality rates of most Australians, and most Australians are no longer poor or socially marginal by any Western standards.

Homo suburbia argues that Australians are a modern people. They suffer from the same causes of death as their middle-class cousins in America or Britain. In this way, the iconography of these images reveal Australia's recent *social mobility* and the corresponding shift in life expectancy and causes of death which are associated with that mobility. *Homo suburbia* has gentrified Australia and highlighted that country's genteel deaths – private, interior, and medical.

This gentrification of Australia's population is also associated with the widespread acceptance of scientific ideas about the world and most particularly an *individualistic, biomedical* view of death. This is the second theme which emerges, particularly from a closer inspection of *Homo suburbia.* The general population of *Homo suburbia* no longer believe that infectious diseases, aside from the well-known exception of HIV/AIDS, are killer diseases for Australians. Most death comes from chronic systems diseases such as cancer or heart disease. Other death, such as suicide or accidents, heart disease or cancer, are at least in theory 'preventable'.

In this way, *Homo suburbia* embraces what Crawford (1980) describes as 'healthism', the ideology which places the focus for change, and the blame for lack of it, on the individual. No significant change is sought in work practices or the design of roads, housing or agribusinesses that might control the actual contexts of health maintenance and death. Unlike the Bushman or the Soldier, *Homo suburbia* does not blame 'the bush' or 'the Hun' for his misfortune. He blames himself, his diet, lack of exercise, his 'inability to cope', his drinking or cigarette smoking. Whilst previously death had been part of men's inability to control the world, now death meant his inability to control himself. For *Homo suburbia*, death is failure, and it is a medically endorsed morality tale.

The final theme which emerges from any perusal of Australia's death iconography is the consistent absence of female images of death. Death in childbirth is not part of the Bushman images of death. Death of women workers during the war is not part of the Soldiering images of death. And *Homo suburbia* assumes, often mistakenly, that same *causes* of death means same *experiences* of death for everyone, gender differences included.

In that way *Homo suburbia* continues the tradition of *patriarchy* that characterizes the life and death images of the Bushman and the Soldier. Australian meanings and experiences of death are consistently gendered in masculinist ways which exclude the experiences and meanings of death for Australian women. But women are not the only group in Australia to have their experiences and ways of death marginalized.

THE ABORIGINAL EXPERIENCE OF DEATH

When noting the Aboriginal experience of death in the context of Australian nationhood we will focus on three aspects of that experience: dispossession, 'disappearance', and disadvantage.

Dispossession and Aboriginal Death

Aboriginal life was irrevocably transformed many years prior to official contact. Epidemics of diseases, such as smallpox, moved along the routes of ceremonial gift exchange. Along the south-east coast of Australia at least two epidemics of smallpox (in 1789 and 1828) decimated the Aboriginal population (Butlin 1993: 102–3).

The high Aboriginal death-rate on the frontier was a result of a complex interplay of social processes. Frontier violence was a persistent feature of dispossession. At times, Aboriginal–settler conflicts reached such intensity that entire regions were seen to be in a state of war. This was the case, for example, in Tasmania during the period 1824–31. There are many counter-heroes in Aboriginal histories who come from these times, such as Pemulwoy of the Eora (NSW) and Walyer from Tasmania (Ryan 1981: 150–1; also Wilmot 1987).

Disease continued to play a prominent role in Aboriginal depopulation. Infectious diseases were a significant cause of death on Aboriginal missions and reserves and some of these had particularly tragic sources and consequences. For example, high rates of sexually transmissible diseases in Aboriginal people resulted in high levels of infertility. And along the coastal regions abutting the Bass Strait, colonial sealers had for a number of decades in the early eighteenth century used Aboriginal women for labour and sex. The death-rates of these women were so high that it resulted in considerable gender imbalance in surviving clanspeople.

The heroic myth of the Bushman obscures much of this history, much of this experience of death, even though its presence is implicit in any contact story from these times. The Aboriginal presence in the Bushman myths is submerged under the rubric of 'nature'. It was the 'wilderness' that was conquered by these rugged pioneers. Much less is said about the impact of white diseases and delinquency in contact situations, 'peaceful' or otherwise.

The Bushman myth trivializes the brutality and devastation of these encounters with Aboriginal people. Furthermore, it portrays Aboriginal people as victims, sometimes violent, sometimes passive to the onslaught of a 'superior' civilization. Its images deflect the fact that the foundation of the Australian nation rests on the violent pacification and subjugation of Aboriginal countries.

Death and the Myth of 'The Passing Race'

Australian colonialism was a continent-wide process and its frontiers were usually multiple and shifting. So much was this the case that in 1888, at the centenary of the first fleet landing, Aboriginal people still lived in North and Central Australia, largely beyond the control of the invaders. At the same time: 'The Australian handbook for 1888 noted that in the "settled parts" the aborigines were now "few and inoffensive" and are fast "passing away". Alexander Sutherland prophesied that another decade would bring the "extinction of the race within Victoria's boundaries"' (Reynolds 1988: 129).

This latter view became prominent as the Australian colonies approached Federation in 1901. In fact, the myth of the 'passing' Aborigine was one of the sustaining foundations of white Australian nationhood. Rendered invisible in national discourse, Aboriginal survivors were also marginalized in the legal and political apparatus of the developing nation–state.

Another consequence of this invisibility can be observed in the paradoxical nature of the myth of the Australian citizen-soldier. The potency of the Soldier mythology of national identity rests on the inferred heroic courage of a virgin (white) nation. Indeed, in a political and legal sense, the Australian nation was relatively young at the outbreak of the First World War – the war that gave rise to the Anzac myth.

However, only by ignoring our early history of conflict with Aboriginal nations can the myth of Australian military history be said to begin here, in the First World War. More people died during the black wars in Tasmania than in any other military conflict (other than the world wars) in Australian history. Reynolds notes this irony:

> In the forging of the Anzac legend there was no desire to link the new tradition, based on overseas engagements, with the much older story of conflict with the indigenous people within Australia. Conceptually, the two traditions were kept continents apart. This separation has influenced attitudes to both Aborigines and warfare. Conflict with the blacks was trivialized, while conflict with enemies overseas was romanticized. (Reynolds 1995: 209)

The myth of the 'passing' Aborigine should have been a reminder to the violence and loss of the early colonies, but the status of the Soldier myth in white Australian narratives would suggest otherwise. These two powerful myths stand as national emblems, paradoxical symbols of the historical amnesia that txook hold in white Australia.

Death as a Mark of Disadvantage

Today, as on the early frontier, death continues to be a central aspect of Aboriginal experience. Aboriginal life-expectancy is approximately twenty years less than that of non-Aboriginal Australians. Aboriginal people of all age groups are at risk of death relative to non-Aboriginal people. Young and middle-aged Aborigines are particularly at risk, with relative risk of death up to ten times that of non-Aboriginal people (Thomson 1991: 37–79).

These differentials reflect somewhat dispassionately the too frequent experience of loss in Aboriginal communities. Premature death deeply inscribes grief and loss as one of the core emotional and symbolic components of the colonized condition. One consequence of this is a historical consciousness that conflates the contemporary experience of death with the overwhelming loss of life associated with the process of dispossession. In this context, the contemporary political issue of Aboriginal deaths in custody symbolically resonates with the violence of the early frontier. Death is perhaps one of the most potent experiences that restates and refigures a subjectivity formed out of a colonial tradition of genocide and sexual violence.

Finally, Aboriginal deaths in Australian society are a stark reminder that the deaths in suburbia – private, interior and medical – are confined to those places and the white residents who inhabit them. For Aboriginal Australians, death is more often public, as in custody; or exterior, as from poor environmental conditions. The experience of death is not dominated by medical labels but social ones – violence, poverty, isolation, social and political neglect. For Aboriginal peoples, death is a mark of disadvantage – the very antithesis of urban comfort and life-style.

CONCLUSION

Australia's unofficial national anthem *Waltzing Matilda* sings the praises of a man who flouts authority and chooses death rather than submit to it. A song with a woman's name, the lyrics privilege a man's story about death, asking who will dance with Matilda after he is gone. Matilda is behind the song, not in it. And that is, as we have tried to show in this chapter, also the story of the Australian way of death. Behind the great myths about Australian identity are other voices that are crucial to that identity, but often these are kept marginal or silent because they shed a penetrating, revealing, critical light.

There has been, and there continues to be, a masculinist, European tradition of death in Australia but it has dominated the Australian imagination at a cost. That cost can be seen in the way broader experiences of death are hidden away from popular view. The hidden nature of that broader cultural experience of death serves to remind us, yet again, that dominating images of death reflect dominating influences in life itself. For national history and identity, the politics of death reflect the politics of everyday life.

REFERENCES

Butlin, N. (1993) *Economies and the Dreamtime: A hypothetical history*, Cambridge: Cambridge University Press.

Collins, D. (1798) *An Account of the English Colony in New South Wales*, Sydney: A.H. & A.W. Reed [Reed Edition, 1975].

Crawford, R. (1980) 'Healthism and the Medicalisation of Everyday Life', *International Journal of Health Services*, 10, 3:365–89.

Freeland, G. (1985) 'Death and Australian Civil Religion', in M. Crouch and B. Huppauf (eds.), *Essays on Mortality*, Kensington: University of New South Wales.

Gilbert, A.D. (1987) 'Old Age and Death', in G. Davison, J.W. McCarty and A. McLeary (eds.), *Australians 1888*, Sydney: Fairfax, Syme & Weldon Associates.

Kemeny, J. (1986) 'The Ideology of Home Ownership', in J.B. McLoughlin and Margo Huxley (eds.), *Urban Planning in Australia: Critical readings*, Melbourne: Longman Cheshire.

Lake, M. (1992) 'Mission Impossible: How men gave birth to the Australian nation – nationalism, gender and other seminal acts', *Gender and History*, 4, 3:305–22.

Maher, C. (1986) 'Australian Urban Character: Patterns and processes', in J.B. McLoughlin and Margo Huxley (eds.), *Urban Planning in Australia: Critical readings*, Melbourne: Longman Cheshire.

Reiger, K. (1991) *Family Economy*, Ringwood, Victoria: McPhee Gribble.

Reynolds, H. (1988) 'Aborigines', in G. Davison, J.W. McCarty and A. McLeary (eds.), *Australians 1888*, Fairfax, Syme & Weldon Associates.

Reynolds, H. (1995) *Fate of a Free People*, Ringwood, Victoria: Penguin.

Ryan, L. (1981) *The Aboriginal Tasmanians*, St Lucia: University of Queensland Press.

Thomson, N. (1991) 'A Review of Aboriginal Health Status', in J. Reid and P. Trompf (eds.), *The Health of Aboriginal Australia*, Sydney: Harcourt Brace & Jovanovich.

Welborn, S. (1982) *Lords of Death: a people, a place, a legend*, Fremantle: Fremantle Arts Centre Press.

Wilmot, E. (1987) *Pemulwouy*, Sydney: Casselton.

2 Secular, Savage and Solitary: Death in Australian Painting

Lesley Fitzpatrick

INTRODUCTION

The relationship between art and death is so well established, it is generally accepted that an artist's work is more likely to win acclaim after the artist's death. As well as this commonly accepted link, the relationship has been explored at another, more complex level. There is a wealth of evidence to support the notion that images encode messages that express ideas and emotions for a society (see for example, Albrecht 1976; Fischer 1976; Zolberg 1990). As Geertz notes, the symbols used to hold and communicate cutural meanings include language, art, myth and ritual and they 'function to synthesize a people's ethos – the tone, character, and quality of their life, its moral and aesthetic style and mood – and their world view – the picture they have of the way things in sheer actuality are, their most comprehensive ideas of order' (1973: 89).

While many analyses of art acknowledge the role of social conditions, they ignore its role as an expressive and symbolic medium (Lyotard 1989; Mitchell 1980; Nemerov 1980; Wilson 1981). Art can manifest univeral and transcendent qualities for the culture for which it is resonant (Wolff 1983), because it uses symbols to encode identifiable associations that may be 'filled with long extensions of meaning' (Scholl 1984: 19).

All societies seek to integrate and understand the experience of death within the framework of their social system and cultural values (Blauner 1977: Charmaz 1980; Kearl 1989). Many studies (see for example, Ariès 1974, 1985; Boeckl 1990; Tashjian and Tashjian 1974) illustrate the role art plays in providing insights into cultural responses to death and in supporting and maintaining social structures. To date, research into the meaning of death within the Australian context has not used artworks for enlightenment. Rather, it has focused on exploring individual reactions to death (Aveling 1985; Griffin and Tobin 1982; Kellehear 1990), statistical analyses of mortality and morbidity records (Gandevia 1978; Lancaster and Gordon 1988), studies of cemeteries and memorials (Birmingham 1973; Dalkin 1974; Gilbert 1980), and examinations of death-related industries (Waterson and Tweedie 1985). In general these studies uncover similarities to, or confirmation of, expressions and attitudes to death evident in other European cultures.

Despite the European origin of the colonial Australian settlers, the unique social experiences that have contributed to Australia's history are likely to have influenced the way death is understood and portrayed. To explore this contention further, this chapter looks to art to enhance our understanding of the cultural meaning of death through the discussion of a study (Fitzpatrick 1993) which examined the portrayal of death and dying in a sample of 100 non-Aboriginal Australian paintings.

BACKGROUND

The collective attitude of the living towards death is of unique significance in shaping a nation's ethos, social structures and organizations (Blauner 1977; McManners 1981). An important dynamic in shaping responses to death is the dialectic between individual consciousness, social structures and cultural values (Charmaz 1980). One outcome of this process is the development of myths which vary from culture to culture, and provide cultural paradigms that 'explain natural phenomena, guide individuals through life, assign them their place in society, and connect them with the spiritual forces of the universe' (Krippner 1989: 3). Kellehear (1984) notes that the constructs that fill conceptual gaps regarding death are not purely existential, but are grounded in cultural and historical meanings. Furthermore, the structures that hold authority in relation to death influence the process of dying and the understanding of death. Kessler (1985) sees death as indicative of the rift between society and nature: the challenge lies in its acceptance as part of the natural order rather than the final transition from one social status to another. Hüppauf (1985) extends Kessler's analysis by emphasizing the natural life-cycle. He notes that in premodern European society, death was linked to social and religious beliefs, but following the Englightenment, magical and religious views of life were replaced with more rational belief-systems.

Among the most well-known studies that use art to explore sociological notions of death are those of Philippe Ariès (1974, 1985) who charted changing attitudes to death in Europe from the Middle Ages to modern times. Ariès concluded that artworks carry messages about the way death is perceived and about the ideal or socially prescribed way of managing death. He termed this ideal the 'good death'. The concept of the 'good death' is common throughout history and to many societies (Geertz 1973; Kellehear 1990; Kessler 1985). Despite criticism of Ariès's work (Houlbrooke 1989; McManners 1981; Whaley 1981), his notion of 'good death' has prompted many explorations of the concept. The dynamics of the 'good death' are clearly illustrated in McCray Beier's study (1989) of its development and maintenance in seventeenth-century England. McCray Beier identified ritualized attitudes and responses that ensured that the spiritual and temporal world were in order prior to death. For example, preparation for death was of paramount importance – the model death did not come suddenly; it took place at home and included deathbed speeches. The ideal pattern of dying was of patience in the face of trial, and final quiet sleep in the Lord after a difficult but successful struggle with bodily pain and spiritual temptations (Houlbrooke 1989).

There is a wealth of evidence in the literature of unique responses to death in other cultures (Geertz 1973; Humphreys 1981; Kessler 1985), but there is no evidence that this has occurred in Australia. In 1985, Aveling studied a series of letters written by members of the Bussell family during the mid-nineteenth century. The letters detailed deaths that were not typical of colonial Australian deaths which were often sudden or violent (Gandevia 1978: Lancaster and Gordon, 1988; Thomson, 1989; Welborn, 1982). The descriptions reflect an ideal and echo the 'pious peaceful and public' (Aveling 1985: 34) European notion of 'good death'. Gilbert's (1980) study of Australian cemeteries, gravestones and epitaphs also attests to this desire to recreate aspects of the European response to death. Likewise, Kellehear (1990), found evidence of the 'good death' existing within contemporary Australia, where terminally ill individuals retain a measure of control over the social processes related to their dying.

THE STUDY

While the 'good death' is a common thread in the European and Australian literature, the quest for distinct symbols and social meanings of death within the Australian context prompted me to turn to art for evidence of a discourse that is missing from our current understanding. I examined 100 non-Aboriginal Australian images related to death and dying. The images were restricted to those created by artists with a European background in deference to the essential difference between the cultures and social experiences of Aborigines and European Australians (see Chapter 1). The study was limited to figurative art – abstract art is fundamentally art that expresses experience, while figurative art attempts to narrate and communicate a shared reality (Scholl 1984).

Published images of artworks were selected as an appropriate data source – having weathered the selection processes of critics, authors and publishers, they enjoy an imprimatur of cultural recognition. After browsing through books on Australian artists, a selection was made of paintings on the subject of death or dying. In the case of artists who have produced many works on the subject of death, a representative grouping of their *oeuvre* was chosen. Individual works were selected for their richness of suggestion, acknowledged significance to Australian culture and contrast with other works. The emerging patterns, repetitions and variations in the artworks drove the discovery of links, themes and interpretations which were then grouped under four themes: social factors and death; the land and death; social rituals and gender roles; and perceptions and images of mortality. In this chapter, only a small number of images will be discussed – those that are well known or exemplify the features of the main themes. Assuming a lack of familiarity with the images on the part of some readers, a brief description will be included.

SOCIAL FACTORS AND DEATH

The earliest Australian images of death are linked to social conflict and focus on the deaths of convicts, Aborigines, bushrangers and dissident social groups in the colonial settlement. Within weeks of the arrival of the First Fleet, three convicts were executed for theft and desertion (Sweeney 1981). This occasion was painted later by Liardet (*c.* 1875) and was the first of many images of death by hanging. Invariably, the images are set in a landscape and depict a hanging, spearing, shooting, ambush or battle, or portray a corpse that has met death through one of these means. The colonization of the land and the subsequent displacement of the Aborigines led to many deaths by hanging, shooting and spearing – violent, sudden deaths expressive of overt aggression. Thus, there emerges a strong theme of conflict (and the ultimate resolution of death) in representations of the relations between the original inhabitants and the colonials, which continues to find expression in the work of contemporary artists (for example, Sidney Nolan's *Death of Captain Fraser,* 1948).

Other early images highlight death due to cultural and class tensions, often related to the established animosity between the English and the Irish. The transplantation of the values and bigotries of England to the new colony was compounded by the fluid nature of the settlement which facilitated the movement of people (including ex-convicts) from one social grouping to another through land acquisition and the accumulation of wealth. Given the conflict of interest between the continued prosperity of the Establishment and the political and social rights demanded by the settlers, suppression of political and cultural dissidents was imperative. The images of hangings and battles with bush-rangers (highwaymen) and miners are the most obvious illustrations of this struggle.

The clash between the Kelly gang and the police is the most well-known example of the conflict between bush-rangers of Irish decent and the predominantly English Establishment. Paintings on this theme indicate the emergence of dynamic – the community's admiration for the bush-rangers and the eulogizing of their struggle with the law. The colonial artist William Strutt painted one of the first works on this theme, *Bushrangers on St. Kilda Road* (*c.* 1880–87), in which several travellers lie dead following an attack by bush-rangers. The glorification of the bush-rangers and their defiance of the law becomes more evident in the artworks of recent times. Tucker's *Metamorphosis of Ned Kelly* (1956) shows Kelly wearing his metal armour and mounted on a skeletal horse, rearing against a barren landscape. The work infers that, despite death, the legend of Kelly has triumphed over the hostile land.

The friction between the military rulers, convicts and free colonists is also expressed in the images of battles. The most well known of these was fought on the gold-fields at Ballarat, where miners had been agitating for the abolition of mining licences and political rights, including adult male suffrage. Henderson's *The Eureka Stockade Riot, Ballarat* (1854) is one of several works on the theme of battles between the law enforcers and the settlers.

The early struggles around law, class, wealth and race have had a profound and ongoing influence on the portrayal of death in Australian art. They provide powerful, continuing themes (for example, in the work of Sidney Nolan and Albert Tucker) and are strongly associated with a sense of Australian nationalism. But, while their input has been important, these factors have not been solely responsible for shaping the Australian experience of death. The actual and perceived power of the land and nature has also been crucial in this process.

THE LAND AND DEATH

Early Australian images of death invariably include the land as a significant visual element pointing to an important theme in the Australian discourse on mortality. There is a sense of solitude, emotional isolation and inhospitable harshness – the land is often characterized as forbidding, alien and vast. Within this group of paintings the subject-matter often focuses on a corpse or skeletal remains (human or animal); the death caused by exposure to the elements or through natural disasters such as bushfire, drought or flood. Without the protective structures of civilization, humans are represented as insignificant and powerless against the elements, and both human and animals appear to be equally likely to fall prey to the harshness of the land.

The first obvious group of artworks that focus on the theme of death in the bush relate to the period of exploration and settlement by the explorers and the overlanders (pioneers). This was clearly a very hazardous business given the size of the continent, the scarcity of water and the limited understanding of survival skills appropriate to the Australian bush. Based on these images, motivation for venturing into the bush was no protection against death. Explorers seeking fertile land met similar fates to those driven by personal advancement. The ill-fated Bourke and Wills expedition provides a focus for Australian artists reflecting on death in the bush. Strutt's *Bourke's Death* (1861) relates the discovery of the explorer's body in the outback while another of his works, *Dingo Devouring Wills' Remains* (1861), provides a more strident picture of the savagery of inland Australia for the explorers. Contemporary paintings on this theme are evident in the work of Sidney Nolan (*Perished*, 1949) and Albert Tucker (*Death of an Aviator*, 1942).

As well as the deaths of famous explorers, many works depict anonymous settlers who perished on their way to the goldfields or in their quest to open up land for farming and other activities. S.T. Gill's *Grim Evidence* (undated) illustrates the discovery of the skeletal remains of a man, his dog and horse. Likewise, Gill's *Unlucky Digger That Never Returned* (1892) and Strafford's *The Gold Seeker* (1851) are indicative of works of this genre and show unfortunate prospectors who met death through starvation and thirst on the way to the goldfields. The theme of death in the bush continues in more contemporary works. Arthur Boyd's *The Shepherd/The Stockman* (1944) depicts a mounted drover (shepherd) emerging from a thicket of river gums into a clearing where rotting trees merge with a dead human, expressing the power of nature and the landscape and the transience of humans who meet their deaths through it (Philips 1967).

In the treatment of the deaths of the explorers, the gold seekers and the overlanders, three dynamics emerge. The first is a significant visual component and relates to the power of nature and the landscape as a major factor in relation to death. The second characterizes death as solitary; the person facing it alone. The third theme depicts the unexpected discovery of the corpse in the bush; a common experience during the days of early settlement (Welborn 1982).

SOCIAL RITUALS AND GENDER ROLES

Social roles and rituals portrayed in the works illuminate the culturally acknowledged roles of women and men in relation to death. Images of social rituals focus on burials held in bush settings which imply an essential aloneness, both physical and social, in the Australian experience of death. Significantly, the social rituals are limited to those after death; there are no depictions of the period of the person's dying. The absence of religiously related themes represents a profound difference to European images of death. While the finality of death is clearly implicit in the images, there is no suggestion of a religious or transcendent encounter. This infers a conceptualization of death as a natural event. The shape of the coffin or tomb emerges as a recurrent symbol in the images – the waiting grave, the coffin, bodies portrayed as coffin-shaped, and images of entombment are common.

Gender roles are polarized: men die and women grieve for them. Frederick McCubbin's well-known *A Bush Burial/The Last of the Pioneers* (1890) exemplifies works of this genre: a woman, man and child gather in a clearing while a neighbour reads the final words over the open grave. The archetype of the stoic woman and the caring mother are very strong, although the artworks are silent about the role of women as care-givers to the dying. There is a sense of the transitory presence of men in life, while women bear responsibility for life's continuation through the care of children. Longstaff's *Breaking the News 1887* provides an illustration of this archetype. The painting depicts the newly widowed woman, with an infant in her arms, being told of the death of her spouse in a mining accident. The image, like many other similar works, infers that women's lives are shaped by the actions of men. Images of women are imbued with a sense of bravery, not in relation to physical deeds, but in terms of endurance and suffering.

The deaths of men and the grief of women are strongly connected, although the depiction of grief responses varies. The woman is portrayed as quiet and accepting as in Dobel's *Dead Landlord* (1936), mechanically brushing her hair while the corpse of her husband lies in the foreground. Alternatively, surviving women express unbearable anguish. For example, the young, grief-stricken bride in Arthur Boyd's *Mourning Bride I* (1958) throws herself upon her husband's open coffin. In most cases the grieving is personal rather than social, with the mourning woman depicted alone with the corpse or coffin.

The roles and significance ascribed to women and men in regard to mortality point to an overwhelmingly masculine discourse. Using the yardstick of the types of death portrayed by artists, the deaths of cultural significance are those of men engaged in risk-taking pursuits. These are the counterpoint around which the women's roles and responses pivot. The absence of depictions of women's deaths within the artworks is linked to the social definition of the their role – they appear to be considered insignificant and unworthy of recording. Given the hidden and largely unacknowledged role of women in the settlement of Australia, the dearth of images is not surprising in earlier artworks. However, the lack of women's deaths as subject-matter in more recent works can only be explained by the continuing patriarchal nature of the art establishment which impedes the voices of artists who express the experiences of marginalized groups (Albrecht 1976).

PERCEPTIONS AND IMAGES OF MORTALITY

It is evident that Australia's secular society does not look to religion to give meaning to death. The artworks locate the meaning for mortality in the life-within-death cycle of nature. Boyd deals with this theme in a range of works; in *The Beach* (1944) a figure in pursuit of the life-giving sun hovers above a floating coffin in a confrontation of life and death symbols. In Boyd's *Cemetery II* (1944) the life-within-death metaphor provided by the seasons is stated more directly; the flowering tree of spring is on one side of the corpse, while a leafless winter tree is on the other.

Metamorphosis, or the regeneration of life, is a strong theme in Australian representations of death, although the preferred symbols contrast with those of other cultures. Rather than the religiously inspired symbols of the sun, winged souls, and skulls favoured by the American Puritans (Tashjian and Tashjian 1974) and the Europeans (Ariès 1985), the symbols of regrowth, flowers and the seasons used by Australian artists indicate a response that perceives death as a natural rather than a religious event. In Boyd's *Drowned Bridegroom* (1958–59) and *Bride Reflected in a Waterhole* (1957–58), a bunch of flowers grows out of the ear of the corpse. Boyd uses this symbol again in *The Mourners* (1942) which features a butterfly on the cheek of the cadaver. Metamorphosis and the regeneration of life emerge as the reasons death can be borne and integrated as a meaningful end to life. There is a sense of the life-claiming and sustaining fertility of nature. This is evident in Boyd's *The Shepherd/The Stockman* (1944), which is imbued with an overwhelming impression of regeneration as the dead stockman gradually decays, becoming part of the bush and earth that surrounds him. Davida Allen introduces another angle on the continuation of life in her drawing *My Father is Dead – I Weep for Him, 9* (1983). In this image her father's corpse touches her infant daughter through the coffin, giving a sense of the continuity of life through subsequent generations.

The linking of mortality with nature in the Australian images of death supports Kessler's (1985) view that the discontinuity of social life needs to be consolidated into natural continuity – symbolic systems attempt to unify life and death into an understandable but not mutually exclusive system, in order to establish cyclical, cultural time modelled on nature's seasonal rhythms. The recognition of nature's role in death is understandable given that European settlement of Australia occurred in the context of the Enlightenment, and supports Hüppauf's (1985) view that the scientific rationalism of this intellectual movement replaced magic and religious understandings of mortality.

THE GOOD DEATH

The images in the study imply that the essential differences in the early Australian experience of death have promoted a unique cultural expression of the 'good death' in Australian art. Echoes of the European ideal of the 'good death' are very faint in Australian images of death. While suggestions of it arise in paintings on the theme of burials, the fundamental barrier to the portrayal of an Australian version of the traditional European 'good death' is that invariably the individual is portrayed alone, and already dead. Thus, rather than the interaction with the dying or dead person being the focal point, Australian images of death focus on the corpse and the grieving survivors. Solitary deaths are the antithesis of the European 'good death' (Ariès 1985), which is framed around a continuum that begins with the realization that a person is dying and ends with the social rituals of burial and other commemorations. In the Australian artworks, the typical portrayal of a solitary corpse truncates the social and ritual interactions associated with the European notion of 'good death'. There are no portrayals of deathbed farewells, religious ceremonies, caring for the dying person, or deathbed blessings or speeches – just the finality of death. Instead of being '*pious, peaceful and public*' (Aveling 1985: 34), death is characterized as *secular, savage and solitary*. It is an unprepared for, almost pagan event, which acknowledges the power of nature, not religion.

The traditional European 'good death' can be seen as a construction that reflects the concerns of the European middle class, embracing the notion of self-determination and control (even in death). It is built on the underlying assumption that the person is able to influence the manner and timing of their death, has family and friends to engage in the designated social rituals and has financial, legal and religious responsibilities to be settled. The Australian construct of the 'good death' evident in the images appears to be the opposite of the European construct. This does not imply that these social and religious rituals are alien to past or present Australian deaths, as studies by Kellehear (1990) and Aveling (1985) describe deaths that mirror the accepted European notion during the time of early settlement and in current social practices.

However, the images of death in the Australian artworks present an alternative understanding and experience of mortality. There is little sense of self-determination regarding the timing and experience of death. It is depicted as a relentless, unexpected, solitary event. The images give credence to Marcuse's theory (1959) that many individuals have little control over the manner and timing of their deaths. They imply that Australian individuals, particularly convicts, Aborigines, and settlers who were not members of the ruling elite, had little control over the manner, place and timing of their deaths.

Geertz (1973) and Krippner (1989) see the development of cultural myths as a crucial process in linking the experience of mortality with a culture's understanding of the fundamental purpose of life. While a cultural myth requires a universality that reflects a collective social construction, the everyday experience of dying is essentially about the last activities of and reflections on an individual's life. It is evident that these artworks do not simply record the experience of death in Australia, but they also express the construction of cultural myths. They do not reflect the broad range of causes and experiences of death, the most obvious omissions being death through illness and old age, which have been effective killers of Australians during the two centuries of European settlement (Lancaster and Gordon 1988). By focusing on images of men who die confronting the law or the bush rather than more ordinary encounters with death, death is transformed from an individual experience to a cultural myth.

Humphreys (1981) maintains that cultures appear to construct an ideal of the 'right' configuration for an exemplary death which reflects conceptions of virtue and the overall shape of human existence, rather than common experience. This cultural construction is based on social and historical factors that are modified by perceptions and understandings of the ultimate nature of mortality. Humphreys note that 'It is *after* [his emphasis] the "demographic transition", when they are becoming less frequent, that such deaths acquire especial cultural significance' (1981: 262).

The cultural myths that have developed around particular experiences of death serve to explain, eulogize, and promote admiration and acceptance of the Australian struggle with life and death. The most succinct examples of these are the images of the explorers and the bushrangers. The explorers epitomize the struggle with the land; the bushrangers, the struggle against the Establishment. These images and experiences of death have caught the collective cultural imagination and elucidate the Australian experience in a way that differentiates it from other cultures.

CONCLUSION

The Australian construct of the 'good death' apparent in the artworks is a masculine discourse that reflects a stoic acceptance rather than a denial of death, and a recognition of the influence of social structures and the natural environment in the experience of death. Metamorphosis provides a culturally embraced understanding of mortality and is expressed through symbols of nature, images of growth and decay, the rhythm of the seasons and cultural myths. Some works express an understanding that the regeneration of life can occur in ways that are not physical; for example, the essence of an individual's life may live on through cultural myth, as is the case of the bushranger, or through the lives of subsequent generations.

The themes that emerged from the artworks parallel those in other disciplines that have explored Australian historical and social conditions and cultural expressions (see Astbury 1985; Clark 1962; Howard 1984; Patience 1990; Ward 1978).

Australian social history and literature abounds with evidence of the establishment of cultural identity and the development of myths through the metaphors of the struggle with the land and activities such as exploration, bushranging and farming. Although the study examined a limited collection of images, they provide a portrait of a unique perception of death within the Australian culture which is a critical development for a broader understanding of an Australian sociology of death. The dissident voice of the Australian 'good death' manifested in the images does not undercut the existence of its European counterpart in Australian society. Rather, it indicates that different conceptualizations of mortality based on different experiences of death may exist side by side, and suggests that there are other unheard voices regarding death in Australia.

REFERENCES

Albrecht, M.C. (1976) 'Art as an Institution', M.C. Albrecht, J.H. Barnett and M. Griff (eds.), *The sociology of art and literature – a reader*, New York: Praeger Publishers.

Ariès, P. (1974) *Western attitudes to death: from the Middle Ages to the present*, Baltimore, MD: Johns Hopkins University Press.

Ariès, P. (1985) *Images of man and death*, Cambridge, MA: Harvard University Press.

Astbury, L. (1985) *City Bushmen: The Heidelberg School and the Rural Mythology*, Melbourne: Oxford University Press.

Aveling, M. (1985) 'Death and the Family in Nineteenth-century Western Australia', in P. Grimshaw, C. McConville and E. McEwen (eds.), *Families in colonial Australia*, Sydney: Allen & Unwin, Inc.

Birmingham, J. (1973) 'Nineteenth Century Tombstones', *Australian Society for Historical Archaeology*, 3, 1:4–9.

Blauner, R. (1977) 'Death and Social Structure', in C.O. Jackson (ed.), *In passing: the vision of death in America*, Westport, CT: Greenwood Press.

Boeckl, C.M. (1990) 'Baroque plague imagery and Tridentine church reforms', Ph.D. thesis, University of Maryland, College Park.

Charmaz, K. (1980) *The social reality of death: death in contemporary America*, New York: Random House.

Clark, C.M.H. (1962) *A history of Australia: from the earliest times to the age of Macquarie*, Melbourne: Melbourne University Press.

Dalkin, R.N. (1974) *Colonial era cemetery of Norfolk Island*, Sydney: Pacific Publications.

Fischer, J.L. (1976) 'Art Styles as Cultural Cognitive Maps', in M.C. Albrecht, J.H. Barnett and M. Griff (eds.), *The sociology of art and literature – a reader*, New York: Praeger Publishers.

Fitzpatrick, L. (1993) 'Images of death in Australian art: A sociological analysis', MA thesis, Bundoora: La Trobe University.

Gandevia, B. (1978) *Tears often shed: child health and welfare in Australia from 1788*, Sydney: Pergamon Press.

Geertz, C. (1973) *The interpretation of cultures*, New York: Basic Books, Inc.

Gilbert, L.A. (1980) *A grave look at history: glimpses of a vanishing form of folk art*, Sydney: John Ferguson.

Griffin, G.M. and Tobin, D. (1982) *In the midst of life . . . the Australian response to death*, Melbourne: Melbourne University Press.

Houlbrooke, R. (1989) 'Death, Church and Family in England between the late Fifteenth and the Early Eighteenth Centuries', in R. Houlbrooke (ed.), *Death, ritual and bereavement*, London: Routledge.

Howard, M. (1984) *Shaping a new nation: Australian history and its background to 1914*, Melbourne: Longman Cheshire.

Humphreys, S.C. (1981) 'Death and Time', in S.C. Humphreys and H. King (eds.), *Mortality and immortality: the anthropology and archaeology of death*, London: Academic Press, Inc.

Hüppauf, B. (1985) 'War and Death: the experience of the First World War', in M. Crouch and B. Hüppauf (eds.), *Essays on mortality*, Kensington Studies in Humanities and Social Sciences, No. 1:56–65, Sydney: University of New South Wales.

Kearl, M.C. (1989) *Endings: a sociology of death and dying*, New York: Oxford University Press.

Kellehear, A. (1984) 'Are we a Death Denying Society? A sociological review', *Social Science and Medicine*, 18, 9: 713–23.

Kellehear, A. (1990) *Dying of cancer: the final year of life*, London: Harwood Academic Publishers.

Kessler, C.S. (1985) 'The Cultural Management of Death: individual fate and its social transcendence', in M. Crouch and B. Hüppauf (eds.), *Essays on mortality*, Kensington Studies in Humanities and Social Sciences, No. 1:135–54, Sydney: University of New South Wales.

Krippner, S. (1989) *Mythological aspects of death and dying*, Philadelphia, PA: The Charles Press.

Lancaster, H.O. and Gordon, D. (1988) 'Health and Medicine in Australia, 1788–1988', *Reference Australia*, 2, May: 221–49.

Lyotard, J.F. (1989) *The postmodern condition: a report on knowledge*, Minneapolis, MN: University of Minnesota Press.

McCray Beier, L. (1989) 'The "Good Death" in Seventeenth-century England', in R. Houlbrooke (ed.), *Death, ritual and bereavement*, London: Routledge.

McManners, J. (1981) *Death and the Enlightenment: changing attitudes to death among Christians and unbelievers in eighteenth century France*, Oxford: Clarendon Press.

Marcuse, H. (1959) 'The ideology of death', in H. Feifel (ed.), *The meaning of death*, New York: McGraw-Hill.

Mitchell, W.J.T. (1980) *The language of images*, Chicago, IL: University of Chicago Press.

Nemorov, H. (1980) *On poetry and painting, with a thought of music*, Chicago, IL: University of Chicago Press.

Patience, A. (1990) 'Australia's Hard Culture: Notes for an historical sociology', *Australian Studies*, 14 October: 45–53.

Philips, F. (1967) *Arthur Boyd*, London: Thames & Hudson.

Scholl, S. (1984) *Death and the humanities*, Cranbury, NJ: Associated University Press.

Sweeney, C. (1981) *Transported in place of death; convicts in Australia*, South Melbourne: Macmillan Company of Australia.

Tashjian, D. and Tashjian, A. (1974) *Memorials for children of change: the art of early New England stone carving*, Middletown, CT: Wesleyan University Press.

Thomson, N. (1989) 'Aboriginal Health: A socio-cultural perspective', in G.M. Lupton and J.M. Najman (eds.), *Sociology of health and illness: Australian readings*, South Melbourne: Macmillan Company of Australia.

Ward, R. (1978) *The Australian Legend*, Melbourne: Oxford University Press.

Waterson, D. and Tweedie, S. (1985) 'A study of the Funeral Industry in New South Wales: A preliminary report', in M. Crouch and B. Hüppauf (eds.), *Essays on mortality*, Kensington Studies in Humanities and Social Sciences, No. 1, Sydney: University of New South Wales, pp. 123–35.

Welborn, S. (1982) *Lords of Death: a people, a place, a legend*, Fremantle: Fremantle Arts Centre Press.

Whaley, J. (1981) *Mirrors of mortality: studies in the social history of death*, London: Europa Publications Ltd.

Wilson, F.A. (1981) *Arts as revelation: the role of art in human existence*, Fontwell, Sussex: Centaur Press Ltd.

Wolff, J. (1983) 'Aesthetics and the Sociology of Art', *Controversies in Sociology*, 14, Boston: Allen & Unwin.

Zolberg, V. (1990) *Constructing a sociology of the arts*, New York: Cambridge University Press.

3 Good Girls Die, Bad Girls Don't: the Uses of the Dying Virgin in Nineteenth-century Australian Fiction

Susan K. Martin

The limited story-lines available to a young middle-class woman in nineteenth-century fiction have been frequently mapped. She can marry, she can fall, she can die, or she can indulge in some combination of the three. Along with the dying fallen woman, the dying virgin provides an important site for the working-out of middle-class female subjectivity in this period.

The nineteenth century was also an era with particular sorts of interests in death and disease, reflected in the increasing chronicling, documentation and story-telling around death. Anxieties about death and about the status, identity and sexuality of middle-class women were not simply reflected in the popular fiction produced across the nineteenth century, but were uncovered, explored, resolved and problematized through it. In fiction produced in Australia, intensified anxieties about status and identity produced by the specific colonial situation made such explorations distinctive. This chapter charts some of these explorations in Australian fiction.

Elizabeth Langland (1992) claims, in relation to nineteenth-century England, that 'domestic' fiction played an important role in the production (and exposure) of contemporary ideology and the regulation of class management. She sees the ostensibly leisured middle-class female as hard at work in the onerous job of producing, sustaining and differentiating class positions and 'ensuring middle-class hegemony' (as well as being produced by it) (291). Langland argues that middle-class wives and daughters are vital to these processes, through their central role in the complexities of household management and therefore the management and positioning of 'lower-class' servants, and the lower-class objects of middle-class philanthropy. Like Nancy Armstrong (1987) and Mary Poovey (1988), she sees such regulation conducted within discourse; both in fiction and non-fiction, but also through the management of elaborate systems of signs of various sorts – from fashion to social practices such as visiting.

For Langland domestic narratives partially defuse female power and involvement in class and domestic management by naturalizing it, and making it part of women's 'nature', concealing the skill and work involved. Armstrong, similarly, sees 'a class sexuality that valued people according to intrinsic personal qualities' (74). In both arguments the domestic woman, while doing an extraordinary amount of ideological and physical labour, is depicted as, in Armstrong's words (1987: 79), 'apparently having nothing to do', and therefore in both domestic and class virtues must be located in the personal qualities or 'mental features' of the domestic woman, rather than in physical display or actual signs of the labour undertaken.

I want to offer some preliminary arguments in this chapter about what happens to this figure of the ideal woman in the context of Anglo colonies influenced by this middle-class hegemony in various ways, but not necessarily able to reproduce the conditions of its production – the minute practices of etiquette and behaviour which consolidated middle-class status.

DEATH AND THE VIRGIN

Illness, especially fatal illness, is one way of defusing or muting female power, both social and physical, particularly in situations where involvement in physical labour is not always concealed as it is in British fiction. This I would argue is the case in American and Canadian women's writing, but especially in Australian women's fiction. However, as with other ways of concealing female power in fiction, invalidism can also be a cause of anxiety and discomfort. It focuses on the body as it denies it; confuses the language of the 'pure and innocent' feminine with notions of corruption, contagion and disease. It also mixes up public with private, and for the invalid virgin mixes the notion of the virgin as sealed vessel (Warner 1987: 263) with the Kristeva (1982) abject.

To go one further, to the *dying* female, is to solve some of the problems raised by the invalid female while exacerbating others. The figure of the dying virgin is particularly potent. The *virgin* is a recognizable figure, a subject position which can be placed. Though defined in terms of negatives, lack and fragility it holds intimations of power, autonomy and control. The female virgin is a production which reifies masculinist rights in the Victorian era and works towards subjection, though it may, as Lloyd Davis argues, also provide a position which resists and questions its own cultural values and uses (1993: 10). One way of controlling, and fixing the power and ambiguity of that virgin body is through death. The dead body, Foucault (1973) implies, provides for the post-eighteenth century the illusion of a fixed identity, an ultimate knowableness. The dead virgin promises the ideal if unreal fixed subject – the knowable unknown body and mind, a body which may be explored without violation, a pure female figure defined by and yet transcending her biology. To the extent that the state of virginity can be taken as a state of innocence, including innocence of the knowledge of one's own subjectivity – 'one can only know it by being not it' (Munich 1993: 144) – any use of this figure in an exploration of subjectivity can be seen as subversive.

The two halves of the figure are mutually incompatible. Death removes the virgin body from the sexual economy which defines it. Such a removal can be seen in a number of ways; death for the virgin can be escape from enforced patriarchal definition, *or* perfection in its terms – after all, the only sure virgin is a dead virgin (Munich 1993: 144). Death or dying negates, as it stands in for, the dangerous sexuality of the female. The status of the virgin body as representing the closed system, the intact body, contests the supposedly available and open body produced by death, even as death, literally, breaks the seal, and removes this illusion of closure.

Elisabeth Bronfen (1992) argues that femininity and death are inevitably linked in Western cultures. Both, she claims, are irruptions of the repressed other of these cultures, and images joining the two are part of what she calls a 'dominant cultural image repertoire' (xiii). In her argument the dual threats of death and femininity are defused by representation – and such representation invokes the fantasy of a regained order after the threat (xii).

The narrative moment of death, while it frequently gestures towards the erasure of subjectivity, and indeed towards the impossibility of language and artistic practice (Stewart 1984: 44–5), is also a moment which affirms or instates the subjectivity of the witnesses within the text, and by extension of the reader-as-witness or spectator. Virginity, likewise, can represent this absence – a space defined by masculine desire (Munich 1993:150). In the popular fictions under discussion, while the subject thus doubly erased is always female, the implied reader is also often female, so that even when the dying virgin loses or is denied subjectivity, her loss can be the gain of the female witness/reader. In the colonial fictions where the textual subject is particularly vexing or dangerous, the process may work to apparently neutralize a dangerous model of female subjectivity to the advantage and affirmation of only slightly less threatening models.

Many fictional dying virgins are young women on the brink of sexual maturity. The acknowledgement of the difficulty of narrating an adulthood for the transgressive female child can also be read as the freeing of this threatening subject from repressive models of nineteenth-century female maturity; the sexual economy and gender boundaries which burden the adult female.

The figure of the dying virgin, then, is a site of intersecting anxieties about female bodies, power and weakness, ideal femininity and female sexuality. The deathbed scene, according to Margarete Holubetz (1986) and Garrett Stewart (1984), offers a particular, familiar Victorian narrative programme within or against which such anxieties may be played out.

A great many of the best-remembered dying virgins in the nineteenth century are in fiction by men. In women's fiction the ranks of the virgin dead include Frankenstein's bride Elizabeth in Shelley's *Frankenstein* (1818), Gaskell's Bessy

Higgins in *North and South* (1854–55), Brontë's Helen Burns in *Jane Eyre* (1847), Maggie in Eliot's *Mill on the Floss* (1860), Little Eva in Stowe's *Uncle Tom's Cabin* (1850–52) and Beth in Alcott's *Little Women* (1868–69). The cultural uses of the figure are liable to vary according to the gender of the writer and her distance from the supposed centres of British middle-class culture. For instance, Langland's (1992) argument about the discursive mystification of women's involvement in labour in nineteenth-century British fiction can be seen to work in different ways for the fiction produced in the colonies, particularly British-ruled Anglo-dominated colonies like Australia or Canada. In real terms it is likely, because of the shortage and expense of servants, that many middle-class women in Australia were engaged in forms of manual labour that their British equivalents were not. But the 'real' does not rule fiction, and there are other ideological projects at stake in the fact that nineteenth-century Australian fiction by women depicts middle-class heroines engaged routinely in tasks which would have been coded working-class in most British fiction. The work of maintaining and defining class boundaries undertaken in such texts, then, becomes proportionately more complicated. Likewise the need to invest class characteristics in mystified ideal lady, if the benefits of middle-class status are to be produced and enjoyed in the Australian context, are all the more imperative where heroines are making their own clothes (O'Neill, *Faithful Unto Death* (1886), Lloyd-Tayler, *By Still Harder Fate* (1898), Gaunt, *Kirkham's Find* (1897), Praed, *Outlaw and Lawmaker* (1893)), blacking their own boots (*Outlaw*), baking bread (Chads, 'Plentiful as Blackberries' (1882)), washing their own dishes, personally supervising wash-day, and even herding sheep (Liston, 'How a Woman Kept her Promise' (1869?)) and running tea-rooms (Cambridge, *A Humble Enterprise* (1896)).

DYING VIRGINS IN AUSTRALIA

The dying virgin in Australian women's fiction is often a figure who has transgressed British-defined boundaries, but can be used to justify transgressive behaviour and even appropriate it to the subjectivity of the ideal colonial lady, by, literally, dying for it. A death scene which transforms the dubious colonial girl into the angel of the house and whitewashes either her own former actions, or those of figures paralleled with her, works to the reification of a model of middle-class female subjectivity similar to that posited by Langland. Inevitably it is a model supported by structures even more fragile, fractured and transparent than those described by Langland.

At around the same time as the publication of *Little Women* in North America, Maude Jeanne Franc [Matilda Jane Evans (1827–86)] published *Minnie's Mission.* Franc was the rather prolific author of improving fiction for young women, mostly set in South Australia, frequently reprinted, and apparently popular as School and Sunday School prizes. Ostensibly the most conservative and harmless of fictions, a number of them were concerned, as *Minnie's Mission* is, with temperance.

Minnie Rayton sails from Britain to live with her uncle and aunt on their rural property in Australia. She is frustrated with the scope of her role in life as a young girl, and despite advice that lighting up her uncle and aunt's home is sufficient mission for her, she takes on the cause of temperance as well. Much of the novel is involved with Minnie's rather unconventional pursuit of this mission. She learns to ride and to saddle her own horse so that she can independently gallivant around the countryside converting shepherds and the nearby townspeople to her cause, with the help of her trusty pledge book. In pursuit of temperance she has a number of dubious *têtes à tête* with single young men of the area, including the local doctor, and a neighbour who is positioned as the love interest of the narrative.

She wreaks havoc in her own new home by converting her uncle to teetotalism. Towards the end of the novel she becomes concerned about the imminent return of her as yet unconverted cousin, Harry, so she decides to empty the contents of the wine cellar before he can get to them, and gets up at 2.00 a.m. to perform this 'duty'. This expedition, and the descriptions of the locked cellar, to which only Minnie holds the keys, which must not be entered by Harry, and which holds such dangerous and pungent liquid, is implicitly sexual. Imprudently, Minnie neglects to dress warmly for the expedition. She gets wet feet, and when she is startled by her cousin's arrival she falls down the stairs and breaks her 'ancle' (279). The somewhat archaic spelling here perhaps aligns the 'ancle' with the uncle whom she has also 'broken'.

The sexual ambiguity of Minnie's actions in the rest of the novel reaches its climax in the description of her 'fall' and rescue. The cause of temperance is used in this, as in other nineteenth-century women's fictions, to justify and sanitize behaviour which, if pursued for selfish reasons, would impugn the reputation and class status of the female. In *Minnie's Mission,* at least, death is also useful in reasserting class status as it legislates unprecedented freedoms of behaviour.

The repentant cousin Harry is sobered up from the 'evening's debauch' by the sound of his cousin's screams (281). Having discovered her, 'white and senseless', at the foot of the cellar stairs, he awakens the female servants: 'he shouted, "this is no time for fooling. Miss Minnie is out here – met with an accident – look sharp and dress, and come out, will you?"' (281). They twice answer that they saw Miss Minnie 'go to her own room for the night' (281–2), but they get dressed anyway and one of them goes to check Minnie's room. The trespass involved here is explicitly physical, and specifically sexual and moral. The place for a good, genteel young woman at night is in her room, particularly if her debauched cousin, who may or may not have had 'time for fooling' with the maids in the past, is lurking around. The maids check not the present, unconscious figure at the bottom of the cellar stairs, but the domestic space which should be occupied.

Maids and family come to what might seem the least likely conclusion when faced with the evidence of a barefooted girl unconscious in the cellar, reeking of alcohol, dressed in a wine-soaked nightgown and clutching the cellar keys – they assume she has been sleep-walking. Nevertheless, her subsequent death is sufficient to obscure any threat to her status.

Minnie contracts a fatal chill through her exploits in the cellar (that is, ironically, she is killed by alcohol) and commences to fade away, confident in her heavenly destination, but still anxious about her cousin Harry. This is part of the prolonged death scene:

A few fair flowers lay upon the bed, and Minnie, supported by pillows, rested among them, a fair, but fading flower, drooping fast. . . . Minnie's mission was nearly accomplished, but it seemed as if the spirit lingered yet, to put the last touch to its work . . . .

"Harry." The tender, loving, anxious eyes turned towards him as he entered the room and came and stood at her side.

"Dear Minnie, you asked for me," he faltered, ... What did she want with him?

She feebly clasped his hand; but even as she did so, the gentle eyes closed, and one of the fitful dozes supervened . . . Harry, with one hand still in that gentle clasp, stood still with his face shielded by the other, while more than one tear escaped his eyes. Helen . . . softly laid her hand upon his arm, They were standing so when Minnie, with a faint sigh, once more re-opened her eyes. They rested anxiously upon them.

"Harry, is it yes or no?" she whispered faintly, for life's currents ran very low and tremulously.

"Yes; God helping me!" he exclaimed in earnest tones. "Dear Minnie, I will do what you wish."

A smile of joy came over the dying face like a passing sunbeam. Her eyes looked anxiously round towards the writing-case on the drawers.

"The book," said Jessie, sobbing; "The pledge-book, she wants that, Here it is, I will bring case and all to the bed." She spread it open before Harry. Minnie glanced lovingly up at him again. "Sign," she said, "read and sign." He read it through blinding tears, and the name that followed, tremulously as it was written down, was written in prayer.

The smile that came again to the pale lips was beautiful to behold. "Mission is ended," she whispered. "Bless God for it! . . . Helen, you will be Harry's bride now? you will watch over and help him now?" [*sic*]

Helen Campbell bent low over the dying one, kissing her fondly, whispering back, "Dear Minnie, I will."

"It is nearly over; I am nearly home. How sweet is rest!" and the dark eyes gently closed again. . . . There she lay, passing away to her rest in the full glory of womanhood.

> Yet, even as a ripe shock of corn, for the harvest of her life was over, her work was done, and of her most assuredly might be recorded, "She hath done what she could."
>
> But there was yet something to be done – a farewell to be taken of each. . . . How tenderly those adieus were spoken one by one! . . . She turned at last to Dr Leigh. He was standing watching her by the side of Edwin and his wife. The anxious look came back into her face.
>
> "Dear Edwin – doctor – will you not grant a last wish – for Minnie's sake – sign." The words came with evident difficulty; but they were words that must be said. It had flashed to her mind that her work was not yet done, that more remained behind: it was this; oh, could they deny her?
>
> They could not. Edwin bent down and whispered, "Darling Minnie, I will;" and firmly in sight of the fading eyes he dashed his pledge. The pen was taken up by the doctor. Slowly and deliberately he wrote, as though weighing the value of every letter.
>
> "Thank you, dear Minnie, for remembering me," he bitterly exclaimed, as he threw it down again, and turned away.
>
> "Thank you, doctor. My mission is fully ended God help you all to follow me, Jesus only – can – help – you – save you! Good-bye!"
>
> They were Minnie's last words . . . .
>
> Minnie's mission on earth was over; she had gone to the place where the mansions prepared were awaiting her, where the triumphant songs and the crown and the palm-branch were to be her portion . . . there she would await the arrival of those who were to be the stars in her crown – jewels to shine resplendent to all eternity! (289–92)

There follows a prolonged and tacky description of the laying-out and funeral of Minnie, and the secret bereavement of her would-be spouse. A scene such as this operates to neutralize any anxiety raised by the over-active and over-assertive Minnie in the rest of the novel. Her previous nightgown scene was one in which she, wild-eyed and with her hair down, confronted her drunken, violent uncle and commanded him to stop abusing her aunt and to give up drink.

Trespasses, literal and metaphorical, are erased by an ending which affirms Minnie's class and feminine status by asserting her sure entry into the celestial hierarchy. Displays of power unsuitable to a middle-class girl, and acts of class coercion are defused by a scene in which Minnie is displayed as apparently powerless. Unable to walk, barely able to speak, flowerlike, delicate, dying, virginal and prostrate, she becomes the ideal passive, domesticated woman. Her fate is both payment for and palliation of her sins.

In context the death scene does work this way, but there are also counter-narratives in operation. As in a number of fictional Victorian death scenes, there is a potential sexual charge in the gathering at the female's bedside of a collection of spectating male relatives. The way in which the dying virgin becomes the passive object for the male gaze here is partly deflected by the control that virgin exercises. Instead of fading gently away, and leaving, as the narrative states several times, 'the rest of her mission to God', Minnie repeatedly revives sufficiently to issue orders which, because of her privileged position as the dying subject – the subject about to abdicate subjectivity – it is barely possible to refuse. Thus, in her state of near death, she achieves those things which she failed to achieve in life, despite all that energetic horse-riding. She extracts signatures for her pledge book from her two cousins *and* the doctor; and coerces her best friend into marrying her now pledged cousin. In Britain in the late 1860s 'dying declarations' held at least a quasi-legal status (Barnard 1990: 173). Potentially Minnie's requests are further empowered by a form or moment of female speech which commands patriarchal recognition (see also Bronfen 1992: Chapter 5).

The narrative nature of the pressure to temperance is stressed here in the final persuasions of a temperance novel, by the call to 'read and sign'. In that they are affirming and signing Minnie's text here, they are affirming not just Minnie's mission, but Minnie herself, forcing the witnesses of her death scene to witness not just her erasure, but her affirmation through a text (the pledge book), which it is stated will live on after her death. There is an evident equation between the novelistic text and the internal text of the pledge book. Minnie's mission as textual construct is to continue to revive at the point of death and closure and demand that those who read will 'sign'.

Minnie's virgin death frees her from the alternate plot set up for her in the narrative. The matrimonial narrative, which sometimes has a similar function of palliating female class and gender transgressions, is displaced by the death narrative, which in this case provides the heroine with an uncompromised glorious and powerful future.

Thus virgin Minnie dies out of the narrative, into apparent ultimate closure. The text removes its protagonist not so much into the oblivion of unknowable death as into the assured hearts, flowers and crowns of an elect heaven, which is beyond the temporal.

I do not wish to draw any huge national conclusions from the contrast between *Minnie's Mission* and its American contemporary, Louisa M. Alcott's *Little Women* (1868–69) but rather to make some trans-national claims for the anxieties exposed. The death of Beth in *Little Women* is one of the better known virgin deaths of popular women's fiction. The novel is frequently read as providing options for middle-class white female subjectivity, in that it maps out four diverse female trajectories towards adulthood in the four March daughters (Murphy 1990). Depending on your reading of these four, the dying virgin Beth provides a saving example which enables the somewhat more transgressive pathway of the creative, angry sister Jo, who is explicitly paired with her; or Beth provides an illustration of the literally fatal consequences of becoming the ideal domestic woman of the period – literally in-valid, self-abnegating to the point of annihilation. The most useful reading is to see the dying Beth as part of a continually unravelling text in which Beth is offered up, *both* sincerely and insincerely, as an example of what Murphy (1990) calls 'terminal goodness'. Here, Jo's resistance to Beth's erasure, as well as her adoption of Beth as role model, work constantly against each other in a narrative friction which makes the text, and the death, enduringly compelling.

If Beth embodies one respect of nineteenth-century female subjectivity, then Minnie carries several contradictory aspects and, it might be argued, is a character who has to die because of the impossibility of their coexistence in the one body. In

Little Women the death of the ideal domesticated woman enables the tracing of an alternate female subject through Jo.

In later Australian women's novels, such as Augusta O'Neill's *Faithful Unto Death* (1886), the dying virgin is used more explicitly to enable the career and affirm the subjectivity of her more transgressive female counterpart. At the same time the body of the dying virgin, Lily, is fetishized by a still contradictory narrative which privileges the attractions of the perfected dead female body, while simultaneously arguing for the rights of the imperfect desiring woman, Lulu.

Probably the most famous dead virgin in Australian fiction of the nineteenth century is Judy of Turner's *Seven Little Australians* (1894), a character who parallels *Little Women*'s Jo in tomboyish disobedience, but is not provided with a useful double to die in her stead. She exhibits features of ungenteel vigour – she walks 77 miles to escape her ladies' boarding school, scythes the grass single-handed (a feat which has certain sexual connotations), constantly resists patriarchal authority, and engages in ambiguous class transgressions in her persistent adoption of an Irish accent, which aligns her with much-maligned working-class Irish servants, such as their own Bridget (98). She is briefly welcomed back into the domestic fold so strictly policed by the extreme patriarch Captain Woolcot, during a bout of illness, which renders her, like Alcott's Beth and O'Neill's dying heroine Lily, temporarily possessed of a variety of ideal feminine features – passivity, obedience, frailty and silence. When she breaks out again, however, she is immediately squashed by a falling tree, and dies a poignant death.

This is a death readable as punishment for insufficiently concealing the construction and exercise of a subjectivity contrary to patriarchal interests. As with some other dying virgins, such as Minnie, it also saves and expunges Judy from a threatening sexuality, prefigured early in the novel in her real name, Helen, and her father's fear that 'she would be shipwrecked on rocks the others would never come to, and [her 'restless fire'] would flame up higher and higher and consume her' (22).

CONCLUSION

While the dying was used in similar ways in English-language fiction from Britain and elsewhere, the imperatives of increasingly powerful and persuasive middle-class ideologies, in conjunction with the various configurations of class, gender, sexuality and work in Australia, arguably made some particular uses of that potent figure attractive. There is nothing which can be named 'a middle-class nineteenth-century Anglo-Australian female subject'. I agree with Fiona Giles that that position was under anxious negotiation in the second half of the nineteent century for the white population in colonies like Australia, but disagree that, for women at least, this was negotiated so directly through difference in relation to its English source, and opposition to the indigenous population. I would argue that these subjectivities were produced more through subtle manipulation of available models than through opposition, and relied more heavily on the stabilizing possibilities of that mythical ideal woman.

The sanctity of English-defined virgin subjects could enable the legitimation of a variety of more colonial behaviours, and if necessary, that figure could still be killed back into perfection at the last moment, having released in life possible subjectivities not entirely shut down with her death. By the end of the century the use of the dying virgin to negotiate the status and identity of middle-class women in fiction was being replaced by more radical interrogations of the figure of the lady and her usefulness. Even where that figure was affirmed, there was a growing tendency to revive the sickly virgin to enjoy the more earthly rewards of her affirmed status.

REFERENCES

Alcott, L.M. (1983) [1868–89] *Little Women*, New York: Signet.

Alcott, L.M. (1985) 'Behind the Mask', in *Behind the Mask and Other Stories*, London: Hogarth Press.

Armstrong, N. (1987) *Desire and Domestic Fiction: A Political History of the Novel*, Oxford: Oxford University Press.

Barnard, S.M. (1990) *To Prove I'm Not Forgot: Living and Dying in a Victorian City*, Manchester: Manchester University Press.

Bronfen, E. (1992) *Over Her Dead Body: Death, Feminity and the Aesthetic*, Manchester: Manchester University Press.

Brontë, C. (1973) [1847] *Jane Eyre*, Harmondsworth: Penguin.

Cambridge, A. (1896) *A Humble Enterprise*, London: Ward, Lock & Bowden.

Chads, E.A. [E.A.C.] (1882) 'Plentiful as Blackberries', in *Tried as Pure Gold and Other Tales*, Melbourne: Cameron Laing.

Davis, L. (ed.) (1993) *Virginal Sexuality and Textuality in Victorian Literature*, New York: State University of New York Press.

Eliot, G. (1986) [1860] *The Mill on the Floss*, Harmondsworth: Penguin.

Foucault, M. (1973) *The Birth of the Clinic: An Archaeology of Medical Perception*, trans. A.M. Sheridan Smith, New York: Pantheon.

Franc. M.J. (1888) [1868] *Minnie's Mission: An Australian Temperance Tale*, London: Sampson, Low, Marston, Searle, & Rivington, 'New and Cheaper Edition'.

Gaskell, E. (1973) [1854–55] *North and South*, Oxford: Oxford University Press.

Gaunt, M. (1988) [1897] *Kirkham's Find*, Ringwood, Victoria: Penguin.

Holubetz, M. (1986) 'Death-Bed Scenes in Victorian Fiction', *English Studies*, 67, 1: 14–34.

Kristeva, J. (1982) *The Powers of Horror: An Essay on Objection*, trans. Leon S. Roudiez, New York: Columbia University Press.

Langland, E. (1992) 'Nobody's Angels: Domestic Ideology and Middle-Class Women in the Victorian Novel', *Periodical of the Modern Language Association*, 107, March: 290–304.

Liston, E, (1936) [1869] 'How a Woman Kept her Promise', in *Pioneers*, Adelaide: Hassell Press.

Lloyd-Tayler, N (1898) *By Still Harder Fate*, Melbourne: George Robertson.

Munich, A.A. (1993) 'What Lily Knew: Virginity in the 1890s', in L. Davis (ed.), *Virginal Sexuality and Textuality in Victorian Literature*, New York: State University of New York Press, pp. 143–57.

Murphy, A.B. (1990) 'The Borders of Ethical, Erotic, and Artistic Possibilities in Little Women', *Signs*, 15, 3: 562–85.

O'Neill, Mrs. H. [Augusta] (1886) *Faithful Unto Death: A Novel*, Newcastle, NSW: W.T. Poulton.

Poovey, M. (1988) *Uneven Developments: The Ideological Work of Gender in Mid-Victorian Britain*, Chicago: University of Chicago Press.

Praed, R. (1988) [1893] *Outlaw and Lawmaker*, London: Pandora.

Shelley, M. (1971) [1818] *Frankenstein*, Oxford: Oxford University Press.

Stewart, G. (1984) *Death Sentences: Styles of Dying in British Fiction*, Cambridge, MA: Harvard University Press.

Stowe, H.B. (1982) [1850–52] *Uncle Tom's Cabin*, New York: Viking Press.

Turner, E. (1988) [1894] *Seven Little Australians*, Ringwood, Victoria: Penguin Puffin.

Warner, M. (1987) *Monuments and Maidens: The Allegory of the Female Form*, London: Picador.

4 Prayers to Broken Stones: War and Death in Australia

Phillip D'Alton

THE FALLEN HEROES
Brosnan J.
Bennett F.
Daisley W.
Frew R.J.

A sandstone column perhaps three metres high, set in a small courtyard and screened from the road by the shrubs and trees that have grown up since the last 'greening of the suburb' took hold. Marble paving and marble covering the low plinth upon which the column is set and, at waist height, a series of basins on each of its four sides.

Hall A.F.
Logan J.
Morrow W.B.

There is a marble rectangle above each basin and, cut into the stone, long columns of names in alphabetical order. Three of the rectangles are crowded and bear an identical legend at top and bottom; 'These Answered The Call' heads the lists, while 'God Bless Them All' rounds them off. A hundred and eighty names in all.

Penn L.
Seale S.S.
Wilson L.W.

On the fourth face the names are more spaced and the legend is different. Heading the list of twenty-four names;

ten of which appear above: 'The Fallen Heroes' and, below the last name, 'Lest We Forget'.

The column does not taper as it rises but ends in a flat top with a series of open funeral wreaths; the sharp edges of the sandstone carving faded and blurred, and above, a life-size statue of an Australian soldier standing at ease.

There is one additional marble fixture on the memorial. Set below one of the basins it states: 'Erected by public subscription in honour of fellow citizens who gave their lives and of those who gave their services in the interests of humanity during the Great War 1914–1919.'

There is no single style to Australia's memorials to the Fallen Heroes. Some have soldiers standing at ease, on guard or attention; and there are others where the soldier has his rifle reversed and, hands folded on the butt, bows his head forward in sorrow. Many are simple four-sided columns tapering to a square-cut point; the lists of names incised in gold or black; and there are others that follow the civilian way of death with the column itself broken off, the traditional representation for a life ended before its time.

The memorials themselves are to be found in virtually every country town and many of the older city suburbs across the whole of Australia. In fact there are more memorials to the soldiers of the First World War, per head of population, in Australia, than in any other country in the world (Wilson 1995).

Although they do not conform to a single style, there is one physical feature that most of them do share, and that is their age. Most were built in the early 1920s to commemorate the first of the modern wars; modern in the sense that the level of involvement of the population either directly in the armed forces or in the civilian sphere was unprecedented, and their number reflects the size of the impact.

Out of a total population of less than 5 million, 330,000, one-fifteenth, served overseas in the armed forces and 64.8 per cent of them became casualties; the highest proportion of casualties in the British Empire. The memorials are a physical expression of the scale of the fighting and the casualties and, in calling it the Great War, reveal their naivety to more recent generations who know enough to number them (see Bean 1972).

The Second World War was more protracted; six opposed to four years, the social dislocation as great, with one person in ten in the armed forces and one-eighteenth of the total population serving overseas. Casualty rates were slightly better, with only 14.5 per cent of overseas service personnel killed compared to the 20 per cent of the First World War, but in real terms that still amounted to 27,073 fatalities. Furthermore, with Japanese troops in New Guinea and Japanese planes bombing the north, the felt physical threat was far more immediate than it had been in the earlier conflict.

Yet when it came to an end, there was no comparable explosion of monument construction to rival the 1920s. Some new monuments were built, and the Canberra War Memorial, the national repository for our encapsulated view of military death, began to take on its present form but, for the most part, the spatial location of our memorials shifted firstly to the cinema and then to the television screen. Furthermore, the use of film for propaganda purposes had, after an initial reluctance on the part of some countries, been extensively developed by all of the combatants during the course of the First World War.

An echo of that earlier desire to immortalize in stone is to be found in the First World War memorials; like the Woolgoolga and District Memorial on the north coast of New South Wales, which has additional plaques for the Second World War: 'The Following Made The Supreme Sacrifice', and underneath a list of names.

The transition from physical to media representations is typified in a monument, but not an old one, located in the main street of Dorrigo. A rectangular block of shiny metal is raised a few centimetres off the ground to give it a light but solid aspect. The top of the block is slightly hollowed and, moving into the excavation, is a soldier leading a donkey on which another man is sitting. No dates and no explanations are given and, incised into one side of the block and picked out in gold is the legend: 'To Our Glorious Dead.'

This modern-day monument is a bridge between earlier, tangible representations and more modern essentially electronic ones, because it poses the question of what is being represented rather than the form that the presentation takes.

If we turn again to those 'Great War' monuments then

there is a consistency that runs through all of them, not in the form but the content. These answered the call, God bless them all, lest we forget, the supreme sacrifice, of these our fallen heroes, our glorious dead.

Beyond the 'physicality' of our images of war, tangible or intangible, the tone of their presentation provides insights into the functions that they serve. In order to mobilize a population, and for modern wars to be fought, images of warfare must conform to a number of criteria that transmute the essentially nightmare qualities of the experience for the participants, into affirmations of socially positive values.

'They were brave to the end against odds uncounted, they fell with their faces to the foe', a fragment from *Lest We Forget*, epitomizes the split between the real world of individuals struggling to come to terms with the combat environment; where the individual has been characterized as an ant scurrying around amongst a large number of descending boots, and a portrayal that turns those same individuals into interchangeable parts in a 'green machine', all apparently motivated by such abstractions as God, King–Queen, spreading democracy and national fervour (see Stouffer *et al.* 1949).

Our images of death and warfare part company with reality when we turn a human experience into an idealized one, and by so doing deny the reality of that combat experience. Death in war becomes iconic, a series of tales which, repeatedly retold, conjures up visions of community, mateship and self-sacrifice. The unlabelled tableau on the block of metal in Dorrigo is, of course, Private John Simpson Kirkpatrick and his donkey, bringing a wounded man to safety during the Gallipoli campaign: 'the man with the donkey'.

Across a time-span of eighty years this well-known Australian image is deemed to be so 'familiar' that it needs no identification; encapsulating the values for which it stands. The public at large does not retain a detailed knowledge of military campaigns; let alone ones that occurred before over 95 per cent of them had been born. What is retained is a few 'pieces' that are highly congruent with the dominant myths concerning warfare at the societal level.

Gallipoli, a military campaign in which Australians were defeated, has a special place in Australian nation-building that lifts it beyond the 'merely' military. It was where Australia came of age, the birth of our nation. Perhaps the symbolism of blood and afterbirth, a part of the process in the creation of new life, was lost on the politicians both then and now.

One does not have to win a campaign to have all the ingredients for a set of socially reinforcing myths. The 'Digger', the archetypal Aussie soldier: tough, laconic, a 'bushy', disrespectful of authority, brave (of course) and, most important of all, a real mate, emerges from that campaign and, with a series of updates, remains our dominant image of the Australian fighting man. The film *Gallipoli*, starring Mel Gibson, offers most of the stereotypes, though its climax, the slaughter of Australians at the Nek in August 1915, is hardly positive about military commanders.

The Nek (especially since the movie), Lone Pine, 'a torn and silent valley and a tiny rivulet, with some blood upon the stones beside its mouth', the man with the donkey and heroism and mateship, 'and a sound of gentle sobbing in the south'.

As we move further away from that moment, how much do we really know about Gallipoli, outside this strange mix of nationalism and pathos? Or, to pose the question in a different way, why do we know so little about the rest of Australia's experiences in the First World War – not an academic's knowledge, nor that of an amateur historian with a penchant for things military, but the common stock of knowledge in social circulation (see Bean 1972)?

After all, Gallipoli was not the end of Australia's military commitment but the beginning of it; the 7,600 killed and 19,000 wounded only one-eighth of the total casualties, most of them in the slaughterhouse of the Western Front. And yet the only other durable image is that of the light horsemen, a story which in fact is intertwined with the Gallipoli story because it was 300 dismounted light horsemen who were killed in the futile charge against the Nek on 7 August 1915.

Our public memories of the light horse are a variant of the 'Digger' with horses added in, an affirmation of the 'outdoorsy' Aussie and his mates, culminating in the successful cavalry charge against Beersheba by the 3rd Light Horse Brigade. The names and numbers are far less important than the sustaining of an image, and in this case one that has been transmitted down through the generations by a series of films, the most recent being *The Lighthorsemen*, released in 1983.

Our images of war and warfare are sustained in our present in the same form as the predominant vehicle for the transmission of information and ideas, the electronic media. It is therefore only fitting that the columns of an earlier time should be first supplanted by books and radio as the carrier of the message and then submerged by film and television.

It does not follow, however, that an increase in either the sources of information, or the volume, works to change our images. As Curran and colleagues (1977) have pointed out, the media works most effectively when it is affirming and sustaining existing beliefs, not in changing them.

Three hundred deaths in a pointless charge, but their toughness and mateship taking them over the top. An affirmation in defeat in keeping with the more general defeat at Gallipoli and also transmogrified into a 'victory'.

Three hundred from a total of 59 342. Is it that those 50 000 others have no story, or is it because the stories from the Western Front make far less socially positive reading?

The grind of combat kills everyone. This is a truth most apparent to the soldiers involved in it, but almost totally opaque to those who have not experienced it. Statistically some do live through it unscathed, at least physically, but that only has meaning outside the combat environment. For the participants, especially during both world wars, the only foreseeable road to life was to be wounded too badly to be returned to duty, or for the war to end, because they were committed for the duration (see du Picq 1921; Gray 1967; Marshall 1947).

Nor was this a uniquely Australian discovery. Robert Graves served with the Second Welsh Fusiliers on the Western Front from 1914 to 1918. During those four years the battalion, which never had a strength of more than 700, suffered 20 000 casualties (Graves 1967). German, French, Russian, Japanese and American, all with the same bitter lesson. The grind of combat kills everyone.

The 'non-war' wars Australia has been involved in since the Second World War perhaps demonstrate that at some level this message has been taken to heart, because endless combat commitment has been replaced by a one-year rotation plan – a 'tour of duty'. During the ten-year involvement of Australia in Vietnam, 50 001 service personnel rotated into and out of the country. For the troops, this meant that the essential combat nightmare had at least a finite end-point.

The presentation of the Vietnam War by the media has to be seen as a total aberration in the portrayal of a conflict while it is in progress. Censorship has always been a part of the reporting of war news. The novelist John Steinbeck, working as a war correspondent during the Second World War, has made the point that the only stories they were able to transmit had to support 'that gaseous thing called the war effort' (Steinbeck 1960). Secrecy, national security, personal and commercial interest and bloodymindedness, are all present in the drive to manage war news and the treatment of war generally, and there are certainly some good arguments for at least a level of control of the media.

Maps of the Nivelle offensive by the French army in 1917 which appeared in Swiss newspapers days before the attack took place, is a suitable example of the need for secrecy regarding pending military operations, but does not address the broader issue of what the public is entitled to know (see Pitt 1962). Are they, for example, entitled to see a 'warts and all' visual record every night on their television screens? In the case of Vietnam, and undoubtedly because the civilian and military authorities had simply not caught up with the visual power of the new technology, the answer was yes.

Vietnam was the television war, and it brought home to the civilian population the essentially repetitious and apparent pointlessness of what was being enacted; in the case of America every night, on their television screens. The mistakes, lies, the problems with 'our Vietnamese allies'; and on and on, undoubtedly the most lifelike account of a war; even overlaid as it was by government sources both here and overseas, churning out their versions of the truth for media consumption, that has been presented both before or since, and that is what makes Vietnam the aberration (see Gabriel and Savage 1979; Hackworth 1990).

Looking at the Falklands and Gulf Wars as visual-news products for public consumption, they are clear evidence of the lessons learnt in Vietnam: not in how to fight wars, but how to manage their coverage in the media (see Glasgow University Media Group 1986).

Wars have to have *meaning*. The sacrifice has to be *for* something. When the coverage of warfare escapes official control the images we see are not affirming of our beliefs but challenging. Losing at Gallipoli was nation-building and a single campaign in a war we won. The losses and privations of the Second World War were supportable because we won again and built on the Anzac tradition. The 'Anzac, Bapaume and the Marne, could ever the old blood fail/No foe shall gather our harvest, or sit on our stockyard rail' (MacKellar 1967). These images of the First World War were later joined by other images such as those of the rats of Tobruk and the fighting on the Kokoda trail.

The Korean War, with a small Australian commitment and 1,526 casualties, was at least a stalemate, but Vietnam – a not only lost but 'suspect' war for a whole variety of reasons – how do you react to that?

With the exception of the John Wayne film, *The Green Beret*, the movies on Vietnam are not offering socially positive messages. The mateship as the glue that holds units together is still there; though restricted to a close circle of friends, but a wider meaning, one that links the activity to something more than sheer survival of self and 'mates', is absent. The characters act out their personal dramas in a space virtually devoid of such abstract symbols as patriotism, saving the world for democracy or stopping the red menace; the moral justifications for getting them there in the first place. What is left is surviving until the end of the tour and looking after your mates.

The Odd Angry Shot and such American movies as *Casualties of War, 84 Charlie Mopek, Full Metal Jacket, Go Tell The Spartans* and *Apocalypse Now,* all display this portrayal of a war which, for the combat soldier at the time, has no meaning, and this is very in keeping with the television portrayals of that war.

If a plethora of competing messages is the hallmark of the public's 'understanding' of the war in Vietnam, the presentation of the Falklands and Gulf Wars in the media carries the hallmark of a production that is fully back under official control. Both were wars fought in places away from large centres of population and access for journalists could therefore be easily controlled.

Only two teams of reporters from the BBC went with the British task force to the Falklands and the media was actively manipulated at home in the UK through what was released as news and picked up by a press hungry for stories (see Glasgow University Media Group 1986). In the media's defence, programmes such as Tumbledown did tell the more human side of the story but, on the whole, there was very little media questioning of what had been, after all, both a successful short war and a media event. The fact that wounded returned soldiers confined to wheelchairs were not allowed to wear their uniforms to church services celebrating the victory, presumably because it would spoil the 'look' of it to both the live and the far larger television audience, somehow seemed to get lost in the general outpourings over the victory (BBC 1992).

Despite the quantum leap in information-gathering and reporting systems in the 16 years between the end of the Vietnam War and the Gulf conflict of 1991, the quality of the flow, as opposed to the quantity, has diminished. With the army locked away in the desert, the military itself became the only pipeline for information to a breathlessly waiting group of television corporations who, having gone to 24-hour a day coverage, had nothing to offer but stock footage and a series of talking heads, and whatever the authorities chose to release to them.

The style of presentation, and one that was echoed fairly faithfully in the media, was that of a video game; a hymn in praise of military technology where a suitably demonized enemy of the verities of democracy and freedom is defeated and driven out of a country he has invaded. Hardly surprising that the 50 000–60 000 Iraqis who died in the war were labelled 'collateral damage'.

When the authorities have a firm control on the dissemination of information, the message about the nature of war is far less ambiguous (see Anon. 1968; Chomsky 1969). War is both politically correct on the social level and, despite the sacrifices it entails, ennobling on the personal level.

The War Memorial in Canberra, the centralized repository

of our images of death and warfare, is more an affirmation of the positive messages and symbols to be culled from warfare, rather than a condemnation of its waste and brutality or, for that matter, an exposé of the real world of combat.

The numerous dioramas from the First World War, for example, present a picture of Australian soldiers all performing positive acts: charging, shooting, advancing along trenches, fighting with bayonets against Turk and German, manning defensive positions and guarding prisoners. The issue does not revolve around an attempt to show that Australians are 'bad soldiers' because this is *not* the case. The problem is that these idealized portrayals of combat deny the real world of the individuals it seeks to explain. Soldiers are not interchangeable bits or smoothly functioning cogs in a camouflaged entity called an army. To assume that they are serves clear social functions and, in simplifying the public's perception, moves us further away from a genuine understanding (see du Picq 1921; Keegan 1975; Marshall 1947; Stouffer *et al.* 1949).

One other thing missing from these dioramic visions is that the dead are all intact. The weaponry does not simply kill, it dismembers; so the fallen which appear in these renditions to 'prove' their authenticity are in fact a denial of it. No bodies eviscerated, the gaping body cavities and tumbled internal organs smeared with mud. No arms and legs, or heads, or torn bits of torsos and trunks; heads or limbs as attached optional extras. And no rotting corpses, or long-dead bodies bloated with the gases of corruption and soon to burst. Perhaps the creators of our national shrine felt that those additions would look untidy?

While the dominant presentation of images concerning warfare by the authorities has always stressed its positive aspects, acceptance of them has never been total. During the First World War two Australian referendums on introducing conscription were defeated – one in October 1916 and the other in December 1917. As Odgers (1993) comments: 'It seemed that short of a supreme crisis at home, the Australian people would not support conscription for overseas military service.'

Whether the threat of a Japanese invasion in 1942 would have provided the 'supreme crisis' Odgers alludes to can only be a question of academic interest, because the Australian people were not given the opportunity to state a preference via referendum; conscription was a government-created fact from the beginning of the Second World War.

Although it may seem strange to talk about wars in terms of their popularity, there are popular and unpopular wars. Winning a war both quickly and 'cheaply', in terms of your own casualties, is generally an excellent way to popularize a conflict, and both the Falklands War (for the British), and the Gulf War of 1991 for the Allies, were popular wars.

Vietnam, on the other hand, was and is an unpopular war. For Australia, our ten-year commitment (1962–72) made it our longest war; although, with 425 killed and 2,398 injured, certainly not our costliest in terms of human life. The divisiveness of the war, both in Australia and the USA, stems not only from the drawn-out nature of the conflict but because the reporting of it, the images presented, were far more uncensored than during any other war in our history.

The official 'story' carried with it the standard version of events but, because of media access, there were many other versions around to facilitate alternative 'readings'. Losing a war that was already ambiguous in terms of its meaning to the Australian public meant that the Australian veterans of that war returned to a welcome that was equally ambiguous. The defeat at Gallipoli had been transmuted into the birth of the nation in fire and blood: there was no such uplifting transformation possible for the returnees from our longest war.

In 1987, 15 years after the last Australian troops of the 50 001 who had been committed had withdrawn, Australia finally held a long-delayed welcome-home march across the nation. Across the years leading to the national reconciliation march and up to the present, the Vietnam 'experience' has become a part our general military story through a not unpredictable process. At the political level it is justified as having bought time for the rest of South-East Asia to achieve social stability, and thus the *meaning* of the sacrifice is affirmed.

For the soldiers who took part in the essential combat nightmare, their 'victory' was to have 'fought brilliantly, never losing a battle. (With a) discipline and professionalism (that) impressed the world' (Odgers: 1993: 247). And, the final blending which cements the union with our past: to be the same tough, laconic Diggers who looked after their mates that their fathers and their fathers before them had been.

The transmutation that turns real individuals struggling to survive in the most threatening, man-created, environment on the planet into iconic figures, is a product of an ongoing cultural battle about the meaning of war and warfare. Clearly, it is a battle that can only be fought with free access to information and, if the coverage of the Gulf War is indicative, that is not what we are going to get.

Devine R.
Murray M.
Roberts L.
Watts S.A.

'Because only soldiers actually fight, they understand how much of what is afterwards called glory is but memory trying to put a good face on terror and torment' (Turtledove 1992: 191).

REFERENCES

Anon. (1968) *Report From Iron Mountain*, Harmondsworth: Penguin.
BBC (1992) *Tumbledown*, screened by ABC, July.
Bean, W. (1972) *The Broken Years*, Sydney: Penguin.
Burke, K. (1942) 'War and Cultural Life', *American Journal of Sociology*, 48, 3:404–10.
Chomsky, N. (1969) *American Power and the New Mandarins*, Harmondsworth: Penguin.
Cowley, M. (1955) *The Literary Situation*, New York: Viking Press.
Curran, J., Gurevitch, M. and Woollacott, J. (eds.) (1977) *Mass Communication and Society*, London: Open University Press/Edward Arnold.
du Picq, A. (1921) *Battle Studies*, New York: Macmillan.
Gabriel, R. and Savage, P. (1979) *Crisis in Command*, New York: Hill & Wang.
Glasgow University Media Group (1986) *War and Peace News*, Milton Keynes: Open University Press.
Graves, R. (1967) *Goodbye To All That*, Harmondsworth: Penguin.
Gray, G. (1967) *The Warriors*, New York: Harper Torchbooks.

Hackworth, D. (1970) *About Face*, Sydney: Pan Books.
Keegan, J. (1975) *The Face of Battle*, London: Jonathan Cape.
MacKellar, D. (1967) in *Penguin Book of Australian Verse*, Sydney: Penguin.
Marshall, S.L.A. (1947) *Men Against Fire*, New York: The Infantry Journal.
Odgers, G. (1993) *Army Australia*, Canberra: Department of Defence.
Pitt, B. (1962) *1918: The Last Act*, London: Cassell & Co.
Steinbeck, J. (1960) *Once There Was A War*, New York: Bantam Books.
Stouffer, S., Suchman, E., De Vinney, L. *et al.* (1949) *The American Soldier*, 2 vols., Princeton, NJ: Princeton University Press.
Turtledove H. (1992) *The Guns Of The South*, New York: Ballantine Books.
Wilson, R. (1995) *Architecture In Australia*, 2BL interview, 9 September.

5 The Legacy of Suicide: the Impact of Suicide on Families

Mary Fraser

In 1855 the poet and balladeer Banjo Patterson penned a song which was destined to become the unofficial national anthem of Australia. 'Waltzing Matilda' underlines many elements in the colonial society of that day. Class-conflict, the oligarchy of the landowners and the justice system and the ethos of rugged individualism are all themes in this song about a swagman caught stealing a sheep by a waterhole. It is also a song which glorifies suicide because the swagman chooses death by drowning rather than surrendering himself to the troopers. 'Waltzing Matilda' highlights the fact that suicide rates in nineteenth-century Australia were higher than in England (Welborn 1982: 17). Ever since then suicide has been a significant way of dying for Australians.

The aim of this chapter is to examine the impact of such suicides on the families that remain, an impact which has often been described as the 'legacy of suicide'. The discussion presented here is based upon focus group interviews with four families and a total of sixteen participants. Each of these families had experienced a suicide of a family member in the two years previous to the interview.

THE LEGACY OF SUICIDE

> Parting is all we know of heaven
> And all we need of hell
>
> (Emily Dickinson, Poem 176, reproduced in Reeves 1959: 99)

For many people in a post-suicide situation there is a sudden

Table 5.1 Legacy of Suicide

Main Features
(1) Support (initially)
(2) Lack of support (later)
(3) Normlessness
(4) Suicide – a very different grief
(5) Irrevocability of the impact of suicide
(6) Management of child survivors
(7) Stigma

and for the most part unexpected shattering of their lives. In addition to the grief and loss associated with the death of a close relative there is an extra burden for the family members of a suicide victim. Part of that burden is the altered social world in which they find themselves. Their private sorrow has a public aspect, and their grief and adjustment to it must be lived out within a social context which has little supporting structure or understanding of their plight. In conducting the interviews certain themes have emerged, and are grouped under the heading of the 'legacy of suicide'. These themes are summarized in Table 5.1.

INITIAL SUPPORT

Consistent with the research of Dunn and Morrish-Vidners (1987–88), there was support of one kind or another for all those people interviewed. By far the strongest support for all those interviewed was found within the family. This was sometimes within the family of origin or the family acquired by marriage. Friends were also a great support. Sometimes it was just one other person, like a neighbour, who gave reliable and consistent help. At other times it was a single situation, such as the example quoted by Barry:

> I am probably one of these fools who thinks he doesn't need any help . . . I was working away at the time and, I thought everything was rosy and I broke down one night with a guy I hardly even know . . . he was a most unlikely sort of guy but he was probably as good as anybody. I just

> needed somebody, you know. That was outside the family and it came as a bit of a shock to me because I didn't see it coming. It was like catching a cold. Boom, it hit you. (Barry)

There were a variety of agencies and services which were also helpful but there were none that all families found helpful, with the exception of the police. All those interviewed who had contact with the police found them helpful and supportive. Most, but not all, found hospital staff accommodating. Undertakers, in some instances, were extremely helpful but not so in others. The same was true for workers such as counsellors and social workers. It is important to note that although most of those interviewed came from roughly the same geographical area, a variety of different services were used with families utilizing agencies in surrounding regional centres. There were some examples also of occasions when people found agencies not only unhelpful but also obstructionist and uncooperative, as in this situation: 'We wanted to see Peter but the undertaker kept saying, "He looks terrible you shouldn't go and see him", but he hadn't seen him after the autopsy, he just didn't want to get him out and prepared before time' (Sue).

LACK OF SUPPORT

While it was obvious in all the interviews that there was support for the survivors, especially within the family and within some agencies and organizations, it was also apparent that others failed to understand the situation of those bereaved. Often acquaintances, work colleagues, parents of children at school with the grieving children did not respond in ways that indicated an understanding of the anguish and bewilderment suffered by survivors. Examples of this are the responses of Sue's acquaintances who thought she ought to be 'over it' by now; Lisa's workmates who looked the other way when she returned to work; and Liz's experience with the mother of her son's friend who was horrified when he said his father had shot himself. Dismissal of the suffering of the bereaved, the ignoring of those so affected and the expressing of horror at the mode of death have served to add to the burden carried by those who have had a family member commit suicide.

NORMLESSNESS

> I found that in the early stages my own doctor, John Blank, was very good. I liked him. No bullshit but I got to a stage where I needed to know if I was handling things right. I was sort of bluffing my way through things with the kids. I wanted someone who knew all about it to lay it out for me and all they could say at [a community mental health service] was you're doing great, keep up the good work. I wanted some real support and constructive advice but they glossed what I said over. I felt patronized, perhaps they didn't know how to help but they're supposed to be the experts. I felt very angry. (Liz)

This excerpt is an example of a theme that was evident through all the interviews. People after a suicide often do not know how to behave. There appears to be little in the way of social norms governing either the behaviour of survivors or that of the community at large.

As Liz said of the agency with which she had dealings, 'perhaps they didn't know how to help me'. Liz felt she needed guidelines to assist her in helping her children cope with their father's death but she found none and was thrown back on her own resources.

Claire was the only interviewee to use the term 'normlessness': 'It's the normlessness of suicide in the end. There are very few rules and regulations. You are not sure how to act, or how others might react, you can feel lost and uncertain.' Her brother James expressed similar sentiments:

'Because it's been a tabooed subject, you don't talk about it. That's really dangerous as well, because people don't know the rules, not that rules can tell you how to feel but rules do give you guidance as to what you're feeling is normal.' Sue spoke of wanting to see other people who had suffered a suicide to 'see' if they were normal and of not knowing what is appropriate for grieving. Lisa, in another interview, also spoke of her experience at work: 'I'd walk into work (after Tom died) and they'd sort of look away.. it's just that they didn't know what to do or say to you' (Lisa). The time for grieving was also discussed. And while this is not relevant only to suicide, people felt only they could determine what was appropriate for the period of mourning. Contacts with other people who felt that 'enough' time had elapsed caused confusion and pain for those affected. Once again the sense of what is 'normal' for the mourning of suicide is not clearly defined, adding to the burden of grief. Many interviewees saw this as a denial of their loss.

SUICIDE IS DIFFERENT

In all of the interviews everyone felt that suicide was a 'different' kind of grief. Most of those involved had experienced other close deaths, several had had sudden and tragic deaths, but these people felt that suicide was very different. One family felt that suicide was similar to other griefs but even though they said this, it was conceded that there was more questioning. There was a real fear that those involved with a suicide would have to disclose it to others and then discuss it.

> Other deaths leave questions but in the end you accept it. Suicide, you go through the same things but you're always running out of reasons. You're still going through those questions but the answers aren't there. That's something I don't dwell on too much. How could he have done it? There's an extra dimension. It's the loneliness of taking your own life. (Brad)

Because some of the people interviewed see suicide as a different form of grief to any other they were reluctant to discuss it with others. Lisa hated people asking her why, at her age (26), she was a widow. This had an effect on her interactions with others: 'and you think, how am I going to explain this. And then you sort of say oh no, I'm a widow, and you think "Oh God, don't ask any more questions, please don't". It makes you just want to disappear.'

Harriet also felt the effect of suicide on how she believed others saw her:

'I found that it took me a while to go up the street and then I did feel people were saying, there's Mrs Jones, there she goes. I felt a real nervousness, especially with someone who knows about the suicide, but I'm also nervous with someone who doesn't know in case I have to tell them' (Harriet). Paul, in another interview, felt this way:

'It was normal, you know, when Dad died, because he had a heart attack. And you don't like it but it's a normal way to die. People get old and die. Yeah, with Dad's death there was no anger but with David's it was different. It was more complicated' (Paul).

IRREVOCABILITY OF THE IMPACT OF SUICIDE

There was also evidence that suicide had an irrevocable impact on the lives of those involved in the interviews, in varying ways. This was felt to a greater or lesser degree through interactions with others. 'Since Peter died from suicide I've noticed that every day I wake up and I'm thinking about it, something about his suicide is going through my mind. Once I only thought about it if I heard it on the news. I'm always talking about it to Geoff (husband) now' (Sally). For the children of the families, suicide is now a common topic of conversation.

'It's an ongoing thing isn't it? Like our kids sit talking on the floor, playing a game or something, and someone will say suicide, that's when you kill yourself, isn't it? You know what I mean, every week there is something' (Louise).

SUICIDE AND CHILDREN

Dealing with children in a post-suicidal situation was an important issue in all the interviews. Parents and close family had little in the way of guidelines. Those concerned were very conscious of adding to the trauma of child survivors.

All the families interviewed had young children and they believed that their discussions with their children on this subject were very important. Most of the families felt that an open and honest 'telling of the story' was important both to the child's acceptance of the situation and their own ongoing relationship with their children.

> All the kids talk about it the whole time. My kids do and that's the other thing, every time they do I think to myself thank God we told them the truth because if I hadn't I would be thinking what did I tell them last time. They ask me and I tell them. Michael asked me something the other day. When I told him he said "That's what you said last time" and I said "But that's the truth." (Liz)

One very poignant incident recalled by Lisa illustrates both the normlessness and the problem of how to deal with the issues surrounding the death of a parent through suicide. Erin was five years old when this incident occurred. It happened after a child at school told her that her father was in hell because he had shot himself. Lisa had been very open and honest with her daughter, never telling her too much but answering her questions honestly.

> I said to Erin, your daddy was a good daddy, he would do anything for anyone. If anyone needed help your daddy would be there, and good people always go to Heaven no matter how they died. . . . we were sitting on the couch one night and she said to me, "Mum there's things I understand and things I don't understand." I said well what things don't you understand and Mummy will try to answer them. And she started asking questions. She said did my Daddy really love me? I said your Daddy thought the world of you Erin. I said your Daddy just loved you so much. I said he wrote Mummy a note and he put in that note how much he loved you and he wanted you to remember always that he loved you. And then she wanted to hear the note. And I said, oh God, I don't know if this is the right thing or not. And I said, it's a very very sad note, do you think you can cope with that? "Yes, Mum", she says. So I went and got the note and we were sitting there on the couch and I started to read it to her and it gets to the part where it said please tell Erin how much I love her and that I always will. I looked at her and she's got tears running down her face and of course I started.

And we just cried, and cried and cried and she said oh Mum I've got a sore throat but she has been fantastic ever since.

STIGMA

Throughout all the interviews there was an undercurrent of an idea, mostly mentioned indirectly, and often inferred by the various participants. This was the notion of stigma. Most of those interviewed, if asked directly, rejected the idea that they had been stigmatized, but in telling their stories this issue emerged. Some comments indicate a sense of stigma: 'it took me a while to go up the street and then I did feel people were saying there's Mrs Evans, there she goes, you know . . . she lost her husband in a car accident and now her son-in-law committed suicide'. Sue also likened her situation to that of someone with a contagious disease. Lisa felt people were looking at her and thinking, 'She pushed her husband to kill himself.' Sue also spoke of children at school harassing her 5-year-old daughter because of her father's suicide. Lisa also spoke of her desire to 'mark' herself in some way, by chopping off her finger. This idea of self-stigmatization was apparent to a less dramatic extent in other interviews. In one interview a person denied that he experienced any stigma but felt that 'other people out there have a problem, but not us'.

In another interview, John summed up his attitude in the following words:

> I know that the stigma of suicide was in my mind, you know. I mean, I never got it back from anyone but I had that feeling inside, from early socialization, I suppose, that feeling that suicide is such a failure, and so I felt it was copping out but the reality of stigma, other people didn't reinforce that at all, it was within me. (John)

DISCUSSION

When there is a suicidal death in a family the members of that family are at risk of becoming heirs to the painful legacy of suicide. The elements of this legacy are complex and affect people differently.

While this study confirms some elements of the previous research it also strongly suggests other possibilities regarding the social experiences of people in a post-suicide situation. Many of these experiences fall under the heading of the previously discussed 'legacy of suicide'. In this section I will discuss some ideas based on the findings of this study which might explain this legacy.

Ethic of the Individual

An issue for many of the people in this study which confuses the issue of stigma is the notion of the right of the individual to make certain choices about his/her own life. In contemporary society there is still strong evidence of the Protestant ethic with its emphasis on individualism (Charmaz 1980: 254). In relation to suicide this ethic is very apparent, competing with older, perhaps darker cultural forces in responding to this complex phenomenon. On one hand we have an act which can produce enormous opprobrium and on the other, can be seen to epitomize the notion of the individual's right to make choices about his or her life. This has created profound ambivalence for many people interviewed in the study. People appeared to be struggling with the contradiction between the open and public sanctions *against* suicide and the paradoxical support for the principle that the individual has a right to decide how they will live, and die.

Lisa said of her husband, 'It's not wrong on Tom's behalf that was his choice, sure, but look at what he has put everyone else through, like his family and me and his little girl.'

Claire expressed it this way: 'Andrew had control of his outcome you know, his death was intentional he chose it. Death by some other means would have been different. But ultimately Andrew had done it by choice. I respect that he has the right to make choices.' Her brother James also believed in the concept of choice but found that choice difficult to accept:

> Well I view it as a fairly legitimate choice but I think the situation was really evil . . . I think it is obviously unfair to

> those left behind, I mean not so much on us but more a fear for his kids . . . actually I thought that it was unfair on us and on our families I think, yeah sure, Andrew did that as a choice, but I think it was a rotten choice.

This conflict is very confusing for families as it centres around the negative value and stigma attributed to suicide; the social costs of this action on families and the simultaneous respect and even defence of individuals to make choices in a situation fraught with ambiguity. It is far from clear how individuals or families reconcile this paradox, if indeed they do at all.

Stigma

Dunn and Morrish-Vidners (1987–88) and Solomon (1982–83) also found evidence of stigmatization amongst those close to a suicide victim. Although this study generally supports these findings the issue of stigma is far from clear, with few people actually revealing that they felt stigmatized.

Others did not mention the death to people who did not know of it, whereas they stated that they would have talked about death by accident or sudden illness. There was a sense, in the focus groups, that for those involved the taboo nature of suicide was well internalized. People did not have to be told or have overt sanctions put in place because the stigmatizing nature of the suicidal act appeared to be an attitude that was present already. Even in those instances where people said they had not experienced stigma they were aware of the negative reactions when they brought the subject up with others.

It seems from the present study that there is a strong stigma associated with suicide. This comes both from the wider society and within individual members. As Charmaz (1980: 234) points out, the way people respond to an act such as suicide is based on collective values which in turn rest upon the social structure. Therefore what people think about suicide is related to much broader social values and meanings. The thoughts that John expressed in the previous section about suicide did not come from the suicidal act itself, which in itself is without value, but from the meaning that society attributes to such actions. Although this man attached a sense of stigma to his brother having 'failed' he had derived this attitude from his social world. He was expressing a collective value as it applied to his dead brother and he carried part of the shame attributed to this action within himself. In a recent study Jacoby (1994: 269–70) makes a similar point in relation to epilepsy and stigma: 'Their perceptions of epilepsy as stigmatising were clearly anchored in what they understood to be the commonly held view of epilepsy among the lay community and constituted a major source of anguish among them.'

Suicide and Taboo

The proscribed nature of suicide is something that has been part of Western cultures for centuries. For instance in seventeenth-century England a stake was driven through the heart of a suicide and the burial took place at a crossroads. If the death took place in a house then the body could not be removed via a doorway as this would defile that doorway. Later, victims could not be buried in consecrated ground but had to be buried outside the walls of the cemetery. Because suicide was considered sinful those who committed suicide and those who survived them carried the condemnation and censure of their communities (Farberow 1989: 280).

In contemporary society attitudes towards suicide victims and their families have softened, yet there is still reason to believe that suicide still carries with it a strong taboo which stigmatizes.

Normlessness

The study by Dunn and Morrish-Vidners (1987–88) also commented on the lack of behavioural guidelines for those in their study. However, I suggest that the ambivalence and ambiguity which surrounds suicide and leads to normlessness is a response to the breaking of the suicide taboo and, in fact, that very normlessness is a 'norm'. It is a way of punishing by default, by omission rather than commission. At the same time this normlessness keeps faith with the ethic of the individual. There are no overt sanctions put into place and therefore the right of the individual to make certain choices appears to be preserved. At the same time this act must not be seen to receive approval. The survivors of suicide bear the cost of the violation of the taboo by existing in an environment where there are few rules governing their behaviour or the behaviours of others around them.

There was ample evidence of this lack of social norms in the interview transcripts. For example, Lisa said of her interactions with others:

'They just don't know what to say (to me). I think it makes them feel uncomfortable . . . they probably say I'm sorry to hear about this, I'm sorry about that. I mean, I suppose they don't know how you're going to react either. They don't want a blubbering mess, do they?'

The normlessness observed in this study supports Dunn and Morrish-Vidners (1987–88: 200) when they say: 'Lacking social acceptance, the suicidal act does not lead to a predictable or patterned social response, since behaviour linked to disapproved acts does not give rise to fixed norms. As a result, people do not know how they are supposed to act towards those grieving a suicide.'

Normlessness and Children

An area of concern in the normlessness of suicide relates to child survivors. Many of those interviewed felt a lack of guidelines when it came to dealing with the children who remained. This added to the burden already being carried by families. It could also be interpreted as a social sanction applied to survivors. Suicide has been a part of Australian society since its inception and yet little has been set in place to support families dealing with this traumatic experience. People were unsure about a range of issues, from how much to tell a child, to not condemning the parent who had committed suicide while disapproving of the act. The lack of direction or choice of directions for families is an additional hardship for families, albeit one imposed by default. There was little available to the respondents of this study by way of support or education for the surviving parent.

According to Charmaz (1980: 274), the traumatic experience

of suicide on children may be damaging unless support is available. Children do not have the same psychological capacity to cope with the feelings generated by suicide as adults. According to Klagsburn, 'Children of suicides have a higher than average rate of suicide, not because the tendency towards suicide is biologically inherited, but because they grow up with a heritage of guilt, anger and a sense of worthlessness' (*Grief after Suicide* 1993).

Parents surviving suicide because of the difficulties they are encountering themselves often look for support in helping their children. The fact that little exists for them means they have to struggle alone and with limited resources.

CONCLUSION

Family members of surviving a suicide inherit a legacy which has significant implications for their social interactions with others. The suicide taboo leads to stigma which is sometimes self-imposed and sometimes applied by others. Conflicting with this taboo is the ethos of the individual which supports the idea that people have the right to make certain choices about their lives, even the right to choose death. This apparently insoluble problem is resolved by normlessness, a situation with little in the way of social norms governing the behaviour of self or others. This 'norm of normlessness' allows a type of punishment by default while still keeping intact the ideology of individual autonomy. This drama, which is played out against a backdrop of the role of death in a modern industrial society, can often leave survivors in an existential wasteland.

REFERENCES

Borges, J.L. (1985) *Selected Poems 1923–1967*, Harmondsworth: Penguin.

Charmaz, K. (1980) *The Social Reality of Death*, Reading, MA: Addison-Wesley.

Dunn, R.G. and Morrish-Vidners, D. (1987–88) 'The Psychological and Social Experience of Suicide Survivors', *Omega*, 18, 3:175–215.

Farberow, N.L. (1989) 'Attitudes Towards Suicide', in R.F.W. Diekstra,

R. Maris, S. Platt, D. Schmidtke, G. Sonneck (eds.) *Suicide and Its Prevention, The Role of Attitude and Imitation*, Leiden: E.J. Brill.

Flanagan, M. (1991) 'Suicide', *The Age*, 1 February.

Grief After Suicide (1993) Maryborough, Victoria: Central Victorian Community Health Service Inc.

Jacoby, A. (1994) '"Felt Versus Enacted Stigma: A concept revisited": evidence from a study of people with epilepsy in remission', *Social Science & Medicine*, 38, 2: 269–74.

Range, L.M. and Calhoun, L.G. (1990) 'Responses Following Suicide and Other Types of Death: The perspective of the bereaved', *Omega*, 21, 4:311–20.

Reeves, J. (ed.) (1959) *The Selected Poems of Emily Dickinson*, London: Heinemann.

Solomon, M.I. (1982–83) 'The Bereaved and the Stigma of Suicide', *Omega*, 13, 4:377–87.

Welborn, S. (1982) *Lords of Death: a people, a place a legend*, Fremantle: Fremantle Arts Centre Press.

6 Death and the Great Australian Disaster

Beverley Raphael

There has been a long history of disasters in the Australian context, many going back over the thousands of years before European settlement. Natural disasters have affected all societies and the powerful forces unleashed by them have always brought threat to the survival of communities or groups. Such events are often the cause of large-scale death and destruction, come unexpectedly, and strike randomly. The 'wise men' or 'soothsayers' of the culture or group will seek to explain or predict, so as to protect against these adversities. Disasters, by their very nature, almost always bring confrontation with death and often massive deaths. All societies seek to interpret these deaths; why some, be they individuals or communities, are 'chosen', and others not; and in these interpretations, omens also are sought. Frequently the deaths, or destruction of home, possessions, crops, village, are seen in terms of 'punishment': for these deaths and losses are untimely, and some are affected and others are not. The search for meaning and interpretation is common to all affected by these disasters, which are often viewed as 'Acts of God'. This search for meaning appears in both highly civilized and primitive communities, although these interpretations may be more hidden and less conscious in the former, less conscious, and more direct and overt in the latter.

In Australian communities natural disasters such as fire, flood storm, cyclone or drought have seen scenes of devastation and brought with them confrontation with death. It seems such deaths were incorporated in the natural order of things, both with indigenous narrative history before settlement and in records afterwards. These natural disasters took on greater meaning when they affected major centres of human settlement, and, of course, in more recent times, with extensive media coverage. For these reasons the destruction and often death inherent in them have been highlighted.

'Man-made' disaster is a broadly-based term referring to those major incidents where man is involved in the causation of the disaster or where the technologies of man have in some way failed, perhaps also in interaction with natural events in some instances – for instance, a plane crash in adverse weather conditions. Inherent in the definition is the concept that these are in some way caused by man, either through negligence or failure, or in other instances direct malevolence. Deaths are a common feature and may lead to the 'disastrous' definition of the incident or occurrence.

War and civil conflict represent the ultimate in man-made catastrophe, and Australia's role in such disasters has usually been 'offshore', with the exception of the initial violent invasion, and in some instances 'war', with the takeover of aboriginal lands and with the subsequent treatment of these indigenous Australians. These deaths were not seen as significant originally, because of the failure to understand the nature of aboriginal culture and the mistaken view of these people as barbarians.

The denial of death, except in its romanticized form, and the distance from wars, so that the soldier died abroad – the 'tyranny of distance', as Blainey has called it – all lead to popular assumptions that 'it can't happen here', that the disasters that ravaged other countries, be they natural or man-made, would not affect the 'lucky country'. This meant that Australians were, as a nation, until relatively recently ill-prepared to deal with disasters and their consequences; and as individuals usually failed to take precautions to protect themselves or their families – for instance, from bushfires, even in situations where risk was known to be high, precautions were defined, and such disasters had occurred previously. The popular notion of 'she'll be right mate' reflect the sense of personal invulnerability which is relevant for each individual, but frames this in its particular Australian context.

Some deaths have taken on the aura of personal disasters and popular preoccupation with these, or their prevalence as causes of death, may highlight their disastrous nature. Such individual deaths, because of this, have also shaped

Australian awareness of and response to death, in evolving ways. And here too the media have played a significant role in 'presenting' the death, just as they have 'presented' major disasters. Examples of these personal disasters are deaths of community figures and leaders, deaths from HIV/AIDS; deaths from breast cancer; the high level of motor vehicle-accident deaths; and more recently the high level of suicide deaths among young males. Apart from breast cancer, the majority of these premature deaths are much more frequent among young men and are presented with special poignancy of the loss of these young male lives and promise. The deaths of younger women, for instance with breast cancer, have also been presented in heroic and suffering terms, but here the theme is often, as elsewhere, that of 'women and children', and the presentations reflect the woman's contribution as mother that is lost, and little of her own life, career and other contributions is likely to be considered. Thus in these personal disasters there are gender themes which represent, in terms of death, some of the broader values of the strongly patriarchal themes of the society.

DISASTER DEATHS – THE ANONYMOUS DEAD

It is interesting to look back over some of the documented natural and man-made disasters that have affected Australia in the last two centuries. Carroll (1977) reviewed these and examined catastrophes as diverse as the Castle Hill rebellion of 1804; the wreck of the *Dunbar* in 1857; the Bulli coal-mine disaster of 1887; the Brisbane floods of 1893; the influenza epidemic of 1918–19; the Black Friday Victorian bushfires of 1939; the bombing of Darwin by the Japanese in 1942; the *Voyager/Melbourne* collision in 1964; the Westgate Bridge collapse of 1970; the Darwin cyclone of 1974; the Granville rail disaster of 1977. And there have been a significant number since, including the Ash Wednesday bushfires of 1983 in South Australia and Victoria; the Kempsey and Grafton bus crashes of 1989; the Newcastle earthquake of 1989, and mass shootings in Melbourne 1987. In all of these the dead are described, in records such as Carroll's, as '83 dead', for instance. Rarely are the deceased described in terms of whether they are men and women, except for the first presentation in newspapers, or other media, where identity and identification is made – subsequently they are anonymous, unless they are all men, when it may be recorded, for instance, that 64 men died. Thus it would appear that the dead of disasters are distanced and denied, and become anonymous.

As to why these deaths should become so 'anomymous', it may be that by their nature their sudden, untimely and unexpected nature, they are more threatening. They confront every individual's sense of personal invulnerability, and the more so because they are multiple, many at one time. And they are threatening because they have happened, not to the bad, or the ill, or the old, but to others like the self.

And when deaths *are* defined by identity and gender, we often find men at work, men and their place or occupation as part of the identity of these disaster deaths – 'miners' or sailors', for instance. On the other hand, women's deaths are often defined by the role as mothers – for instance, with their children if these have died, or as 'mother of two'. While such categorizations are not universal, they are frequent, and as with personal disasters, they reflect the gender themes of the society as a whole.

DISASTERS AND THE DEFEAT OF DEATH

Much emphasis is, quite naturally, placed on the prevention of death in disaster, the rescue and who is saved. The rescuers are portrayed heroically and great emphasis is placed on stories of the rescue and, often, the ways in which the rescuers have risked their own lives. This portrayal of heroes again shows the powerful role of men in the emergency, police and other services, and strongly endorses their priorities for the rescue of women and children. These powerful images of 'helper' and 'rescuer' are presented in stereotypes emphasizing the powerfulness of these roles as opposed to the weak and helpless victim. This achieves a number of purposes: it reassures the helpers of the value of their role and may serve to protect them from feelings of inadequacy, uncertainty and failure; it emphasizes their potency as defeaters of death. Thus it is another frame of reference by which the shocking and massive nature of disaster deaths can be distanced and denied. However there is a darker side to this denial, as will be discussed below. For the impact of these disaster deaths on the workers who deal with them may lead to stressor effects with adverse outcomes for well-being.

IMAGES OF DEATH AND DISASTER

A critical aspect of disasters is the massive interest they attract from the media and the images by which they are therein immortalized. These images of death have also had significant influence on Australian awareness of and response to death.

Several aspects are relevant. Firstly the visual media, particularly television, provide visual and other immediate images of the disaster as it happens, or as the rescue proceeds. The deaths are there and personalized, although individual bodies are covered for the propriety of anonymity. Each watcher may think: 'is that my loved one? or may vicariously experience the threat, dread and relief, or watch with horror and fascination. Death by disaster is brought to the living-room, with its directness, randomness, and massive nature. People may talk about, face and deal with death more directly because of this, and this has certainly been the case to an increasing degree, as television has portrayed these events with increasing colour, clarity and reality over the last four decades. Not only is local disaster portrayed, but also the more massive disasters of other peoples, other worlds, with deaths in numbers so great that they become meaningless alongside smaller Australian populations.

Most vivid of death portrayals in the media – disaster deaths not of this country, but of others, which have influenced the Australian awareness of death – have been the images of Vietnam and, more recently, the vivid bombings of Bahrain and the Gulf War and the genocide of Bosnia and Rwanda. These deaths affecting others, not the lucky country, have nevertheless heightened Australian awareness of death and how it could be, or could have impacted on Australians directly. Where they have been personally involved, for instance, peacekeeping soldiers who have been to Somalia and Rwanda, Australians have been psychologically traumatized by the deaths they viewed. Refugees in Australia from the former Yugoslavia, as well as many other war-torn countries, have been similarly affected.

Another aspect of the publicization of disaster death has been the convergence of those who come to a disaster site to watch. These are often so great in numbers as to interfere with the rescue operations. However, many are critical of this 'vicarious' indulgence in death and call those who watch ghouls. This watching serves many purposes, from the wish to master vicariously the mystery and horror of such unexpected deaths to the unconscious indulgence of one's own destructiveness. It serves both negative and positive ends and the balance may vary in individuals. Ultimately, however, to watch reinforces the value of one's own life and personal survival – perhaps even to the level of guilt, survivor guilt at the joy one feels at having survived instead of others, who have died – perhaps in one's place. Whatever, this phenomenon of vicarious mastery of death through the deaths of others is common, and represents one aspect of death awareness that is heightened by disasters.

Grief is also thrown into public awareness at the time of disaster. The multiple deaths cause grief for affected communities and families. The media informs of these, shows images of grieving families and calls for compassion and support for those who have lost loved ones. Memorial ceremonies are encouraged, become public statements and events, and are presented as appropriate communal responses to the deaths and losses that have occurred. In this way the public nature of disaster deaths and the grief accompanying them have provided foci for awareness of those realities of death and grief, and the normality and appropriateness of open grieving. This facilitation has not occurred in isolation however, because it has been alongside similar changes in Australian and other Western societies with the increased understanding of and openness about grieving. Self-help movements for special griefs, such as death of a spouse, sudden infant death, and death of a child, have all represented social processes of change in grieving patterns and in support for grief, and have taken place internationally, and in Australia.

Nevertheless the particularly evocative and distressing nature of multiple deaths in disaster is a special focus for community interest and has led to increased recognition of the naturalness of support and even professional counselling to facilitate grieving. This is so much so that in the most recent years, it is stated and recognized that grief or trauma counselling should be automatically provided in such circumstances.

The publicity of disasters, both internationally and nationally, has also led to a demand for compassion for those affected by such traumas and death. Questions have arisen recently as to whether undue and repeated exposure to disaster leads ultimately not to greater sensitivity but rather to numbing, cutting-off, and 'compassion fatigue'. This lies alongside the question as to the effects of television and other such processes, whether they promote violence or enhance recognition of other lives, as opposed to making reality and fantasy boundaries less clear and thus these deaths 'unreal' and of no personal significance. There is as yet no scientific answer to these questions.

DISASTER DEATHS AND MENTAL HEALTH

Disasters have been an increasing focus for mental-health research in Australia and this disaster research has been at the forefront internationally. It has focused on two key aspects of disaster deaths and has increased understanding of the impact of disaster deaths or disaster life-threat on others, through the 'encounter with death' *per se* as well as through understanding of grief (Raphael 1986).

The evolving research processes and the associated mental-health service implementation have been reviewed elsewhere (Raphael and Meldrum 1993). This highlights understanding of how disaster deaths and threat of death during disaster subsequently impact on well-being, for instance, effects of a 'mortality stressor' as compared to the relocation stressor on mental well-being of people evacuated after the Darwin cyclone, the former causing early effects. McFarlane (1988) was able to show the role of threat of death in contributing to acute post-traumatic stress reactions experienced by volunteer bushfire fighters after the Ash Wednesday fires of 1983. The difficulties of dealing with the gruesome and mutilating deaths of others has been shown to be a specific stressor affecting workers involved in rescue and recovery operations (Raphael *et al.* 1983–84), especially when these deaths are multiple. Here the images may be of 'row after row of grey bodies laid out in the morgue', 'bodies crushed like sardines' or of smell of death at a rescue site. These images of death may lead to nightmares, flashbacks and hyperarousal, perhaps to the level of Post-Traumatic Stress Disorder, both for rescuers after a major disaster, or for emergency workers after the smaller disasters of everyday life, such as motor-vehicle accidents.

Nevertheless it has been the work of disaster research that has consolidated this awareness of the psychologically traumatic effects of threat of death and personal encounter with death. This awareness was highlighted by Stretton's recognition after the Darwin cyclone of the long-lasting effects of 'scars on the mind'. It is now considered appropriate to provide briefing and debriefing, as well as counselling, in an attempt to prevent these adverse effects, or psychological scars, from developing. Over recent decades disaster-related research on the effects of death stressors has led to these understandings and to the provision and public sanctioning of such support services.

This has been particularly relevant with respect to emergency services. These services have a strong 'macho' ethos and militaristic tradition. They have usually been heavily male-dominated with a culture that anything can be dealt with; that there will be no emotional response. And in this context death also was seen to have no effect. This culture of denial meant that many men who were affected emotionally could not admit any such distress to themselves or to others. Casualties in terms of stressor effects nevertheless occurred, and still do. This male culture of denial prescribed, for instance, silent coping, heavy drinking, or aggression to deal with effects and to shut out memories of the deaths that were confronted or the personal life-threat experienced. While this continues to a degree, one result of the research and public awareness has been the lowering of this defensiveness for men and an increasing recognition of the naturalness of stress reactions to such death exposure, and acceptance of support to deal with them. Most organizations now require and provide support for their workers, their men, to help them through these psychologically traumatic experiences associated with disaster deaths.

Another aspect of the mental-health research and response after disasters has been to do with the particular aspects of grief after such deaths where the nature of the types of deaths that occur may make grieving more complex. Sudden deaths; deaths that are untimely, in that they affect people who are often young and well; deaths where there may be difficulties with the bodies being mutilated by the disaster destruction or unable to be found; deaths where there may be uncertainty as to how and why the person was amongst the dead; all these aspects have been established to be associated with greater problems of grieving (Raphael 1983). These are not 'good deaths' (Kellehear 1990). There is no time for preparation, for goodbyes, for resolving ambivalences, for putting affairs in order. In addition social fabric and networks may be disrupted by the disaster, and social support unavailable for the resolution of grief. Studies of disaster bereavements have highlighted these special aspects of death and grief and the problems associated with them in terms of the mental well-being of bereaved survivors (Singh and Raphael 1981).

Societal response has progressively changed with disasters in Australia over the last decade from a situation where counselling support was seen as an intrusion, to a recognition of needs, and special counselling for those who have faced death, or lost loved ones. For instance in the Newcastle earthquake, and in the Australia Post shooting in Melbourne, extensive counselling programmes were implemented, indicating the public and organizational acceptance of these death issues.

Further indication of changed public attitudes lies in the memorial ceremonies for grief and for the dead that are now part of many communities' responses in the post-disaster phase. There may also be recognition of the recovery from deaths in community rituals, theatre, art and writing. These latter are important because they indicate community empowerment to overcome the disaster deaths and not to be eternally 'marked' by the aspect of disaster.

The themes of death still symbolize, however, values of society and one further change of significance is that related to recognition of effects on children. At the earlier times children would have been viewed as significant only in terms of effects of parents. The studies, research and clinical work evolving over the last twenty years have changed this. It is now recognized that children have been affected by death, by both exposure to death and life threat, by the deaths of others and by grief. Specific programmes now encourage children to discuss openly such issues of death, to act out concerns and to write and respond through books, school work, discussion and other formats, to deal with the impact of such stressors. Thus attitudes to and understanding of the effects of death on children has been highlighted by disasters. While this has undoubtedly been occurring on a wider scale and with other aspects of death and children, the public nature of disasters, the focus of community response, and the awareness of the traumatic impact of death, have all created an environment which has promoted the institutionalization of these altered provisions in care for children, for example in schools, families, or in other systems (Wraith and Gordon 1993).

DEATHS OF WAR

If war is the ultimate disaster it is important to note a growing, if ambivalent, change in attitudes to the deaths of war. It was, fifty years ago, the expectation that the returning soldiers of the Second World War would have been unaffected by the deaths they confronted; the threat of their own death as a constant; the gruesome deaths of comrades; the deaths they inflicted on the enemy. If they dwelt on these deaths they were told to put them behind them 'like men'. If they were distressed by them in ongoing ways they were seen as being personally inadequate, not being 'man enough'. These attitudes were challenged by the understandings that arose following the Vietnam War, first in the USA and then later in Australia. It has progressively become accepted that the costs of war lie not only in the body count of deaths, but in the impact of death on those soldiers who survive the combat, and that the extent of exposure to death in combat (threat of death and the deaths of others) directly and linearly predicts some death of the soul for those so savagely exposed. This psychiatric morbidity has been one recognized legacy of war, and indicates, in its very acceptance, a change in Australian attitudes to soldiers and to war and its consequences.

DEATH AND THE TYRANNY OF DISTANCE

Despite the changes that have occurred, despite the public and displayed reaction to traumatic deaths, individual and disastrous, there is still a distancing from deaths that are 'closer to home'. This is most directly obvious with the multiple deaths of overwhelming disasters in other countries, with distant wars. But it is also a factor for deaths within Australia where the community does not seem to come to terms with the reality of deaths that are socially distant. Higher mortality rates, for instance, with the premature deaths of aboriginal Australians whose years of life are 20 less than non-aboriginal Australians, have not led to effective actions to alter this statistic which in some senses is worsening. The social distance is such as to allow the denial of the significance of these losses, particularly when considered alongside racism and other discrimination. So that community attitudes that call for good health, and an end to premature deaths, still carry a social value which gives inadequate priority to the deaths of the socially distant. This appears most grossly for aboriginal Australians, but also as well for other disadvantaged groups, for although social justice is a political priority, in reality some lives are still seen as of greater value, some deaths a greater priority for prevention.

CONCLUSION

Disasters and the public attention to them have both focused some heightened awareness of death and its impact, and lessened some Australian denial. But these deaths too are framed by the social contexts of Australia: care is given, response is empathic, men may now fear death and women grieve. Death is vividly real, feared, fought heroically, but still not a close and accepted fact for the 'lucky' of the 'lucky country'.

REFERENCES

Carroll, B. (1977) *Disaster, Horror and Fear in Australia,* Sydney: Bacchus Books.

Wraith, R., and Gordon, R. (1993) 'Responses of Children and Adolescents to Disaster', in J. Wilson and B. Raphael, *International Handbook of Traumatic Stress Syndromes,* New York: Plenum.

Kellehear, A. (1990) *Dying of Cancer. The Final Year of Life,* London: Harwood Academic Publishers.

McFarlane, A.C. (1988) 'The Longitudinal Course of Posttraumatic Morbidity. The range of outcomes and their predictors', *Journal of Nervous and Mental Disease,* 176: 30–9.

Parker, G. (1977) 'Cyclone Tracy and Darwin Evacuees: On the restoration of the species', *British Journal of Psychiatry,* 130: 548–55.

Raphael, B. (1983a) *The Anatomy of Bereavement,* New York: Basic Books.

Raphael, B. (1983b) 'Psychiatric Consultancy in Major Disaster', *Australia and New Zealand Journal of Psychiatry,* 18: 303–6.

Raphael B. (1986) *When disaster strikes,* New York: Basic Books.

Raphael, B. and Meldrum, L. (1993) 'The Evolution of Mental Health Responses and Research in Australian Disasters', *Journal of Traumatic Stress,* 6, 1: 65–89.

Raphael, B., Singh, B., Bradbury, L. and Lambert, F. (1983–84) 'Who Helps the Helpers? The effects of a disaster on the rescue workers', *Omega,* 14, 1: 9–20.

Singh, B., and Raphael, B. (1981) 'Post Disaster Morbidity of the Bereaved: A possible role for preventive psychiatry', *Journal of Nervous and Mental Disease,* 169, 4: 203–12.

7 Is There a British Way of Death?

Glennys Howarth

INTRODUCTION

If we are to consider singularly 'British' deathways we ought to be describing rituals common to three distinct countries and cultures: Scotland, Wales and England. Yet whilst there are many common legal and bureaucratic procedures required at death, commonality is not so clear in the case of cultural rituals. As in many other areas of political, social and economic processes, so in death the three countries which constitute Britain are assumed to share the cultural characteristics of the dominant country – that is, England. In death, as in life, however, this assumption is perverse since Scotland and Wales maintain traditional, national and regional rituals.

So, if it is difficult to talk in any meaningful way of a British way of death let us instead concentrate on the English way of death, for it is the culture of the English which is deemed to dominate common perceptions of 'Britishness'.

Despite increasing multi-culturality in the daily intercourse of English society, many aspects of social life for people of minority status are marked by discrimination and prejudice. Counter-intuitively perhaps, in the social organization of death, marginality has not been equated with inferior rituals. Indeed, it is often assumed by the dominant voices in the new open discourse on death that ethnic minority groups have somehow sustained more meaningful funeral rituals – long since lost to mainstream English society (Hockey 1996). Members of funeral reform groups and bereavement counselling professionals are keen to learn from the deathways of minority ethnic groups both within and outside England who have retained their traditional rituals. By contrast, the English way of death is repeatedly depicted as cursory, privatized, emotionless and meaningless (Albery *et al.* 1993;

Spottiswood 1991; Walter 1990; Young 1996).

Modern English deathways tend to be perceived as lacking individual control over funeral rituals, by professionalization, bureaucracy, brevity of ceremonies, inadequacy of mourning customs, and as culminating in privatized and pathological forms of grief. Before examining the accuracy of such portrayals let us first pause to consider this apparent loss of meaningful rituals; for if we have now lost meaningful rituals we must once have enjoyed them. It is difficult to encapsulate a definition of 'meaning' but it seems likely that in order for death rituals to be meaningful in any emotionally satisfying way they must be *understood* and internalized by the participants. Furthermore, a lack of meaning assumes a lack of quality and commentators often relate this to a loss of tradition (Walter 1994). Time-worn ceremonies where mourners know and understand the procedures, play their roles without prompting and fulfil the ritual expectations of others, are perceived as inherently meaningful.

In search of the English way of death, this chapter will concentrate first on the Victorian period. Nineteenth-century obsequies are characterized as expressive and flamboyant, entailing elaborate codes of mourning (Curl 1972; Morley 1971). The first mention of inadequate mourning of funeral rituals appears in the twentieth century and often laments the loss of socially prescribed mourning procedures, which once furnished guides to appropriate behaviour, enabling the bereaved to grieve and their friends and relatives to support them during that time (see Gorer 1965; Pincus 1976). Having presented the conventional picture of death in the nineteenth century the discussion will re-examine this portrait and question the extent to which these Victorian trends were enjoyed by all sectors of society. Finally, contemporary deathways will be considered in order to shed light on the assertion that, as a result of professionalization, English deathways have become shabby and meaningless.

FROM RURAL TO URBAN DEATHWAYS

Perhaps one of the most well-known and abiding images of the traditional English way of death is that captured around

1750 in Gray's 'Elegy Written in a Country Church-yard', in which the reader is lulled by the peace and tranquillity of the churchyard, nestling in the idyllic English countryside.

> The Curfew tolls the Knell of parting Day,
> The lowing Herd winds slowly o'er the Lea,
> The Ploughman Homeward plods his weary Way,
> And leaves the World to Darkness and to Me.

One of the clearest messages in the prose is that even in the class-divided society of England at that time, death was the great leveller.

> The Boast of Heraldry, the Pomp of Pow'r,
> And all that Beauty, all that wealth e'er gave,
> Awaits alike th'inevitable Hour,
> The Paths of Glory lead but to the Grave.[1]

This was written of a period prior to industrialization when funerals for the majority of people were organized by the community, the parish coffin borrowed as temporary housing for the corpse and the procession to the churchyard met at the lich-gate by the priest.

The realities of mortality which lay behind this somewhat romantic representation of death are difficult to assess with any degree of certainty. What is certain, however, is that the ideal was soon to come to an end. With the Industrial Revolution came large-scale migration from the countryside into urban centres in search of work, wages and a measure of independence. Much of England's 'green and pleasant land' soon gave way to urbanization and industrialization which resulted in the creation of an urban working class who gave up the plough and learnt to live and die in the shadow of the 'dark satanic mills'.[2] Rapid growth of the towns and cities was concomitant with, and stimulated by, the emergence of an entrepreneurial class – *nouveaux riches,* keen to separate themselves both spatially and socially from the mass of labouring poor.

Despite advances in technologies of production and increased wealth for the new middle classes, death was never far away. Towns were harbours of disease with repeated outbreaks of tuberculosis, typhoid and cholera attributable to polluted water supplies and insanitary and overcrowded living conditions. In London, ignorance of the hazards associated with human decay led to contamination of the Thames by putrefaction from cemeteries located on the banks of the river. For the time being, death appeared to continue to play the role of the great leveller, taking rich and poor, young and old.

The most striking and memorable representations of death in nineteenth-century England are probably the flamboyant funeral processions and the elaborate extra-mural cemeteries with their exquisite architecture. Death rituals were largely designed and controlled by the Church and the undertaking industries. Whilst the former decreed the style of liturgy and dealt with the spiritual requirements of the deceased and the survivors, the latter handled all the material provisions for an 'appropriate' funeral and for mourning attire. Strict codes of mourning, varying according to rank and social status, stipulated the appropriate funereal expenditure and regulated every detail from the correct length of black crêpe to the proper number of mutes, feathermen and horses' plumes (Morley 1971). The code also decreed the length of time the bereaved should remain in black garb and the precise stages at which they must shed their mourning clothes as they returned to normality – the desired end for all except Queen Victoria, who chose to wear her widow's weeds to the end of her days.

After the passing of the 1850 Metropolitan Internment Act extra-mural cemeteries were created to provide burial space for all the urban centres. The first notable London cemetery, consecrated in 1832, was at Kensal Green, closely followed by Norwood in 1837; Highgate in 1839; Abney Park, Brompton and Nunhead in 1840 and Tower Hamlets in 1841. Burial in cemeteries was invariably expensive and a Romantic Movement fashion ordained the purchase of an impressive monument to mark the status of the family and proclaim the great loss suffered. Inhumation in these private graveyards was soon viewed as a symbol of wealth. Kensal Green, a favourite with the rich and famous, became a promenading centre for nineteenth-century society and its monuments a source of spectacle and wonder.

So in envisaging the English way of death in the nineteenth century we broadly invoke an image of an individual dying a 'good' and pious death at home surrounded by family and friends. The significance of this 'good death' is well documented (Beier 1989). After death, the family would consult the undertaker and associated traders such as the carpenter and draper and, adhering to suitable criteria accorded to their social status, they would purchase an expensive and flamboyant funeral service. The horse-drawn cortège would wind its way through the city streets to the distant cemetery where the deceased was laid to rest amid much pomp and ceremony; the monument subsequently erected served as a detailed and intricate reminder of the individual's accomplishments in life.

Towards the end of the century, however, death began to go out of fashion (Jacobs 1899). With greater emphasis placed on nutrition and a better understanding of public health and sanitation, the 1870s witnessed a decline in the mortality rate. So much so, that for the first time in history, wealthier sectors of society could expect their offspring to outlive them (Mitchison 1977). As death began to weaken its grip on life Romantic representations associated with the beautiful death also began to lose sway. The pomp and ceremony came to lack its former lustre and death gradually became a much quieter affair. Public-health reformers, who played an important role in 'taming death' (Ariès 1981) were also hard at work denouncing the extravagance of funeral expenditure and the avarice of the undertaking industries. Although the First World War greatly accelerated the curtailment of elaborate death rituals (Wilkinson 1996; Jupp this volume), the trend had already been set in motion by the turn of the century.

Today, almost a century later, funeral reformers continue to condemn what they regard as exorbitant funeral expenditure (see Office of Fair Trading Report 1989) but are now simultaneously concerned with what they perceive as the loss of meaning in English funeral rituals. Loss of meaning is usually related to the professionalization of deathwork (Clark 1982), to the loss of individual control over the ritual preparation of the body and organization of the funeral (Spottiswood 1991), and to the perfunctory manner in which the ceremony is conducted (Walter 1990; Young 1996). The thrust of these criticism is that the modern emphasis on bureaucracy and expertise has demoralized and disempowered a whole nation.

RITUALS THROUGH OTHER EYES

One of the enduring impressions of England is that it subscribes to an entrenched hierarchy of social class – the 'rich man in his castle – the poor man at the gate'. It is my assertion, however, that what has been perceived as the English way of death – so frequently depicted as having its heyday during the Victorian period – is little more than a celebration of the death rites of the English middle classes. Indeed, despite the efforts of the nineteenth-century Reform movement which emerged in the latter part of the century and sought to rescue the urban labouring poor from extravagant expenditure on funeral rituals, 'meaningful' rituals were not stripped from the working classes. The latter bear a different relationship with death than do the middle classes – surviving in overcrowded, slum dwellings took the romance out of death for a class of people on whom death fed disproportionately to their wealthier counterparts (Winter 1982). Higher-status funerals captured the attention but they were not the experiences and rituals of the English working classes. Proselytizing middle-class funeral mores to the working class only partially succeeded as less affluent communities came to adapt their traditions and to combine Victorian flamboyance with simpler customs consistent with the modern practices engendered by the twentieth-century medicalization and professionalization of death.

To explore this thesis let us return to our description of nineteenth-century death rites and consider the extent to which these rituals were typical, and question whether the English are quite so disempowered in death as conventional wisdom would lead us to believe.

The literature exploring the concept of the 'good death' – an apparently central feature of earlier death rites – rarely questions whether dying according to these religious criteria was relevant to the deaths of members of the urban lower classes. It is assumed that although the poor had little or no access to the literary representations which modelled the 'good death' – religious texts, novels, children's rhymes and stories, and so on – the ideas pervading these media would be accessible to them through religious teaching and popular culture (Walvin 1982). There is scant evidence for this assumption. Indeed, if we scrutinize texts which portray the nineteenth-century urban poor, it seems that religion may not have been at the forefront of their lives. Drawing from Mayhew's work (1861–62), for example, many of the labouring poor may not have benefited from the services of the clergy in helping them to achieve, or even contemplate, the good and pious death.[3]

Cemeteries, although elaborate in some quarters, had other less attractive areas of consecrated ground. For every grand mausoleum erected, hundreds of paupers were buried in common graves, the 'respectable' poor buried in unmarked plots or marked only by a small numbered stone. Nor did the working classes parade to the cemeteries in grand horse-drawn carriages swathed in black crêpe and escorted by truncheon-carrying attendants. These were unquestionably the preserves of wealthy Victorians. The ways of death of the English working classes were far more modest and less obtrusive affairs.

Although all social classes had regular and frequent experiences of death in the nineteenth century, the frequency of exposure increased the lower down the social hierarchy one looked. The decline in the mortality rate in the latter part of the century (a crucial factor in modifying funeral rituals) was more significant for higher-status groups than for the poor. The depreciation in fertility which accompanied and emphasized this improvement had negligible impact on the families of the poor until after the First World War (Mitchison 1977). For them there was no fall in infant mortality rates until the early twentieth century. For working-class people large families continued to be the norm. Death was not 'unfashionable' for the poor – it continued to be a significant fact of life until the 1930s.

Indeed, it was just as death was going out of fashion for people of higher social status, that the respectable working classes, through the creation of burial clubs and the help of trade associations, were increasingly able to afford 'decent' funerals – rather than pauper burials – and they were not about to give that up. The 'decent' funeral which fitted the pockets of the working class was a far simpler affair than that usually conceived of in representations of the funerals of this period – the code of mourning demanded far less expenditure from lower social classes. Cassell's *Household Guide* of 1874 prices a funeral for 'a gentleman' at between £200 and £1,000, compared to a handsome £4 expected of a member of the labouring classes (Morley 1971). For the poor the lengthy distances to the new extra-mural cemeteries had added a further obstacle to their ability to acquire a 'decent' burial and escape the stigma of a pauper funeral or worse still, dissection at the hands of the surgeon or anatomist (Richardson 1987). Their predicament resulted in the success of the burial club movement. Weekly payments were made for each family member and in the event of death (provided a minimum premium had been paid), the claim against the club guaranteed meeting funeral costs. The importance of burial clubs for the poor is emphasized by an account of working-class lives before the First World War:

> A working man and his wife . . . are likely to lose one or more of their children. The poorer they are, the more likely are they to lose them. Shall they run the risk of burial by the parish, or shall they . . . insure each child as it is born, at the rate of a penny a week? If they decide not to insure, and they lose a child, the question resolves itself into one of borrowing the sum necessary to pay the funeral expenses, or of undergoing the disgrace of a pauper funeral. The pauper funeral carries with it the pauperization of the father of the child – a humiliation which adds disgrace to the natural grief of the parents. More than that, they declare that the pauper funeral is wanting in dignity and in respect to their dead. . . . This may be sheer prejudice on the part of poor parents, but is a prejudice which richer parents . . . if confronted with the same problem when burying their own children, would fully share.
>
> (Pember-Reeves 1979: 67–8)

Class differences in mortality rates and the attainment of decent burials were social factors either overlooked or of little interest to middle-class reformers of Victorian genteel society who were strong in their reprobation of an urban poor who, in their view, squandered their meagre resources on elaborate funerals. One of the most renowned campaigners for reform, Charles Dickens, was vociferous in his condemnation of the squalor of urban graveyards, of the greed of undertakers, and of the capriciousness of the working poor in their extravagant expenditure on funerals. Another reformer, Edwin Chadwick, in his 'Supplementary Report on Interment in Towns, 1843', recommending extra-mural cemeteries, concluded that £4–£5 million was "annually thrown into the grave". A not insubstantial element of this sum, he stated, was accounted for by the funerals of the poor. This expenditure was berated by more fortunate sectors of society who readily digested the cliché that the working class would rather see their children starve than undergo a pauper's burial. Furthermore, reports appeared in newspapers and journals of people hoarding corpses until they were able to meet the costs of the funeral.[4] This revelation not only offended the middle-class sense of decency but heightened the fear of contamination by the diseased poor. The latter had to be persuaded to limit their unreasonable expenditure and the funereal exhibition which stood as a reminder of the way in which death had come to rule life (Howarth 1996a).

Let us now turn our attention to contemporary funerals.

CONTEMPORARY FUNERALS: THE LEGACY OF THE VICTORIAN REFORMERS

In perceiving modern English death rituals as meaningless the focus of commentators is often on the time spent in the crematorium – a cursory twenty minutes – viewed as token and institutionalized ritualism. We may speculate that the success of the nineteenth-century reformers in reducing flamboyance and expense has resulted in abridged and inconsequential funeral ceremonies which are no longer able to luxuriate in time, expense and spectacle. Yet to concentrate only on the funeral ceremony is apt to mislead because it fails to take much account of rituals which accompany and surround death, such as community responses; visits of sympathy from relatives, friends and colleagues; the use of flowers as expressions of sorrow and loss; wakes; funeral teas; and so on. For although the ceremony in the crematorium chapel may have become the focal point of death for some, this is not a generalizable experience.

Moreover, for some time it has been regarded as tasteless to view the body of the deceased; as better to cremate rather than to bury (religious preferences notwithstanding); to avoid using the funeral company's mourning cars when travelling to the crematorium (in other words, to dispense of the funeral cortège and meet the coffin at the crematorium); to disperse quickly after the ceremony, perhaps only meeting with other members of the family for tea and drinks when they have travelled great distances. Like the cultural condescension with which the middle classes once viewed the trinity of ceramic flying ducks on the living-room walls of working-class homes, the ostentatious funeral has for the middle classes became a thing of the past – and with it, meaning in funeral rituals has evaporated. In other words, the opportunities for mourners, friends and relatives to openly demonstrate their loss, to present a show of affection for the deceased, and to display their feelings to the whole community have been discarded on grounds of social status and good taste. The rejection of emotional exhibitionism has led to the disappearance of many traditional customs from the funerals of members of the wealthier sectors of society. Simple marks of respect such as the closing of curtains and the doffing of hats as the cortège passes are assumed to be things of the past.

Yet although these deathways may be lost to a middle class who have culled their emotional worlds in search of rational, tasteful practices, they have not necessarily been excised from all sectors of the working classes where traditions tend to linger and retain their cultural significance (Pickering 1974). Although there is clearly a growing preference for simple funerals – not least prompted by financial necessity – many have kept a taste for show. It is not necessary to attend the funerals of ethnic minority groups in England to observe meaningful death rituals. They are also alive and well among many members of the white working classes. In my study of funerals in the East End of London (Howarth 1996b), a traditional working-class area of the metropolis, I witnessed much which contradicted the assertion of contemporary funeral reformers that the English way of death is impoverished. Visits of respect to the bereaved family, for example, continue to be important in these working-class communities. Viewing the body of the deceased is usual in this area of London, and, according to numerous professionals, this practice is commonplace in other regions of England. Whole families are likely to visit the funeral director's premises to say a last goodbye; some come in groups for support, others come alone and may visit again and again before the funeral.

Funeral flowers have come to be considered an expensive and evanescent expression of sympathy – better to donate the money to a medical charity associated with the death. Yet the ritual gift of flowers continues to have symbolic significance in working-class funerals. They show sympathy for the bereaved; they are used as tokens of the esteem and affection felt for the deceased. They may also be used as representations of loss, for example, when floral tributes are constructed in the shape of an 'empty chair'. The relatively new ritual of depositing flowers at the scene of a sudden or tragic death is a method by which people can express sympathy for others whom they may not personally know.

On the day of the funeral families are unlikely to agree to meet the hearse at the crematorium. Indeed, if there are sufficient funds and enough mourners they may hire a number of mourning cars to ensure that the cortège is striking and impressive. Resurgent interest in the horse-drawn hearse and carriage is further evidence of working-class desire to give their loved ones a 'good send-off'.

During my ethnographic study of funeral behaviour I observed many mourners who rejected the emotionless way of grief. They have hurled themselves into the grave in open and unashamed expressions of anguish and torment, poured beer over the coffin in celebration of the deceased's erstwhile joys in life, screamed, wailed, laughed, cried, argued, fought each other and cursed the deceased. Displays of emotion were by no means lacking.

CONCLUSION

In a detailed and persuasive attack on the romanticism of authors, such as Ariès and Gorer, who regret the passing of Victorian mourning practice, Cannadine argues that 'the conventional picture of death in the nineteenth century is excessively romanticized and insufficiently nuanced' (1981: 188). Whilst this analysis is undoubtedly accurate it fails to emphasize the extent to which representations of Victorian rituals were overwhelmingly confined to middle-class funeral practice. In critiquing what I have defined as the English middle-class way of death, however, there is a danger of romanticizing working-class rituals – where funerals are redolent of meaning and brimming with satisfaction. Whilst it would be fallacious to represent the English working class as a homogeneous group enjoying colourful and traditional death rites, it is equally questionable whether the dissatisfactions expressed by largely educated and white middle-class commentators are applicable to other social groups in English society. In some ways these contemporary reformers parallel their nineteenth-century counterparts in that discontent expressed with English deathways is premised upon an interpretation of ritual from a dominant social perspective: a reading which focuses on the relatively brief funeral ceremony and neglects the richness of family and community conventions which surround it.

When referring to the English way of death it is not sufficient to rely on manifestations of authority, on the medicalization of dying or on the professionalization of funeral services, all of which are seen by social observers as depriving people of the opportunity to control this important ritual. The myth that we now live in a classless society effectively renders members of less powerful groups invisible, silencing their ways of life and death. For if England dominates the other countries of Britain in assumptions about cultural characteristics, the dominant voice of England and the perceived deathways of the English remain those which emanate from the England of the white middle classes.

NOTES

1. Extracts from Thomas Gray, 'Elegy Written in a Country Church-yard' reproduced in J. Hayward (ed.) (1978) *Penguin Book of English Verse*, London: Allen Lane, pp. 225–6.
2. Phrases from the English hymn, 'Jerusalem, in C. Hubert Parry (1925) *Songs of Praise*, Oxford University Press.
3. Although it is important to note that we must not assume that the urban poor were a homogeneous group – some were religious, others not; some were regular church attenders, others had no formal knowledge of, or desire for, religious teachings.
4. Many of these reports confused the delay attributable to lack of funds with that imposed by the necessity for Sunday funerals. The working class laboured six days a week, leaving only Sunday free for funerals. If death occurred early, or alternatively too late, in the week to arrange a burial, the corpse would inevitably remain in the house for a number of days.

REFERENCES

Albery, N., Eliot, G. and Eliot, J. (eds.) (1993) *The Natural Death Handbook*, London: Virgin.

Ariès, P. (1981) *The Hour of Our Death*, Harmondsworth: Penguin.

Beier, L.M. (1989) 'The Good Death in Seventeenth-century Great Britain', in R. Houlbrooke (ed.), *Death, Ritual and Bereavement*, London: Routledge.

Cannadine, D. (1981) 'War and Death, Grief and Mourning in Modern Britain', in J. Whaley (ed.), *Mirrors of Mortality*, London: Europa.

Clark, D. (1982) *Between Pulpit and Pew*, Cambridge: Cambridge University Press.

Curl, J.S. (1972) *The Victorian Celebration of Death*, Newton Abbot: David & Charles.

Gorer, G. (1965) *Death, Grief and Mourning in Contemporary Britain*, London: Cresset.

Hockey, J. (1996) 'The View from the West: reading the anthropology of non-western death ritual', in G. Howarth and P.C. Jupp (eds.), *Contemporary Issues in the Sociology of Death, Dying and Disposal*, Basingstoke: Macmillan.

Howarth, G. (1996a) 'Professionalizing the Funeral Industry', in P.C. Jupp and G. Howarth (eds), *The Changing Face of Death*, Basingstoke: Macmillan.

Howarth, G. (1996b) *Last Rites: the work of the modern funeral director*, New York: Baywood.

Jacobs, J. (1899) 'The Dying of Death', *Fortnightly Review*, New Series 72: 264–9.

Mayhew, H. (1861–2) *London Labour and the London Poor*, 4 vols., London: Cass. Mitchison, R. (1977) *British Population Change Since 1860*, London: Macmillan.

Morley, J. (1971) *Death, Heaven and the Victorians*, London: Studio Vista.
Pember-Reeves, M. (1979) *Working Class Wives*, London: Virago.
Pickering, W.S.F. (1974) 'The Persistence of Rites of Passage: Towards an explanation', *British Journal of Sociology*, 25, 1: 63–78.
Pincus, L. (1976) *Death and the Family*, London: Faber & Faber.
Richardson, R. (1987) *Death, Dissection and the Destitute*, London: Routledge & Kegan Paul.
Spottiswood, J. (1991) *Undertaken with Love*, London: Robert Hale.
Walter, T. (1990) *Funerals: and how to improve them*, London: Hodder & Stoughton.
Walter, T. (1994) *The Revival of Death*, London: Routledge.
Walvin, J. (1982) *A Child's World: a social history of English childhood, 1800–1914*, Harmondsworth: Penguin.
Wilkinson, A. (1996) 'Death and Two World Wars', in P.C. Jupp and G. Howarth (eds.), *The Changing Face of Death: historical accounts of death and disposal*, Basingstoke: Macmillan.
Winter, J. (1982) 'The Decline of Mortality in Britain 1870–1950', in T. Barker and M. Drake (eds.), *Population and Society in Britain 1985–1980*, London: Batsford Academic.
Young, M. (1996) 'What a rotten way to go', *The Guardian*, 31 January, p. 2.

8 Women, Death and *In Memoriam* Notices in a Local British Newspaper

Sheila Adams

Death and *In Memoriam* notices are inserted in a local newspaper at a time of emotional distress, when the death of a close relative or friend disrupts the continuity of a social and personal life-history threatening the ontological security of the bereaved. This chapter will suggest that these notices help the bereaved to maintain and re-establish a sense of social and biological continuity in their life-histories. The notices are inserted within the context of a shared framework of reality which, at the turn of the century, was informed by the ideology of motherhood. This change in emphasis was associated with a significant restructuring of the notices in the twentieth century.

The chapter outlines the methodology used to analyse the notices and its limitations and a short description of the socio-economic and religious background of the inhabitants of Coventry, an industrial city in the British Midlands. The accessibility of the local newspaper, the *Coventry Evening Telegraph* (*CET*), to its potential market of readers and inserters of the notices is discussed, before looking at the ways in which the restructuring of the notices reflects the changing status and value of the role of the working-class wife and mother.

A Death notice informs the reader of a death and, after 1930, the time and place of the funeral. An *In Memoriam* notice is inserted to mark the anniversary of the death; or after 1950, the birthday of the deceased. The notices inserted in the local newspapers for the month of February in every decade from 1850 until 1980 were analysed. Unfortunately the geographical boundaries used to collect the statistics for the city's population, mortality rates or circulation of the newspaper do not correspond. It was not possible to relate the number of notices to any of these statistics. The increase or decrease of *In Memoriam* notices in relation to Death notices are expressed as a percentage of the Death notices, e.g. in February 1980, 686 *In Memoriam* notices are expressed as 179 per cent of the 383 Death notices; the duplication of *In Memoriam* notices is ignored, e.g. 1,100 insertions in 1980 refer to 686 persons.

It was not possible to look at ethnicity in relation to the notices. The surnames suggest that notices are only inserted by families of United Kingdom origin; although a significant proportion of Coventrians have come to the city from Southern Asia and by 1988 formed an estimated 8.6 per cent of the city's population (Coventry Health Report 1989). This suggests that perhaps older members of the Asian community, who are responsible for funeral arrangements, do not share an identical framework of reality[1] or a sense of the appropriate or acceptable response in certain situations with families of different traditional, cultural and religious origins.

The identification of the deceased's occupation and religion proved problematical; these are rarely recorded in the notices or the local authority records. However, it seems that since the early part of the nineteenth century, Coventry's population has contained a high proportion of the working class. William Ranger, in his report to the General Board of Health in 1849, said, 'since the town has no suburbs, no villa residences, all who are not engaged in trade or professions . . . are obliged to seek a home elsewhere'. By the 1930s the city was noted for 'the middle class exodus to the surrounding countryside . . . it was a prosperous working class stronghold' (Hodgkinson 1970). This characteristic of the city's population, of a higher proportion of working class than the national average, has been retained since the Second World War; the 1981 census showed 46.4 per cent in social classes IIIb (skilled manual workers) and IV (semi-skilled manual workers) compared with a national average of 38.4 per cent (Lancaster 1986).

The membership of the larger Christian churches (Church of England, Roman Catholic, Presbyterian, Methodist and Baptist) in the United Kingdom has declined throughout the twentieth century, from 74.5 per cent in 1900 to 16.8

per cent of the adult population in 1980 (Brierley and Hiscock 1994/95). Nevertheless, 'most, if not all, the British retain some sort of religious belief' (Davie 1994: 69). Davies and Shaw's survey of 1995 suggests that three-quarters of the population believe in some form of afterlife. Jon Davies suggests that the *In Memoriam* notices in a local newspaper are 'a kind of populist, latter-day mass media chantry' (1994: 35), pointing to a belief in purgatory as a continuing relationship between the living and the dead. Alali also suggests, in his analysis of Nigerian notices, that 'direct contact and communication with the deceased' and a 'belief in the personal immortality of the soul' (1993: 119) are indicated by the notices.

However, the insertion of *In Memoriam* notices in the *CET* has declined from a peak of 324 per cent of Death notices in 1930 to 179 per cent in 1980, which might indicate a declining belief in purgatory and the immortality of the soul. However, the response to Dr Marshall's Virtual Memorial Garden on the Internet (Langton 1995) points to the importance for many people of some form of memorial to the deceased. The memorials recall a shared reality and sense of biographical continuity, enabling the individual 'to keep a particular narrative going' (Giddens 1991: 54) and sustain a sense of self-identity.

ACCESSIBILITY OF THE NEWSPAPER

The technology required to gather, transmit, print and distribute the news quickly and in large quantities developed during the second half of the nineteenth century. However, the circulation of a newspaper also depends on a 'literate people who can afford the expense and time to read' (Bertrand 1969). Both the *Coventry Standard* (*CS*), established in 1741, and the *Coventry Herald* (*CH*), established in 1808, were published weekly, and at $4\frac{1}{2}d$ a copy in 1870, were expensive. Their readers were probably members of the literate middle class of the city; the majority of Coventrians would only have had access to the papers in the Mechanics Institute's library, established in 1828, and the free public library which opened in 1873.

'We can only guess at the circulations of most newspapers during the period of secrecy between the 1850s and the 1930s when all but a few jealously guarded the volume of their sales' (Wadsworth 1955: 1). The circulation of national and provincial newspapers increased at the turn of the century, probably due to the decreasing cost of a newspaper and the growing literacy of the population following the Education Acts. By the 1950s 'the British read more newspapers than any other people on earth' (Bertrand 1969: 15); about 611 per 1,000 of the population compared with 353 in the USA and 263 in Federal Germany (UNESCO 1952 in Wadsworth 1955).

The *Midland Daily Telegraph* (*MDT*), later the *CET*, was founded in 1891 and published daily at ½*d*, or about 0.6 per cent of the average weekly wage. By 1930, when the foundations of Coventry's 'boom town prosperity' (Thoms and Donnelly 1986: 24) were laid, it dominated the local newspaper market and had become an 'institution in the city' (Harrison 1991). The majority of the *MDT*'s readers were members of a 'prosperous working class' (Hodgkinson 1970).

THE NOTICES

The average weekly wage for engineering workers in Coventry in 1910 was £2, when a notice cost 1*s* for 16 words and 6*d* for every additional 6 words. A notice of some 25 words cost 2*s* or 5 per cent of the weekly wage. The cost of an insertion seems to have remained around 5 per cent of the average weekly wage to the present day. The number of insertions does not seem to be influenced by cost. However, the daily publication of the *MDT*, which meant a death could be notified within a day or two of the event and a bereavement recalled on the anniversary, does seem to have influenced the number of notices inserted in the paper. By 1915, 23 Death and 58 *In Memoriam* notices were inserted in the daily *MDT* compared with 15 Death and 9 *In Memoriam* in the weekly *CS*.

Death notices increased in the decade between 1930 and 1940, from 73 to 211 insertions in February. This increase does not seem to be associated with the mortality rate in Coventry, which fell slightly from 9.6 per 1,000 in 1930 to 9.3 in 1939 (CHR). The increase may be associated with the rapid rise in the city's population from 167,083 (1931 Census) to 234,000, as revealed by the issuing of ration books in January 1940 (*CET* 16.1.1940). However, this increased population was largely due to the migration of young single men to work in the 'shadow' factories built in the mid-1930s to realize 'Britain's aim to achieve air parity with Germany' (Richardson 1972: 65). It is unlikely that these young men, having left their families of origin in their home towns, would insert Death notices. The increase is probably associated with the deaths of those who had become regular readers of the local newspaper in the early decades of the century and whose families wanted to inform friends, workmates and relatives of a death. A typical Thanks notice reads:

> Mrs Black, 2 Hampton Road, wishes to thank relatives, friends and neighbours, also workmates of the Daimler, the A.E.U. and Stoke Aldermoor Club for their kind sympathy and floral tributes in her sad bereavement
> (*MDT* 3.2.1940).[2]

In Memoriam notices, first inserted in 1890, began to increase just before the First World War, from 42.4 per cent of Death notices in 1910 to 176.3 per cent in 1915. The increase may be associated with the growth of the Spiritualist movement during and after the First World War, which Cannadine sees as 'the private denial of death' (1981: 227). However, only 14 per cent of the 1920 *In Memoriam* notices use the term 'killed', which suggests that the loss of men during the First World War does not account for the increase. It is possible that the working-class people, whose deaths were notified in the 1940s, having become regular readers of the *MDT* in the early part of the century, inserted the increasing numbers of *In Memoriam* notices in the decades between 1920 and 1930 to mark the anniversary of the death of a relative.

The popularity of Death and *In Memoriam* notices was associated with the wider circulation, among a predominantly working-class population, of a daily local newspaper which had become 'an institution in the city and kept people informed' (Harrison 1991). In 1983 it was noted that 'the Family Notices column in the Evening Telegraph attracts more readers than almost any part of the newspaper' (Campey 1983). The insertion of a Death notice became a 'tradition' informing the discourse constructing the shared framework of reality.

FORMAT OF THE NOTICES

Until 1940 between 25 per cent and 35 per cent of the *In Memoriam* notices were laid out in the format of the poem:

> **SPENCER** Treasured memories of a dear wife and mother, who died February 26th 1922.
> Her loving ways and smiling face
> Are happy to recall;
> She had a friendly word for each,
> She died beloved by all.
> Always remembered by husband, sons and daughters.
> (*MDT* 26.2.1940)

By 1950, although the wording is often similar, the poem format is no longer used, and the words follow each other in the same line:

> **BAKER** (Sarah) – Died February 20, 1949. 'A smiling face, and heart of gold, no better mother this world could hold.' Mary, Donald and Else. (*CET* 19.2.1950)

The alternative format was probably introduced following a policy decision by the *MDT* in response to the rationing of newsprint from 1940, a ration imposed by the government after the commencement of the Second World War in 1939 until 1956 (Bertrand 1969). The poetry format does not reappear in the newspaper but is apparent in the examples of *In Memoriam* notices held at the *CET* in 1995. The 41 examples are kept to help people choose a notice but the format is rarely used.[3] Of these examples, 71 per cent mention 'God'; however the word only appeared in

20 per cent of the notices inserted in 1980.

The majority of notices are composed by reference to back copies of the paper, and written out at home. The wording is not cut or altered to reduce the cost of the insertion, unlike other forms of advertising. The notices, like those appearing in Nigerian newspapers, 'do not include the flaws of the deceased' (Alali 1993: 122). When, on very rare occasions, the notice does not follow the accepted format, the *CET* will suggest alternative wording or refuse to publish a notice seen as inappropriate and likely to cause offence to other readers.

Death notices are now inserted by the funeral director. Some families have the notice written out ready for insertion, but the form and wording is usually discussed and agreed by the family and funeral director.

Death and *In Memoriam* notices are composed by reference to previous notices and/or the expert knowledge of the funeral director, within the context of their own specific traditional and cultural framework of shared reality or awareness of the appropriate public response to a death.

RESTRUCTURING OF THE NOTICES

Until the last decades of the nineteenth century Coventry's economy was dominated by the traditional crafts of ribbon-weaving and watchmaking. Both industries entered a period of slow decline after 1860 when foreign ribbons could be imported free of duty (Thoms and Donnelly 1986). By 1869 only 20 ribbon manufacturers were left in the city, compared with 120 firms in 1826. Many Coventrians left the city to seek employment in the Lancashire cotton textile industry and the new elastic web-weaving factories in Leicester (Smith 1946). Working-class Coventrians could not afford to buy or insert a notice in the local newspaper.

Marriage, until the passing of the Married Women's Property Acts of 1870 and 1882, suspended the being and legal existence of a woman. All her property, the control of her body and children passed into the control of her husband. The identity of the middle-class woman was rooted in her relationship to the male head of household. 'Wives, children, servants, labourers, all could be described in the language of paternalism as the dependants and children of their father, their master and their guardian' (Davidoff and Hall 1987: 21). This is reflected in the notices inserted in the later half of the nineteenth century, which identify men by their occupation or social position, and women and children by their relationship to the male head of household:

> On the 16th, aged 43, Mr John Charles Peters, school master of the Free School, Chilvers Coton (*CS* 25.2.1870).
> On the 2nd last, aged 65, Elizabeth, wife of George Bennett, of Much Park Street, in this city (*CS* 15.2.1850).
> On the 20th inst, aged 14 months, Annie Eliza, only child of Mr F W King, Little Park Street (*CS* 17.2.1860).
> On the 12th last, aged 75, Frances, youngest daughter of the late Mr Thomas Allen, woolstapler, of this city (*CS* 22.2.1850).

The notice informed business colleagues and acquaintances of a death. There is no suggestion of personal or family loss. The middle-class woman and mother is invisible in the notice, reflecting the suspension of her being and legal existence on marriage. The notices, in their affirmation of the value and status of the middle-class male head of household, confirm a shared patriarchal framework of reality.

Throughout the second half of the ninenteenth century, the predominantly middle-class, feminist movement in Britain gradually became more organized, with a higher public profile, in the campaigns to repeal the Contagious Diseases Act of 1864; for the Married Women's Property Act of 1870; and for women's suffrage from the 1860s (although this was not achieved until 1928). The activities of these middle-class women were reported in the local press. The Editor of the *CH* saw the enfranchisement of women as inevitable. 'There are arguments for and against women's suffrage, but there is no argument that will break down persistency in a cause not obviously absurd, and which is supported by reputable political authorities' (*CH* 10.11.1906). Middle-class women were apparent in the discourse which informed a shared framework of reality.

The Married Women's Property Acts of 1870 and 1882

gave women the right to control their earnings and any wealth they might acquire. These acts may be seen as foreshadowing the recognition of a married woman's legal existence and joint responsibility as parent. The first Death notice in which a child is identified in relation to both parents appeared in 1880:

> NUGENT – On the 4th inst, at Victoria Road, Tamworth, after a year's suffering, Helen, aged 7, a beloved child of John and Hannah Marshall Nugent. (*CS* 13.2.1880)

This form of Death and *In Memoriam* notice for children was the accepted form by 1910. The notice acknowledges that both parents have lost a child, although the joint responsibility of parents was not recognized legally until the 1925 Guardianship of Infants Acts.

'The campaign to glorify, dignify and purify motherhood and to transform this image into reality began in earnest soon after the Boer War' (Lewis 1980: 13). The poor physical condition of the average army recruit for the Boer War of 1899–1901 and imperial rivalry between European nations heightened fears that Britain did not have the fit and healthy manpower necessary to compete successfully on the battlefield or in industry (Jones 1986). The high infant mortality rates – one out of every eight healthy babies died within the first year – were seen as a waste of life and manpower and understood to be a 'failure of motherhood'. Working-class women were 'in the greatest need of instruction' (Lewis 1980: 19). In December 1905, Coventry Health Committee appointed a Health Visitor to visit houses and give 'instructions as to keeping the house clean and sanitary, as to the feeding and rearing of children, in order to prevent the large infant mortality' (*CH* 15.12.1905).

Coventry's economic fortunes began to change in the last decade of the nineteenth century with the development of the bicycle and motor-vehicle industries, machine-tool manufacturers, Courtaulds, the Coventry Ordnance works and the General Electric Company. Wages were high and attracted many migrants (the majority being single young men) into the city, and the population increased from 46,563 in 1881 to 106,349 in 1911. Many working-class Coventrians could now afford to buy and read the local paper regularly – in 1906 the *MDT* had a daily circulation of some 10 000 copies.

The newspapers reflected the attention given to the role of the working-class mother during the first decade of the twentieth century and, for example, reported:

(a) The question of extending the cookery accommodation (in elementary schools) should be considered, so that it may be possible to give each girl a longer course in the important subject (CEM 23.11.1904).
(b) The appointment of a Health Visitor.
(c) Education (Provisions of Meals) Act 1906 as 'so many working class children, through no fault of their own, were not able thoroughly to take advantage of education . . . due to improper feeding' (*CH* 29.3.1907).
(d) The exclusion of children under five years from public schools as their proper place was at home (CEM 4.5.1908).
(e) Education should aim to teach children 'to appreciate the benefits of a clean and healthy body rather than turning out dirty citizens when they grow up' especially as 'they were supposed to be training an imperial race' (*CH* 18.6.1909).
(f) Dispensing with the services of married women teachers after 31 July 1909 to stimulate the employment of certificated teachers reinforced the notion that 'a woman's sphere was at home looking after the rising generation' (*CH* 30.4.1909).

Suffragette meetings, which were frequently noisy and disturbed, received extensive coverage. The majority of suffragettes believed women were 'the natural custodians of childhood' but argued that maternal values should be extended into the world outside the home (Lewis 1984: 105). At one meeting in Coventry, Miss Gladice Keevil suggested that the interference of politicians in the home justified the interference of women in politics. 'Babies were emphatically women's business, and if babies were the business of politicians then politics was the business of women' (*CH* 21.11.1908). The papers also encouraged women to be good housewives by printing 'Hints for the Home' with information about the treatment of colds, cleaning white lace, airing clothes, drying damp rooms, and so on.

The press, health, employment and education policies, maternity and child-care provision all stressed the value of the working-class wife and mother in preserving the life and health of the child. The infant 'can only be saved by the mother' (Herbert Samuel, MP, in Llewelyn Davies 1984). This discourse informed the shared framework of reality shaping the working-class man's view of his wife and the children's view of their mother. In 1920 a Death notice might read:

> **WALKER** on the 14th February 1920, at 20 Drapers Fields, Anna, the dearly loved wife of Arthur Walker, aged 58 years, after a painful illness. (*MDT* 16.2.1920)

and an *In Memoriam* notice:

> **WATSON** In loving memory of our dearly loved mother, Eliza, who passed away at 8 Eden Street, Feb. 15 1919. Ever remembered by Flo, Albert and Fred. (*MDT* 16.2.1920)

The working-class woman was loved and valued, and she became visible in the notices, which reflected the social value of her role as wife and mother. In 1920 *In Memoriam* notices represented 180 per cent of Death notices, of these 21 per cent were inserted for a mother and 9 per cent for a father. The role of the mother in the working-class family assumed a greater value than that of the father in the eyes of the children, whose physical life and health depended on her. It seems that 'the hope of working women's groups and middle class women's organisations that the new emphasis on motherhood', would improve the status of mothers' (Lewis 1980: 20) was realized.

The decrease in infant mortality rates between the two world wars was associated with a declining concern with the physical survival of children. However, 'the ideology of motherhood survived. By the 1950s the emphasis shifted from the physical to the psychological needs of the child' (Lewis 1980: 225) and the 'new ideal of the small family' (Weeks 1989: 202). The change in emphasis to the small intimate family is reflected in the heading at the top of the column, which became 'Family Notices' by 1990. The new heading implies that 'births, marriages, deaths, in memoriam and thanks' – the former headings – are primarily the concern of the family unit.

Since the 1950s 'psychology has been instrumental in constructing the ways in which motherhood is seen' (Phoenix and Woollett 1991: 13). As John Bowlby said in 1953, 'it is essential for mental health that an infant or young child should experience a warm, intimate and continuous relationship with his mother' (Bowlby 1987: 13). The child-care and motherhood manuals of the 1960s and 1970s, written by doctors and psychologists, describe motherhood as a special, creative and positive experience characterized by loving relationships within a happy, nuclear, stable family. The nature of motherhood is constructed as crucial for women and mothers are understood to carry 'the responsibility for the normal development of the well-adjusted individual' (Marshall 1991: 83). By 1980 a Death notice might read:

> **SMITH** – Edith Ann, 15 Arthur Street, Coventry, loving wife of Albert, loving mother of Leslie, passed peacefully away in hospital, aged 75 years, on Thursday February 21. Funeral service on Tuesday, February 28 at Canley Crematorium, commencing at 1.20 pm. Deepest sympathy by all the family. Flowers to the Cooperative Funeral Service. (*CET* 23.2.1980)

and an *In Memoriam* notice:

> **DEWSON** (Mary) In loving memory of a dear wife, Mum and Grandma. Always loving, gentle and kind, what a beautiful memory you left behind. From husband, Arthur, daughter, Florrie, Harry and family. (*CET* 4.2.1980)

The wife and mother is identified by the loving and caring quality of her relationship with individual family members. The altered emphasis of the 'ideology of motherhood' to psychological care is reflected in the notices.

The notices ascribe to mothers the qualities of 'loving' and 'caring' associated with the good, normal mother in the social construction of the 'ideology of motherhood'. The notices reflect an ideology which understands that the responsibility of the loving and caring mother is to facilitate the development of her child into a normal, well-adjusted adult (Freud 1962). 'Any flaws of the deceased' (Alali 1993: 122) or qualities which conflict with the ideology are omitted. The acknowledgement of any flaws in the mothering experienced by the child would imply that the child was not a well-adjusted adult. The sense of social and biographical continuity rooted in the shared reality and the 'capacity to keep a particular narrative going' (Giddens 1991: 54) would thus be threatened.

The notices are written with reference to a shared framework of reality and facilitate the ability of the individual to maintain a sense of social and biological continuity during a period of transition following a death. The notices of the second half of the nineteenth century reflected the shared reality of the value and status of the middle-class male head of household and the suspension of his wife's existence. The social continuity of his biographical narrative was maintained in the notice. In the early part of the twentieth century the ideology of motherhood informed the shared reality. The value of the mother in the physical and psychological care of her child is reflected in the notices assisting the bereaved individual to maintain a sense of biological continuity and identity in the construction of their family history.

NOTES

1. Giddens (1991) discusses the concept of a shared framework of reality and the reflexive understanding of self-identity in terms of his or her biography.
2. In order to protect the identity of the deceased and family, all names and addresses, etc., have been changed.
3. Semi-structured interviews were conducted with members of staff at the *CET* who assist members of the public in inserting notices and advertisements in the paper. The wording of advertisements, e.g. items for sale, jobs, services offered, etc., will often be altered to reduce the number of lines used and therefore the cost.

REFERENCES

Alali, A.O. (1993) 'Obituary and In-Memoriam Advertisements in Nigerian Newspapers', *Omega*, 28, 2:113–24.

Bertrand, C.J. (1969) *The British Press*, Paris: OCDL.

Bowlby, J. (1987) *Child Care and the Growth of Love*, London: Penguin Books.

Brierley, P. and Hiscock, V. (eds.) (1994/95) *UK Christian Handbook 1994/95*, London: Christian Research Association.

Campey, R. (1983) 'Your CET', *Coventry Evening Telegraph*, 18 October 1983.

Cannadine, D. (1981) 'War and Death, Grief and Mourning in Modern Britain', in J. Whaley (ed.), *Mirrors of Mortality*, London: Europa Publications.

Coventry City Council Minutes (CM).

Coventry Education Committee Minutes (CEM).

Coventry Evening Telegraph (*CET*), 1950–1980.

Coventry Health Reports (CHR).

Coventry Herald (*CH*), 1850–1930.

Coventry Standard (*CS*), 1850–1930.

Davidoff, L. and Hall, C. (1987) *Family Fortunes*, London: Hutchinson.

Davie, G. (1994) *Religion in Britain since 1945*, Oxford: Blackwell.

Davies, D. and Shaw, A. (1995) *Reusing Old Graves*, Crayford, Kent: Shaw & Sons.

Davies, J. (1994) 'One Hundred Billion Dead', in J. Davies (ed.), *Ritual and Remembrance*, Sheffield: Sheffield Academic Press.

Freud, S. (1962) *Two Short Accounts of Psycho-Analysis*, Harmondsworth, Middlesex: Penguin Books.

Giddens, A. (1991) *Modernity and Self Identity*, Oxford: Polity Press.

Harrison, J. (1991) *Coventry Evening Telegraph*, Special Edition, 5 February 1991.

Hodgkinson, G. (1970) *Sent to Coventry*, Bletchley: Robert Maxwell & Co.

Jones, G. (1986) *Social Hygiene in Twentieth Century Britain*, London: Croom Helm.

Lancaster, B. (1986) 'Who's a Real Coventry Kid', in B. Lancaster and T. Mason (eds.), *Life & Labour in a 20th Century City*, Coventry: Cryfield Press.

Langton, J. 'A fallen soldier attains immortality on the Net', *Sunday Telegraph*, 8 October 1995.

Lewis, J. (1980) *Politics of Motherhood*, London: Croom Helm.

Lewis, J. (1984) *Women in England*, Brighton, Sussex: Wheatsheaf Books Ltd.

Llewelyn Davies, M. (ed.) (1984) *Maternity*, London: Virago.

Marshall, H. (1991) 'The Social Construction of Motherhood', in A. Phoenix, A. Woollett and E. Lloyd (eds.), *Motherhood*, London: Sage.

Midland Daily Telegraph (*MDT*), 1900–1940.

Phoenix, A. and Woollett, A. (1991) 'Introduction', in A. Phoenix, A. Woollett and E. Lloyd (eds.), *Motherhood*, London: Sage.

Ranger, W. (1849) *Sanitary Condition of Coventry and the Sewering of the*

City, Report to General Board of Health held in Coventry City Record Office.

Richardson, K. (1972) *Twentieth Century Coventry*, Coventry: City of Coventry.

Smith, F. (1946) *Coventry: Six Hundred Years of Municipal Life*, Coventry: City of Coventry.

Thoms, D.W. and Donnelly, T. (1986) 'Coventry's Industrial Economy 1880–1980', in B. Lancaster and T. Mason (eds.), *Life & Labour in a 20th Century City*, Coventry: Cryfield Press.

Wadsworth, A.P. (1955) *Newspaper Circulations 1800–1950*, Manchester: Norbury, Lockwood & Co.

Weeks, J. (1989) *Sex, Politics & Society*, London: Longman.

9 The Social Construction of Funerals in Britain

Bernard Smale

The perceived reality of funerals in Britain, as presented by funeral directors, is that they reflect traditional beliefs, meet client needs and are dignified and appropriate. Underlying these manifest claims lie the unstated assumptions that they accurately reflect British cultural norms and are 'necessary' in their present form to meet the specific needs of their customers. Funeral directors exist because they have convinced the general populace that occupational specialism is applicable to the private, personal, emotional, transfixing moment of death.

In this chapter the construction of funerals is examined to show how such significant events come to command widespread acceptance. It argues that the perceived 'reality' of a funeral is the consequence of the creative potential of participants, who act 'as if' there is an objective phenomenon, 'the funeral', with an existence independent of each separate construction. Such an argument runs counter to everyday, common-sense assumptions held by most participants. For them a funeral is a taken-for-granted event which requires no philosophical interpretation. It most obviously has a beginning, middle and end, and is open to be labelled 'good' or 'bad' by reference to commonly accepted standards. It is real and factual. The sociological perspective adopted here requires that the word 'reality' is placed in brackets to indicate that any claim to reality is constrained by place, time, belief and individual perception.

Most people take for granted that they inhabit a world that is real. The phenomena of everyday life appear to be patterned in a manner independent of the observer. The 'reality'[1] of a phenomenon is accepted as a given, existing before an observer becomes aware of it and, in naming it, gives it a concrete solidity. A reification takes place in order to be reassured that the physical and social world *is* stable, coherent and ordered, not imaginary, insubstantial or transitory. Yet it is obvious that what is considered 'real' to a person in one social group may be regarded as unreal in another. Berger and Luckmann reinforce this view by grounding it empirically when they write that 'what is "real" to a Tibetan monk may not be "real" to an American businessman' (1966: 15). Thus 'reality' is a social construct open to contending apprehensions and subject to distinctive interpretation. The consequence of accepting the existence of multiple realities is to question the basis of taken-for-granted 'knowledge'. If 'reality' is socially determined then 'knowledge' is also socially created because the term implies *certainty* that phenomena are 'real' and possess specific, identifiable characteristics available to independent verification.

A key concept in understanding how a belief in the existence of an objective world of events can arise is that of 'ideology'. Mannheim (1936) outlines a *general* aspect of ideology which asserts that *all* knowledge expresses a relation between a particular style of social existence and a consequent mode of intellectual production. 'Belief' and 'knowledge' are thereby framed in a boundaried vision, which confines thought and directs action.

It is argued here that it is impossible to see the world, or to think of it, without a specific perspective which gives it coherence and induces a belief that it possesses an existence independent of its observation. Thus what is perceived as 'real' will have 'real' consequences. It follows that the concept, 'funeral', is a consequence of a mind-set which creates an objective reality – a construct to which each physical performance will approximate. Thus funerals are the outcome of social negotiation between people who possess unequal power to influence their production. They operate within an ideological framework and the 'reality' they apprehend does not exist a priori outside their creative potential. They are actors in face-to-face interactions producing performances on the basis of imperfect information. Funerals are to be considered as examples of focused interaction where the patterned adaptation to perceived rules, including conformance and excusable infractions, constitutes a specific form of social order (Goffman 1972). Within each socially situated occasion, termed 'a funeral', there exists a particularly strong defining potential possessed by the funeral specialists. This allows them to exert considerable influence over its construction and presentation.

The following pages outline the manner in which funeral directors in Britain have operated to exploit a significant market position in a competitive capitalist economy.

FUNERAL RITUALS

Anthropological studies confirm that cultures throughout the world, past or present, tribal or industrial, have developed ceremonies to mark the transition from living to dead and to sanction specific styles of performance by the living. Funerals are powerful, symbolic performances which focus attention on significant status transformations. They exemplify van Gennep's (1909) analysis of *rites de passage* whereby powerful sentiments and physical transformations are given symbolic expression. Any organization, association, business or family that can regularly and successfully create, present and direct such an important ceremony is in a dominant position *to define* appropriateness and significance for inexperienced mourners.

Funeral directors throughout Britain are complacent about the service they provide, considering it to be client-orientated, tasteful, dignified, efficient, skilful and representative of 'traditional' beliefs. It is argued here that the general presentation of funeral ritualism is in practice tawdry, lacking in sensitivity to individual needs, unnecessarily routine in operation, excessively expensive and self-perpetuating. As Johnson (1996) observes, 'The average British funeral is a miserable and disappointing affair . . . the contemporary funerals lacks meaningful symbolism, dignity, adequate time and comfort for those who mourn . . . such an unsatisfactory funeral may, nonetheless, cost in excess of £1000' (Dead Citizens' Charter, 1996). Funerals in Britain do *not* reflect cultural 'folk' history, nor do they respond accurately to the practical and social needs of the bereaved. Rather, funerals are staged performances in which a specific occupation acts as producer and director in order to maintain economic profit and occupational prestige. Adopting business stratagems to exploit a lucrative market, they have been nationally successful in creating a demand for their services. Until recently they have fostered impressions of local, person-orientated, family businesses committed to a form of social service in which profitability was presented as a necessary concomitant of satisfactory service.

The construction of this public front, the background stratagems and the current changes in ownership and financing need to be examined.

THE BRITISH FUNERAL

A funeral is a dramatic performance staged to emphasize specific concepts. Within each performance status transformations are formally confirmed and potentially disruptive emotions given acceptable discharge. Funerals do not just happen idiosyncratically – they are created, circumscribed and stage-managed. They may, therefore, be subjected to critical evaluation like any other performance in which actors seek to convince audiences, and themselves, of their authenticity and competence. Those who produce funerals exert a subtle and influential defining potential which may, or may not succeed. To call the performance 'a funeral' is more a *post-hoc* confirmation of a director's skill than it is a 'dignified' representation of death. As Young (1996) contends: 'The average modern British funeral is a disgrace. Providence cannot have laid it down that this is how we should bury our dead' (1996: 2).

A successful funeral will transform a cadaver into an ancestor, relic, spirit or memory and will create a social space in which the bereaved may move, with reluctance, resignation or acceptance, to new social roles. Simultaneously, viewing audiences and loose assemblies become focused mourners, selectively herded into prescribed places and available for capture as potential customers. Funeral directors are transformed from virtual to actual specialists as they ensure that all potential difficulties are neutralized. They create consensus in performances where individualism could hinder smooth progress from act to act. All involved in the production belong to this significant occasion and play suitable roles where situational proprieties are so highly significant that they become guides to appropriate behaviour and discourse. Such patterned behaviour creates the dramatic performance which sustains an illusion of historical authenticity. The possibility of underlying rules (surviving from previous ages) being non-existent is unlikely to occur to participants who are actively collaborating to create the 'reality' of rule-governed necessity. It is quite possible that this is of no great importance to them – playing the game *as though* it were authentically rule-governed may be sufficient. Existentially, however, the 'reality' does not exist without the constant exercise of directorial definition and active audience participation.

FUNERAL DIRECTING

Funeral directing resembles other occupations requiring a situational face when controlling the space, movement, time and talk of those they are nominally expected to serve. The marshalling and controlling techniques used by uniformed police at demonstrations; the firm direction of first-time publics by gowned ushers in courts of law; the hushed verbal control exercised by cathedral vergers over milling visitors – from each officiating occupation there emanates an unmistakable controlling virtue. Whilst each seeks to set boundaries to social encounters, the significant difference between funeral directors and other defining bodies lies in their prominence in what is essentially a ratification ritual. This ceremony defines and, formally or informally, *endorses* important changes in status, role relationships and self-definition. It is the role of the director to produce a ceremony in which transformations, or relocations, emerge *without* undue participant awareness. Baptismal, initiatory, betrothal and marriage rituals openly demonstrate and celebrate a significant change in status and social behaviour. Bereavement roles are neither sought nor willingly accepted, and few of those who become newly located realize the degree to which they are guided, however benignly, by directors. For example, whilst a bereaved wife is 'virtually' a widow immediately upon her husband's death she is, in a sense, in limbo. The activities and sentiments developed through the funeral ceremony ratify her 'actual' status as widow; by passing through a sequence of events she emerges significantly changed.

An examination of the mourners' choice of coffin will illustrate the extent of funeral-director control. This powerfully symbolic purchase carries, by imputation, the respect, belief, taste and generosity of the bereaved. Biodegradable coffins have been available in Britain since Francis Haydon introduced cheap 'Earth to Earth' coffins in the 1870s, but it is through the high cost of (superficially) strong and durable boxes in the range of £600 to £1,000 that directors receive the greater proportion of their income. They claim that a high mark-up on the approximate retail cost of £50 is necessary to cover all the associated expenses of limousines, workshops, offices and salaries. Expecting mourners to choose coffins in the interquartile range rather than the ostentatious, or the symbolically and monetarily 'cheap' models, directors ensure that the price of these coffins is sufficient to meet their costs and provide the desired profit. One independent director, known personally to the author, only stocks one model as experience informs him that, in most cases, he will successfully steer customers to his preferred choice.

In Britain most mourners never handle a coffin or see the model they choose to buy, as they select it from a catalogue. This item is not closely scrutinized compared with other consumables purchased at a comparable price. Furthermore they do not examine the quality of the chipboard, beading, handles, name-plates, religious symbols and lining material used in its production and would probably be dismayed with the flimsy, cheap and unimaginative materials. Yet, convinced by the director's sales talk, customers regularly buy, believing the coffins to meet every requirement of dignity, taste and expense – in that order.

Sales success is due to the combined effects of six factors which give funeral directors a negotiating skill lacking in their customers:

1. *Image* The creation of an acceptable and trustworthy 'face' which is presented as an outward manifestation of inward moral integrity.

2. *Secrecy* The separation of body-handling activities from the public presentation of a funeral ceremony.
3. *Interpersonal skills* The social manipulation of changing audiences in face-to-face encounters.
4. *Commercialism* A commitment to competitive individualism within an open-market economy.
5. *Directorial control* Personal influence over the creation, staging, presentation and 'tone' of the funeral.
6. *Professionalism* Exploitation of clients with needs they do not feel competent to satisfy themselves.

The first four three factors are common to funeral directors in most industrialized, urbanized countries such as Canada, France and the USA; it is the latter two that influence British directors most. They have developed a style of production allowing them to frame the ceremony in a manner which reduces customer choice and maximizes their own 'professionalism'. They assume a degree of paternalism and a social support role which, they claim, eases the customer through a period of difficult transition. This is not the perceived role of directors, who have fully embraced the inherent commercialism of their work. Many British directors are reluctant to openly admit that their chief concern is to make a profit from the goods and services they provide, preferring instead to emphasize their professionalism. Although unjustified, this status is claimed by them acting as if there existed a core of esoteric knowledge, a commitment to public service, special skills and client autonomy (Smale 1985). In Britain they lack the credentials of the 'true' professions, such as medicine, law and religion, which have received state licensing of their activities. Whilst the funeral business sets its own standards of training, provides certification, and has developed associations to influence members' practices and ethics, it does not have the power to deny entry to the occupation, to enforce training, or to subsume other essential occupations such as clergy, embalmers, and crematoria superintendents, within its defining framework. Despite much effort they have not received state approval to have sole control over death ritualism. If they openly acknowledged their commercial orientation and provided quality merchandise with open customer choice they would lose the ambiguity which has imbued the occupation for so long. A similar uncertainty had weakened the self-identity of directors in the USA (Habenstein 1955).

Such ambiguity does not exist in contemporary USA or Newfoundland, where directors present a unified business orientation and provide a wide range of goods in clean, large, well-appointed funeral homes, where the bereaved and mourners have control. They do not provide an agenda for mourners to follow nor a cortège in which to show themselves in decorous solemnity in a public display. Customers pay a high price but gain autonomous control over all aspects of a funeral except direct body-preparation. These directors do lay claim to professional standards (but this is common to almost every occupation from prostitution to police), they avoid however the *moral* professionalism claimed, overtly or latently, by so many practitioners in Britain. In other words, they sell merchandise with honesty and skill but do not presume to *create* funerals.

During the last fifty years in Britain there has been an accelerating take-over of many smaller and medium-sized family funeral firms, where the commercial–professional ambiguity has been most pronounced. As large and economically powerful businesses have taken over smaller concerns, commercialism has become more noticeable. Even though family names retained importance (Chappell, Dottridge, Gillman, Kenyon, Leverton, Shakespeare, Truelove, Uden, to name a few in the London area alone), they were kept as fronts which concealed the movement towards even larger companies. National and international organizations now seek to dominate the entire death-work market by owning crematoria, cemeteries and extensive networks of high street funeral directors. This is the most important development in the funeral industry at the present time, not only because it challenges the entire concept of private family firms offering individually tailored funerals for the locality where they are well known, but because it makes it even more difficult for the customer to influence the content and style of the funeral.

One reaction to the intimidating influence of large multinational companies has been the formation of the Society of Allied and Independent Funeral Directors (SAIF), which seeks to protect the independence of smaller businesses from the predatory advance of large concerns, whether indigenous Co-operative Associations or the free-market companies arriving from France or the USA. The influx of foreign capital is to be expected because it reflects the underlying logic of competitive, free-market capitalist ideology. Entrepreneurial capitalists claim that concentrating resources into strategically located command centres enables them to be channelled efficiently to meet consumer demand, thereby rationalizing both human and material costs. Leaving aside the meaning attached to the term 'rationalization', the consequence of claiming that 'economies of scale' will be beneficial for all concerned has led to goods, vehicles, drivers, bearers, conductors and directors being dispatched from distant centres to supply local needs.

The first face-to-face contact experienced by a prospective customer may be with a receptionist in a local office who merely channels information upwards to a line manager. The conductor or director dispatched for the funeral ceremony itself may be unknown to the customer. Such conditions already operate within some Co-operative Associations and are the most likely outcome of the succession of mergers and 'take-overs' that are restructuring the funeral trade. Many caught up in this transformation, from medium-sized family firms to large companies, claim that this results in a denial of the 'local service' ideal they have so continuously stressed. For example, the long-established family firm of Kenyons of London which serviced the wealthy and the aristocracy was bought out by Hodsons of Birmingham to become Hodson–Kenyon. Twenty-eight per cent of this company's shares were taken up by the French giant, Pompe Funèbre Générale (responsible for 73 per cent of French funerals) and was renamed Pompe–Hodson–Kenyon (PHK), thereby capturing 11 per cent of the UK market. In 1990 PHK shares were bought by entrepreneurs in the USA wishing to expand into Europe. The resulting organization, Plantsbrook Group, had shares distributed in the UK (65 per cent), France (28 per cent), and USA (9 per cent). Because there had been widespread flotation of English shares among several groups, effective control was in the hands of the French. At the same time the Great Southern Group, which owned many funeral firms and crematoria, was captured by US capital; the resulting amalgamation is entitled Service Corporation International (SCI). This powerful organization is estimated to control 17 per cent of the funeral market in the UK, and to own 13 of the 36 privately-owned crematoria. In opposition to this foreign encroachment stand the Co-operative Movement, with a 25 per cent share, and private businesses, with a 58 per cent share of UK funeral businesses.

The crucial concern among the indigenous companies is the willingness of local authorities to sell their crematoria to SCI. Their fears are raised by the Secretary of State's intention to press ahead rapidly with a privatization bill which *encourages* local authorities to sell crematoria to private interests. The inducement to do so is that they will be allowed to keep 90 per cent of the income so generated, in contrast to the 50 per cent they had previously been permitted to hold.

According to the pressure group National Funerals College (NFC 1996), the economic power possessed by SCI will enable it to construct a vertical progression from the many funeral firms they own to their own crematoria. About 80 per cent of urban funerals and 65 per cent of *all* funerals use cremation for disposal. Critics agree that in buying up weaker firms and forcing out smaller competitors SCI will create local monopolies. Eventually, they believe, SCI will create a national monopoly because there is no government regulator to check expansion. The consequence, they claim, will be an increase in funeral prices and the demise of small, independent firms. It is possible therefore that the ownership of costly crematoria will become the central issue, with funeral firms providing a steady supply of the 'raw material' for their continued profit.

This is not, however, the only consequence of large, multinational companies seeking to dominate the market. Owners of independent family firms, having formed SAIF, are responding to the threat by urging their members to actively seek public support for the genuine family business committed to local involvement. This attempt to fight off the increasing dominance of SCI is supported by the recent public launch of the NFC (1994), which is actively campaigning against the inherent monopolistic tendency of SCI. The NFC has published a 'Dead Citizens' Charter' (1996) – a consultative document arguing persuasively for far-reaching reform of funeral services, and opposing the increasingly bureaucratic anonymity they perceive to be stifling funeral provision. Criticisms made by the NFC reinforce those made in this chapter, namely that funerals are expensive, tawdry and hurried affairs which fail dismally to meeet the needs of the bereaved, and primarily foster the profits of the funeral firms. Nevertheless, in the 'Charter' there is acceptance of funeral directors as central providers of funerals, and the main recommendations address how they may be made more sensitive to the needs of the bereaved. The contention in this chapter, however, is that funeral directors are central players in the performance and will continue to be significant 'agenda-setters', even if they show more sensitivity to the needs of those who pay them.

The most recent development, that of the funeral supermarket, is set firmly in the mould of competitive individualism rather than large-scale amalgamation, and in due course it may become a significant challenge to multinational companies. The Funeral Centre, opened in Catford, south-east London, in July 1995, was the first funeral supermarket in the UK. Six months of trading have encouraged its joint owners, two funeral directors, to plan a further 60 in cities throughout England. Their press release emphasized public disquiet concerning the secrecy of funeral directors' charges and the stress and discomfort that is experienced by so many mourners when trying to arrange a funeral. In a large, well-lit store with piped classical music and no interference from sales staff, customers are encouraged to browse and select whatever they require. Everything required is on open display, including flowers, tombstones, memorials, statues, urns and coffins, and can be personally handled. Prices are clearly displayed and a complete funeral service can be purchased for 30 per cent less than competitors who, surprisingly, have accepted this supermarket innovation. Here, under one roof, they provide private arranging rooms, chapels of rest, refrigerated mortuary facilities, garaging for funeral vehicles and stonemasonry. Their claim to be demystifying the process of funeral directing appears to be succeeding.

One of the most powerful inducements to shop in any supermarket is not merely price but freedom of choice from a wide selection of openly displayed goods. 'Handling' is an essential element because it carries underlying assumptions concerning personal choice, rejection, comparison, inward calculation and unhurried reflection. Above all there is autonomy – the freedom to ignore the advice of 'the expert'. It is difficult to explain the apparent complacency of the funeral trade to this challenging development. If customer control over every aspect of funeral merchandise is encouraged it may prove to be the cognitive shift necessary to transform funeral directing in Britain. Trading in the next year will show if it is becoming socially acceptable to construct a funeral.

Challenges of a different kind are also emerging. These derive from the presence of new diseases; the ability of young people to influence the death ceremonies of friends; the growth of expressive individualism; and a growing awareness of 'green' and similar environmentally supportive funerals. If these pressures continue, large-scale organizations may find themselves undermined because the 'traditional', conservative, formal presentation favoured by small family businesses, or the uniformly similar productions created by multinationals, are both unsuited to meet changing expectations. Both are antithetical to a growing mood of self-determination which, though tenuous at present, may be strengthened by the open-choice supermarket approach. There is pressure, for example, arising among the partners, friends and peers of people dying from HIV-related illness to take greater, or in some cases absolute, control of the funeral ceremony. They wish to openly *celebrate* a life that was valued rather than tolerate the conservatism of a 'normal' funeral wherein emotional expressiveness is contained. In the recent past many such funerals were commandeered by an unsympathetic family, committed to underplaying the assumption of a 'deviant' life-style. The formal trappings of a conventional funeral prevented friends of the deceased, and especially a same-sex partner, if there was one, from creating a celebratory ceremony. This has been recognized by one funeral director in Kensington, Central London, who caters specifically for those who reject the social and religious conventions so readily accepted by most funeral directors. Colourful, physically exuberant affirmation of life among some gay groups leads them to reject traditional forms of funeral that do not fit their needs, commitments or experiences.

In the forefront of those advocating inexpensive, green, privately organized funerals is the charity pressure group, The Natural Death Centre, in North London. They supply information on a wide range of new ideas for improving every aspect of dying and funeral organization, including the purchase of body bags; ensuring that personal wishes for a funeral ceremony are known in advance by those who will eventually 'make' the funeral; creating a purely secular ceremony; digging a grave and developing a supportive network around the bereaved. The most important contribution, however, is the detailed information on 'do-it-yourself' funerals. Here they show how coffins can be purchased privately, how the dead can be honourably, sensitively and clinically prepared and directors dispensed with. Developing the ideas further, they provide information on constructing a coffin, how to paint and fit it out, and how to carry and transport it. The environmental theme is presented as equally important and coffins can be made of willow, flax, cork or other easily degradable natural materials. Such funerals can be created for as little as £480 (1995 costs), without the aid of a funeral director.

Funeral directors, whether in small family businesses or large multinationals, continue to sell 'tradition' as well as the 'service' and 'goods' that are their stock-in-trade. Once the former claim is challenged and the second is shown to be inadequate and unnecessary, then the supermarket provision of goods on open display could challenge directors even on the sale of merchandise. The concept of 'funeral' may thereby change and the social construction of such important rituals be claimed by participants.

It is argued throughout this chapter that funerals are the public, symbolic manifestations of contending definitions concerning spirituality, physicality, disposal techniques, occupational specialisms, commercialism, profit-seeking and personal, possibly idiosyncratic expressiveness. They are best regarded as social constructs in which personal expressiveness has been restricted, undervalued and overborne by the limiting definitions created by firms, businesses and organizations dedicated to commercial profitability.

The 'reality' held by an individual will illuminate his or her conception of the world; artistic creativity is possibly the most powerful representation of personal vision. Practical group reality develops when many individual realities coalesce. 'A funeral' is one such entity, produced by overlapping realities where one vision is sufficiently organized to produce uniformity. This certainty is now being openly challenged in Britain.

NOTES

1. To put quotation marks around the term 'reality' every time it is used is grammatically and stylistically disruptive. However, it is necessary to do so to focus attention on the implicit assumption that is made whenever the term is used without such qualification.

REFERENCES

Berger, P. and Luckmann, T. (1966) *The Social Construction of Reality*, London: Penguin.

Goffman, E. (1972) *Encounters*, London: Penguin.

Habenstein, R. (1955) 'The American Funeral Director', unpublished Ph.D. thesis, University of Chicago, USA.

Johnson, M. (1996) Preface to the *Dead Citizen's Charter* (Consultative Document), Lincolnshire: The National Funerals College.

Mannheim, K. (1936) *Ideology and Utopia*, London: Routledge & Kegan Paul.

Smale, B.J. (1985) 'Death Work', unpublished Ph.D. thesis, University of Surrey, UK.

The National Funerals College (NFC), (1996) *The Dead Citizens Charter*, Lincolnshire: NFC.

van Gennep, A. (1909) *The Rites of Passage* (1960 trans.), London: Routledge & Kegan Paul.

Young, M. (1996) 'What a rotten way to go', the *Guardian*, 31 January 1996, Society section, 2.

10 Emotional Reserve and the English Way of Grief[1]

Tony Walter

White English people are not prone to wearing their emotions on their sleeves, and they are expected to bear suffering with a stiff upper lip. English men, in particular, are not supposed to weep and hug each other – except on the football field. Does this emotional reserve lead to a particularly English way of managing grief? In this chapter, I identify six different social norms which govern the English way of grief. Since these norms can conflict with one another, my analysis provides a framework for looking at change as well as at continuity. (By 'the English' I refer primarily to those of English descent, living in England; the *British* way of death is considerably more varied than the English.[2])

Any study of grief in England has to refer to Geoffrey Gorer's much-cited *Death, Grief and Mourning in Contemporary Britain* (1965), based on a survey conducted in 1963. My other starting-point is a short passage in *The Loneliness of the Dying* by Norbert Elias (1985). Elias argues that traditional rituals provided a framework within which you could express how you felt (24–8), but nowadays we have become more informal (see also Wouters 1977, 1986), and distrust 'empty' ritual. This would not present problems for the mourner, were it not for the combination of informality with emotional reserve. Denied the old ritual forms in which strong emotion could be expressed in code, mourners now find that emotional reserve forbids any public expression of grief. But are informalization and emotional reserve inevitable in the development of Western civilization (as Elias suggests), or do they characterize some nations more than others (as I will suggest)?

Using Elias's two dimensions of expressive/non-expressive

Table 10.1 Norms for Grief (Selected Western Societies)

	Formal (acceptance of ritual)	*Informal (distrust of ritual)*
Expressive	Ireland Mediterranean countries Orthodox Jews	West Coast USA
Reserved	Scotland Germany Switzerland Finland	England Australia Netherlands

and formal/informal, Table 10.1 sketches how the English way of grief may differ from other modern Western countries and indeed from other patterns within the British Isles.

Table 10.1 provides a rough picture of how certain cultures vary on the two dimensions of expressiveness and formality. The people of Eire, Italy and Greece and Orthodox Jews have clear funeral and mourning customs which ritualize emotion in a way that would embarrass most English people. This is very different from the expressivism of the USA, especially its West Coast, which distrusts ritual. Cultures that *dis*courage the public expression of the emotions of grief range from those that are rather formal in their rituals (Scotland, Germany, Switzerland and Finland) to those that discourage ritual (England, Australia, the Netherlands). If Elias is correct that the combination of informality with the distrust of ritual makes the articulation of grief particularly problematic, then this would seem to apply to this last trio of countries.

Table 10.2 relates the English way of grief to other patterns within the British Isles, and identifies variations *within* the English way. This chapter refers mainly to the lower right-hand box.

Emotions and behaviours following bereavement are many and varied, even within the same person. Psychologists and psychiatrists have tended to order these emotions and behaviours into stages (Kübler-Ross 1970), phases (Parkes 1986) or tasks (Worden 1983); Stroebe and Schut (1995) have analysed them in terms of an oscillation between expressing grief and learning new roles. In this chapter I describe how bereaved English people face varied and sometimes

Table 10.2 Norms for Grief (British Isles)

	Formal (acceptance of ritual)	*Informal (distrust of ritual)*
Expressive	Traditional Irish (North and South) Orthodox Jewish Hindu Caribbean	English: expressive professions
Reserved	English: traditional working class Traditional Scottish (all classes) Royal Family Muslim	English: commercial middle class : detraditionalized working class

contradictory expectations as to how they should feel and behave; this suggests a more sociological way of interpreting the confusing experiences of bereavement.

PERSONAL GRIEF

Gorer claimed that 'the style of mourning in Britain is now a matter of individual choice'. Until the beginning of this century all societies provided rules how to mourn (possibly, Gorer suggests, reflecting the preferred styles of powerful individuals), but in contemporary Britain 'the cultural rules are discarded (so) the varieties of individual temperament will develop spontaneously private behaviour' (Gorer 1965: 64). There is evidence (Wortman and Silver 1989) that there is not one 'grief process' but several, so a norm of freedom could represent liberation from imposed rules of mourning. Certainly in my own experience of loss, from the early 1970s to the present, I have not felt social constraint to grieve in a certain way and I have been aware that others have grieved in different ways from myself.

When given total freedom, however, most human beings do not know how to use it, looking anxiously around to see how others are using their freedom. In the 1830s de Tocqueville observed that Americans, a people who proclaim individual freedom as an absolute value, were actually rather conformist (Bellah *et al.* 1985). Throughout the modern West, teenagers loudly protest their freedom yet ensure they make the same consumer choices as their peers. Bereavement is a stage of life evoking even more anxiety than the teenage years, so we find that even if there are no strong, nationwide norms as to how to grieve, mourners still conform to certain patterns, often learnt within their nuclear family. Bereavement is a time of insecurity, the most unlikely moment for people to become pioneers or eccentrics, as any funeral director will tell you. Bereavement organizations often comment that their clients need to know that their emotions are normal and not signs that they are going mad; they are grateful to be informed that their emotions and responses are within the range of the normal.

Virtually every contemporary British book on grief, however, gives examples of bereaved people being criticized for inappropriate behaviour, indicating that many Britons do not believe that grief is a matter of personal inclination. A widow with a young son and daughter said: 'I just couldn't cope for a long while, there was nothing to do for it. My sister and the minister told me to pull myself together, but I said "What for?" They said I had to for the children, but I still felt there was nothing to do for it' (Marris 1958: 11). If indeed people do have their own preferred style of grieving, it can be very hard for other family members who have a different style. She wants to go out and be with friends, he thinks this inappropriate; she wants to talk and talk and talk, he wants to go for long walks and visit the grave by himself. Couples who thought they knew each other begin to find the other behaving in incomprehensible ways. He remarries before his children have got over the loss of their mother. Gorer (1965: 81, 83) gives similar examples of criticism from grieving relatives and neighbours: indeed he himself implicitly criticizes the style adopted by some of his interviewees.

In so far as there is a norm of freedom to follow personal inclination, this does not mean the grieving are free from social influence. They may seek affirmation, or they may receive unasked-for advice or criticism. Freedom does not exist in a social vacuum.

ANOMIC GRIEF

On examining his interviews, Gorer concluded that for most Britons the abolition of culturally prescribed grieving did not result in personal freedom but a deregulation that left people at a loss. This is the state the French sociologist Durkheim (1952) termed *anomie* – though Gorer did not refer to Durkheim. The only exceptions, Gorer concluded, were the (then very small) religious minorities that lay down clear rules and rituals for mourning.

Gorer argued that mid-twentieth-century Britain had witnessed the demise of Victorian funeral and mourning rituals, leaving a vacuum. David Cannadine (1981) has challenged both Gorer's somewhat rosy view of Victorian mourning and his timing of their demise, but nevertheless affirms Gorer's identification of the importance of the First World War. After the carnage of the war, Cannadine argues, the peacetime death rate continued to decline, funerals became simpler, mourning less elaborate, yet there was a 'massive, all-pervasive pall of death which hung over Britain', and Cannadine writes of 'the inventiveness with which the grief-stricken responded to their bereavement' (230). This inter-war period saw a flourishing of the cult of remembrance, pilgrimages to war graves and spiritualism.

Building on Cannadine, Ruth Richardson (1984) has suggested that each generation this century has had its own socialization into awareness of death. Many of the very old, raised before the First World War, some of them survivors of the trenches, had always known they were mortal – though the upper class were protected as children from the sight of death. The generation raised between the wars seems to have grown up with a horror of morbid ritual, perhaps in reaction to the inter-war obsession with death, yet all too aware that some of their male relatives were missing – and were themselves in turn plunged into the Second World War. It is this generation, I suggest, that is most likely to be characterized now by *anomie.* It is certainly this generation that some of its children now castigate for 'denying' death. (A portrait of this generation in grief may be found in Marris 1958). The post-1945 generation, by contrast, grew up under the abstract shadow of the Bomb, but without direct contact with death – mortality rates were at an all-time low, most deaths occurred in hospital, and children could grow up with the family still complete. Richardson (1984: 51) reckons this generation seems 'less worried by death than the shell-shocked generation born between the wars, children and grandchildren of the Great War's bereaved'. If *anomie* is an accurate characterization of the grief of some Britons, we must be clear as to precisely which generation or generations are characterized by *anomie.*

PRIVATE GRIEF

> The ladies of a bereaved family should not see callers, even intimate friends, unless they are able to control their grief. It is distressing alike to the visitor and the mourner to go through a scene of uncontrolled grief. Yet it is difficult to keep a firm hold over the emotions at such a time, and it is therefore wiser to see no one if there is a chance of breaking down . . . . Even relatives should remember that the bereaved ones will want to be by themselves, and that solitude is often the greatest solace for grief. (Troubridge 1926: 57–8)

> No-one knows my sorrow
> Few have seen me weep
> I cry from a broken heart
> While others are asleep
>
> (*In Memoriam* notice in regional newspaper, England, late 1970s)

I believe the dominant type of grief in mid- to late twentieth-century Britain, starting with the upper classes and then filtering down the social ladder, to be *private* grief. This entails very clear norms which differentiate between what is felt in private and what is shown in public, and is well understood by a people who value emotional reserve. The norm is that grief should be private and not disturb others; it should not go on indefinitely, for this too is disturbing to others. If these are the obligations of the grieving person, the obligation of others is not to intrude upon his or her grief.

Gorer (1965: 113) captures this when he says of the British that 'one mourns in private as one undresses or relieves oneself in private, so as not to offend others'.[3]

This norm is more problematic, however, than may at first sight appear. The norm is not just that you should grieve in private, but that others should know you are grieving – otherwise you might not have cared for your husband/mother/child after all! The task for the grieving therefore is to provide clues that they feel deeply, without actually breaking down in public and embarrassing others. This is a difficult act to achieve. The relative who reads the lesson at the funeral and who momentarily has a catch in his voice but who masters this and continues to read the lesson perfectly; the funeral attender who dabs at a moist eye but who doesn't break down; the widow who answers a telephone call of condolence with the occasional halt in her voice but who continues to appreciate or even enjoy the conversation – all these have mastered the fine British art of grief. Breaking down in the privacy of your own room is fine, though – as Marris's (1958) study of younger widows in the 1950s makes very clear – not in front of the children. This difficulty of pulling off a successful performance could explain why friends and neighbours may avoid mourners, or mourners avoid their friends and neighbours.

The norm that grief should be private makes public appearances problematic, and emotionally charged public appearances such as the funeral can be dreaded. After the funeral, mourners say of the widow on view to all in the front row of the crematorium 'Didn't she do well?' – signifying a successful performance in which she didn't break down but gave off enough signals to indicate she was feeling terrible. The English tend to see the funeral not as psychologically helpful (as many textbooks assert, on the basis of little or no evidence), but as a trial of emotional strength and acting skill to be got over and done with as soon as possible. People who normally avoid mood-altering medication will take valium for this one occasion.

According to stage theories of grief, the funeral tends to occur during the first, numb stage – which experts who want the funeral to be therapeutic may deem to be bad timing. It may be, however, that many people *prefer* to be numb at the funeral as this reduces the chances of their causing a scene; it may even be that some subconsciously choose to keep the numbness going until the funeral. (Mediterranean or West Indian funerals also occur soon after the death, but are not noted for emotional numbness.)

Managing the appearance of a privately grieving self is particularly tricky now that Victorian ritual mourning is no more. Victorian mourning clothes, particularly the middle- or upper-class widow's black dress and veil, hid how she really felt, as did her enforced absence from social engagements. She could have been pleased her husband had died, but no one need know because she was wearing the appropriate clothes and her face was hidden. In the twentieth century, however, the display of grief has to be consciously staged by the individual. Widows and widowers must display that they are upset in more subtle ways, such as the temporarily broken voice or the careful timing and management of meetings with potential future partners.

If private grief makes public performances tricky, private feelings are themselves problematic. The private mourner is likely to experience as much *anomie*, lack of direction and uncertainty as the anomic or personal mourner. If grief is private, how are children to learn about it as part of their upbringing? If all that can be observed in public is the stiff upper lip, how will first-time mourners know what is 'normal'? How will they know whether their feelings are 'normal'? How will they know when they should be 'getting over it'? The answer is that they don't, which could account for the demand for media portrayals of grief, especially portrayals which get behind the public façade to show what the mourner feels in private (Walter *et al.* 1995). It could also account for the growth of autobiographical accounts of loss (Holloway 1990) and of personal revelations in bereavement groups, where mourners share their feelings and experiences with each other.

FORBIDDEN GRIEF

Private grief entails suppression of one's feelings in public, not psychological repression or denial in which the mourner denies their pain to themselves. Indeed, denial is likely to lead to a less than satisfactory performance, in which one appears not to care for the dead. Conscious suppression and unconscious repression, however, are often confused by researchers who take the one to imply the other. But the English norm to hide grief need not mean that grief is forbidden.[4] Many who assert that death and grief are denied in modern society do so on the basis of their absence in public discourse, ignoring the possibility (Mellor 1993) that grief can be absent in public but very present in private.

Some English people, however, do expect mourners to get on with life without grieving, in public *and* in private. Advice that keeping busy helps you through grief, that tears once begun never stop, and that the stiff upper lip is the best way forward are frequently heard.

Another form of forbidden grief is to deny that the person has suffered any loss. Losing a partner in a covert homosexual relationship is one example, losing a mistress or lover is another. Miscarriage and stillbirths were also once in that category – 'just one of those things' the parents must put behind them. This, however, has been challenged in the past decade. Whereas previously a stillbirth would not have received any ritual or personal attention, many maternity units now encourage parents to hold their dead baby and to attend its funeral.

EXPRESSIVE GRIEF

Over the past two to three decades, absent and private grief have been severely criticized by those who consider it psychologically healthy for people to be more expressive. For expressivists, grief proceeds through the working-through and/or expression of a range of feelings – a view often propagated by what Bernice Martin (1981) terms Britain's expressive professions (clergy, social workers, teachers, etc.). Gorer himself is an expressivist, but the most influential expressivist has been the Swiss-American Elisabeth Kübler-Ross, whose best selling text on the stages of dying (1970) was quickly used to describe stages of grief as well. The expressivist revolution in death and dying has been described in some detail by sociologists Lofland (1978), Wood (1977) and Walter (1994). The intellectual origin of the revolution is the Freudian idea of repression; the social origin is the strand in American culture that Bellah *et al.* (1985) term expressive individualism and that emanates in particular from California; and the historical origin is the counter-culture of the 1960s. Almost all the current books and media documentaries on bereavement are produced by expressivists aiming to challenge private, personal and anomic grief. There is a good way to grieve, they believe, and – having captured the media – they are making sure we all know what it is.

That the British have not immediately taken to this new way of grief, indeed to a considerable extent reject it, is in part because – unlike private grief – expressive grief takes little or no account of the distinction between public and private. Expressivists see the expression of grief not as social but as natural; it therefore harmful to repress tears – whatever the situation. Public situations, however, are not natural but are governed by social rules.

All this cannot but leave millions of Britons confused. They are now encouraged to cry, yet are aware that encounters with others are rule-governed and that weeping spontaneously in the supermarket or outside the school gates will disturb others. Expressivists provide no guidance as to when, how, in what manner or with what people it is appropriate to express grief. In many ways the old norm, that you grieve alone while keeping a stiff upper lip in public, is much easier. For the new norm to take hold, the emphasis on tears as psychologically healthy must be complemented by guidelines as to when and where is the best place to cry. Otherwise the anxiety level of people who are bereaved, not to mention everybody else, cannot but rise. This is so in any Western society, but especially so in a society that values emotional reserve – which is why expressivist literature emanating from a less reserved USA may be less than totally helpful to grieving Britons. In Britain the new norm may therefore develop into but a variation of the old – grieve in private (private being extended to include one-to-one encounters with a trusted friend or counsellor), but not in public.

Another area where expressivism comes into direct conflict

with the norm of emotional reserve is at the funeral. Increasingly, textbooks refer to the funeral as an occasion for expressing emotion, yet mourners (and clergy) are often petrified of uncontrollable emotion in funerals. There is in fact no widespread demand for more emotional funerals. Funerals must affirm the mourners' cultural values in order to stabilize their fragile grasp on reality, so the English are unlikely to approve of funerals that challenge emotional reserve. Indeed, the English often criticize Irish funerals for being 'sentimental' or 'wild'. What *is* widely wanted in England, however, are more personal funerals. The English seem to like funerals that capture the personality of the deceased, and criticize those that don't (Walter 1990).

It is clear, therefore, that expressive grief can only enter the English repertoire if it shows more awareness of social norms; in the meantime, it exists in considerable tension with private grief. Theories that consider grief to be a process of working through feelings may not be appropriate for many British people (Walter 1996).

Another way of analysing the private/expressive tension is in terms of the tension between modernity and postmodernity. If modernism entails a clear distinction between the public and the private, postmodernism entails their interpenetration: the invasion of the public sphere by private feelings and meanings, and the control of private feelings by expert systems and theories. I have argued at length elsewhere (Walter 1994) that this is precisely what one finds in expressivist approaches to dying and grieving.

TIME-LIMITED GRIEF

Gorer argued that healthy grieving is time-limited – neither denied, nor prolonged indefinitely. He suggested that time-limited grieving characterizes many traditional cultures, but not all Britons manage it. I would argue that, though many English people grieve for a shorter time than Gorer thought healthy, the idea that grief should last only a certain amount of time is very common in England. This is often found in criticism:

> My family were very nice for about six weeks – very understanding but I was terrible for months afterwards, I used to forget things – I was living in another world, it takes me a long time to get over things. Anyway in the end they just lost patience. My husband was really nasty about it, he said: 'For God's sake woman what's the matter with you, I was never like that when my mother died – it's been *months.*' (Littlewood 1992: 87)

Even expressivists can place a time-limit on grief. There is evidence (Walter 1994: Chapter 8) that bereavement organizations not only normalize diversity but also, and contradictorily, provide clear guidelines as to the timing of grief.[5]

CONCLUSION

In this chapter, I have argued that there is an English way of grief. It is driven by informality and reserve, a combination characterizing especially the less traditional sections of the working class and those sections of the middle class not involved in the caring professions. Informality plus reserve lead to a number of norms, of which private grief is the most important. This norm, however, is difficult to fulfil, and is contradicted by the norm of expressive grief which, arriving across the Atlantic, has sponsors in the caring professions and in journalism. In so far as the English way – as the dominant way of grief in the United Kingdom – is imposed (for example, through the design of crematoria) on ethnic and religions minorities (Firth 1993), further tensions may ensue. To talk of an English way of grief is not therefore to claim that it is unchanging or unproblematic.

NOTES

1. I wish to thank Jenny Hockey, Glennys Howarth, Jasmin Gunaratnam and David Clark for comments on earlier drafts and presentations of this chapter.

2. *Great Britain* consists of England, Wales and Scotland; *the United Kingdom* consists of Great Britain plus Northern Ireland. *The British* are the citizens of the United Kingdom. *The British Isles* consist of Great Britain, Ireland and nearby smaller islands. *The Irish* are those from both Northern Ireland and the Republic of Ireland.
3. Elias (1978) suggests that the hiding of such bodily functions is typical of the civilizing process, but I suggest that its extension to grief characterizes some nations more than others.
4. Ariès, in writing of the modern West in general, seems to confuse forbidden grief (1981: Part 5) with hidden or invisible grief (1974: Chapter 4). My observations of English and American funeral practice suggest that the English may tend to hide grief, while North Americans may tend to deny it (Davies 1996).
5. For an American study of this, see Wambach 1985.

REFERENCES

Ariès, P. (1974) *Western Attitudes toward Death: from the Middle Ages to the present*, Baltimore: Johns Hopkins University Press.

Ariès, P. (1981) *The Hour of Our Death*, London: Allen Lane.

Bellah, R.N. *et al.* (1985) *Habits of the Heart: individualism and commitment in American life*, Berkeley: University of California Press.

Cannadine, D. (1981) 'War and Death, Grief and Mourning in Modern Britain', Chapter 8 in J. Whaley (ed.) *Mirrors of Mortality: studies in the social history of death*, London, Europa.

Davies, C. (1996) 'Dirt, Death, Decay and Dissolution: American denial and British avoidance', Chapter 5 in G. Howarth and P. Jupp (eds.) *Contemporary Issues in the Sociology of Death, Dying and Disposal*, Basingstoke: Macmillan/New York: St Martin's Press.

Durkheim, E. (1952) *Suicide*, London: Routledge & Kegan Paul.

Elias, N. (1978) *The Civilizing Process. Vol. 1: The History of Manners*, New York: Urizen Books.

Elias, N. (1985) *The Loneliness of the Dying*, Oxford: Blackwell.

Firth, S. (1993) 'Cross-cultural Perspectives on Bereavement', Chapter 49 in D. Dickenson and M. Johnson (eds.) *Death, Dying and Bereavement*, London: Sage.

Gorer, G. (1965) *Death, Grief and Mourning in Contemporary Britain*, London: Cresset.

Holloway, J. (1990) 'Bereavement Literature: a valuable resource for the bereaved and those who counsel them', *Contact: Interdisciplinary Journal of Pastoral Studies*, 3: 17–26.

Kübler-Ross, E. (1970) *On Death and Dying*, London: Tavistock.

Littlewood, J. (1992) *Aspects of Grief*, London: Tavistock/Routledge.

Lofland, L. (1978) *The Craft of Dying: the modern face of death*, Beverley Hills: Sage.

Marris, P. (1958) *Widows and Their Families*, London: Routledge.

Martin, B. (1981) *A Sociology of Contemporary Cultural Change*, Oxford: Blackwell.

Mellor, P. (1993) 'Death in High Modernity', in D. Clark (ed.) *The Sociology of Death*, Oxford: Blackwell.
Parkes, C.M. (1986) *Bereavement: studies of grief in adult life*, 2nd edn, London: Tavistock.
Richardson, R. (1984) 'Old People's Attitudes to Death in the Twentieth Century', *Society for the Social History of Medicine Bulletin*, 34: 48–51.
Stroebe, M. and Schut, H. (1995) 'The Dual Process Model of Coping with Loss', paper presented at the International Work Group on Death, Dying and Bereavement, St Catherine's College, Oxford, 26–29 June.
Troubridge, Lady (1926) *The Book of Etiquette*, Kingswood, Surrey: The World's Work.
Walter, T. (1990) *Funerals – and how to improve them*, London: Hodder.
Walter, T. (1994) *The Revival of Death*, London: Routledge.
Walter, T. (1996) 'A New Model of Grief', *Mortality*, 1, 1: 7–25.
Walter, T., Littlewood, J. and Pickering, M. (1995) 'Death in the News: the public invigilation of private emotion', *Sociology*, 29, 4: 579–96.
Wambach, J.A. (1985) 'The Grief Process as a Social Construct', *Omega*, 16, 3: 201–11.
Wood, J. (1977) 'Expressive Death – the current deathwork paradigm', unpublished Ph.D. thesis, University of California at Davis.
Worden, J.W. (1983) *Grief Counselling and Grief Therapy*, 2nd edn, London: Routledge.
Wortman, C.B. and Silver, R.C. (1989) 'The Myths of Coping with Loss', *Journal of Consulting and Clinical Psychology*, 57, 3: 349–57.
Wouters, C. (1977) 'Informalisation and the Civilising Process', in P. Gleichmann, J. Goudsblom and H. Korte, *Human Figurations: Essays for Norbert Elias*, Amsterdam.
Wouters, C. (1986) 'Formalization and Informalization', *Theory, Culture and Society*, 3: 2: 1–18.

11 Why was England the First Country to Popularize Cremation?

Peter C. Jupp

This chapter seeks to show how the rise of cremation in England is a consequence of shifts in social authority and of its promotion by specific interest groups. This is complementary to the process whereby cremation became popular with individual families facing death or bereavement, who, once faced with a practical choice between burial and cremation, chose the latter. That process is discussed far more fully elsewhere (Jupp 1993a; 1993b) and has received some recent confirmation in Davies and Shaw (1995).

THE RISE OF CREMATION

The pioneer of cremation in England was Sir Henry Thompson, the son of a Nonconformist shopkeeper, who rose to be surgeon to Queen Victoria. A member of both the Reform Club and the Athenaeum, he possessed both cultured friends and access to the corridors of power. In 1874 he published 'The Treatment of the Body after Death' (Thompson 1874). He gathered sympathizing friends to form the Cremation Society.

Thompson knew his proposal for cremation would be controversial and he avoided the religious aspects of burial, stressing instead the sanitary and medical aspects of the corpse. The Protestant culture of England knew instinctively that funeral expenditure could not benefit the dead, but families at most levels of society invested in funerals to declare their affection, their identity and their social status. In 1874, certainly, the spheres of economics and sentiment at funerals still seemed firmly fixed.

Habits were, however, on the cusp of change, and three factors are notable here. First, death was being seen increasingly not as the dominion of God but as the province of nature. Developing understanding of the correlations between medicine and diet, health and longevity, all promoted increasingly secular interpretations of mortality (Prior 1996). Second, there began a not unassociated reaction against elaborate ritual mourning, both in custom and costume. In 1889, Davey observed, 'Private mourning in modern times . . . has been greatly altered and modified . . . to suit an age of rapid transit and travel' (Davey 1889: 96). Third, death was not only increasingly postponed, but its location was being marginalized and its visibility impaired. Since the Burial Acts of the 1850s, cemeteries had been relocated at the cities' edge. From the 1880s, closed urban churchyards were subhumed beneath new parks, gardens and playing-fields.

Reaction from religious leaders to Thompson's proposals was divided. Contrasting pastoral and theological concerns were demonstrated by the bishops. The Bishop of Manchester, consecrating a new cemetery in Stockport, commented, 'In the first place, this is a long distance for the poor to bring their dead; in the second, here is another hundred acres of land withdrawn from the food-producing areas of the country for ever.' Meanwhile, the Bishop of London wrote to *The Times*, 'We could not conceive anything more barbarous and unnatural than cremation, and one of the very first fruits of its adoption would be to undermine the faith of mankind in the doctrine of the resurrection of the body, and so bring about a most disastrous social revolution' (*c.* 1874, quoted in *Undertakers' Journal*, 15 October 1911).

Cremationists conducted their campaign in a legal and respectable manner. In 1875 the Cremation Society obtained legal advice favouring cremation, 'provided no public nuisance might be afforded'. The private New Southgate cemetery (North London) offered a piece of consecrated land for a crematorium, but the Bishop of Rochester refused his consent. When the Society formed the London Crematorium Company, and bought land at Woking, the (Conservative) Home Secretary refused permission for a crematorium on the grounds that forensic evidence, especially after death by poisoning, might be destroyed by cremation (Leaney 1989).

The Society settled down for a long programme of advocacy, to persuade Parliament, the law, the funeral and mourning-wear industries, sanitary engineers, officers of health, doctors and clergy of the value of cremation. At this point two unconnected private individuals played an unexpected role.

The mother and wife of a Captain Thomas Hanham had requested cremation after their death. The Cremation Society rejected his use of Woking, whereupon he built his own cremator and performed the cremations. There was much comment in the press but none from the Home Office. Their bluff was effectively called a second time when Hanham was himself cremated in December 1883 (White 1990).

The next month, in South Wales, William Price, a doctor, former Chartist and self-proclaimed druid, attempted to cremate the body of his baby son (ap Nicholas 1940). Price was brought for trial. The presiding judge was James Fitzjames Stephen, brother of Leslie Stephen, the cleric turned agnostic, and member of that Victorian 'intellectual aristocracy' who possessed 'an interest in obtaining reforms which many in the ruling classes resisted' (Annan 1984: 7). Stephen, dismissing religious considerations, concluded that cremation was not an illegal act provided no public nuisance was caused.

LEGAL CREMATION

The Price verdict handed the Cremation Society an unexpected victory. The Society drafted its own code of practice intended to overcome the forensic anxiety of the Home Secretary. An unsuccessful Parliamentary Bill to legalize cremation received 79 favourable votes. Eleven months later, the first legal cremation took place at Woking.

In a long perspective, the 1880s proved a decade in which the avenues for the expression of democracy were being restructured and advanced. In 1888, the Local Government Act transferred the administrative powers of the Justices of the Peace to elected County Councils. This provided a system of elected local government, not only distinct from national government but able to override the competing interests of Boards, vestries and Guardians. Legislation on health and sanitation was a major concern. The Local Government Act provided cremationists with new opportunities to work through local authorities.

Unsuccessful attempts were made to provide local authority crematoria at Tunbridge Wells (1889), Cardiff (1894), Leamington (1896), Hull (1897) and Leicester (1899), but two private crematoria were built at Manchester (1890) and Glasgow (1895). The London boroughs, meanwhile, were confronted by massive problems in the extension and maintenance of their already vast cemetery holdings. A number of London boroughs consulted the Local Government Board to solve the cemetery land problem by the adoption of cremation.

The London County Council, in consultation with the Home Office, drafted a bill to enable local authorities to provide facilities for cremation. Three attempts to pass the Bill through Parliament all faced controversy. Two particularly contentious issues were 'public nuisances' and religious scruples. The 200-yard rule obstructed the building of crematoria within 200 yards of houses, without the owners' written consent. Another amendment freed Anglican clergy from an obligation to conduct funerals involving cremation. The Church had as yet authorized no cremation liturgies. When Dr Price was cremated in 1893, Welsh clergy adapted the service for burial at sea.

The passing of the Cremation Act 1902 was followed by Cremation Regulations, 1903. These acts dealt particularly with forensic issues, requiring, for example, two doctors' signatures for cremation. Yet the new Act neither rescued local authorities nor popularized cremation overnight. The first local authority crematoria were built by Hull (1901) and Leicester (1902), followed by the City of London at Ilford, Leeds, Bradford and Sheffield, all in 1905. They charged lower fees but failed to make headway. Thus no further municipal crematoria were built after 1905, although Liverpool came under public ownership in 1908. Burial was preferred by the majority of religious believes and funeral directors. Traditional attitudes to death, the corpse and the afterlife continued to hold sway up to 1914.

THE FIRST WORLD WAR

The First World War wrought changes in every sphere of social life. It could not but affect attitudes to death and dying, the deceased, and their destiny, to funeral procedures and mourning customs, to the expression of grief and to forms of memorialization (Fussell 1975; Marwick 1965; Wilkinson 1978; Winter 1995). Any summary would be inadequate; three issues are particularly pertinent – religion, grief, memorialization.

Traditional religious interpretations of death were put to hard tests. Combatants learned to cope with the prospect of violent death in superstitious, fatalistic and cynical ways. Their experiences of dealing with severely mutilated corpses challenged beliefs in the resurrection of the body. Many clergy, whilst counselling the dying and bereaved, taught that soldiers, having died in a good cause, went direct to Heaven. This theology eroded the Protestant disjunction between this world and the next, with the assistance of the revival of traditionally Catholic intercessions for the dead, and the revival of (more secular) spiritualism.

The war effected a shift from public to more private expression of grief. The sharpness of wartime bereavement was partly because families, in a pre-war era of declining infant mortality, had learned to expect that children would survive their parents. For the first time, people had to cope with their bereavements without sight of coffin, corpse or funeral parade, even – until after the war – of the grave.

Women had traditionally been the major bearers of death and mourning ritual. Women of every class were so busy in war work that they could not practically continue the traditions of mourning seclusion and ritual. The war also liberated attitudes to marriage, widowhood and family responsibilities. Mourning wear became increasingly unfashionable. With so many husbands and sons dead, fewer people felt they could lay claim to the former social considerations offered to the bereaved. This privatization of bereavement was, paradoxically, strengthened by the publicity given after the war to national mourning (Gregory 1994).

Wartime mortality also affected the class-specific traditions of memorialization. The War Graves Commission (founded

1915) promised soldiers perpetual care of individual graves, with a policy of 'equality of treatment for equality of sacrifice'. The introduction of uniform graves and stones set a public example of orderlines and maintenance of cemeteries, which local authorities, on far more restricted budgets, could not hope to match.

All these affected attitudes to belief and to practice, weakening the traditions of belief, burial and funeral expenditure. They reduced the authority of the Church and lowered the traditional divide between the living and the dead. They reduced the necessity and thereby simplified the level of acceptable investment in marking that divide. They rendered extravagant forms of funeral anachronistic and set precedents for simpler forms of mourning and memorialization. They encouraged the privatization of belief and discouraged the role of community and neighbours in funeral ritual and support. All these factors, in setting precedents for the greater simplicity and lower profile of funerals, would smooth the way for the acceptance of cremation as the simpler form of funeral, once cremation legislation was less obstructive, and its facilities more widely available. Post-war shifts of emphasis within two institutions, local authorities and the Church, would contribute to this, each partly prompted by the Cremation Society.

LOCAL GOVERNMENT

In 1924 the Cremation Society founded the Federation of Cremation Authorities (FCA). Its major target was local government. First, Labour majorities were now being elected, many for the first time, and health and social issues were increasingly important, not least because of the recent enfranchisement of women. Second, the suburbanization of land around cities was rapidly swallowing extensive acres. The Society's motto, 'Save the Land for the Living', was aimed, not at individuals, but at local authorities, who were now considering the cost-effectiveness of cremation.

The FCA spearheaded approaches to the Home Office to revise the cremation regulations, and ease families' choice. One issue addressed was the inadequate number of doctors officially listed to sign cremation certificates, for which, it was complained, unnecessarily high fees were charged. The Cremation Regulations were passed in 1930.

By 1930, 21 crematoria accounted for 0.9 per cent of funerals. These limited facilities were not the sole factor favouring burial. Cremation costs were still beyond the normal purse. Whilst the 1902 Act had empowered local authorities to fund crematoria, they were not allowed to use them for pauper funerals (11 per cent of London funerals in 1938). The 200-yard rule prevented the establishment of crematoria in cemeteries in the old built-up areas. The 1902 Act supported traditional Church procedures in two ways: it supported clergy who opposed cremation; and prevented crematoria being built in consecrated but redundant cemetery chapels.

After 1930 the enormous benefits of providing crematoria became steadily apparent to local authorities, especially to those in cities: in 1935, the cremation rate for cities was 6.2 per cent, and the national rate 1.5 per cent. The first joint conference between the Institute of Burial and Cremation Administration (IBCA) and the FCA in 1932 was a first fruit of public and private collaboration. Increased local authority investment in crematoria after 1935 made the position of the Cremation Society as the parent body of the FCA (GB) somewhat difficult and the latter became autonomous in 1937 as the Federation of British Cremation Authorities (FBCA).

Cremation was promoted as a solution to local government's need for new housing land and industrial sites. Captain Elliston MP commented, 'the London County Council wants a green belt. Currently our cities have a white belt of cemeteries' (*Pharos* 2:1, October 1935: 6). He phrased the alternative of 'either playing-fields or cemeteries'. Meanwhile, town planners began to propose unified control of planning sites as an answer to the cemetery dilemma.

Just as private crematoria made profits, municipal ones realized economies. Between 1935 and 1939, 25 more crematoria had been opened, most by local authorities. Eight of these were in London. By 1939 the cremation rate had reached 3.8 per cent. This suggests that, whilst cremation's growth is correctly and numerically a post-war phenomenon, cremation's basis as a municipal solution to the urban problems of disposal was well-established before 1939.

THE CHURCHES

Shifting beliefs during the war surfaced in 1922 in the Major controversy, which revealed clerical divisions: Major was a leading Anglican clergyman who was accused of discarding belief in the resurrection of the body. Cremation focused attention on the growing conflict between belief and practice. For many parish clergy, cremation could only be a prelude to the interment of ashes in consecrated ground. The bishops, with less recent pastoral experience, more liberal in theology and moving in elite circles, seemed less troubled. Bishop David told the Cremation Society: 'It is already agreed among the best educated Christians that the quickest, cleanest, and most seemly disposal of the dead is provided by cremation' (*Pharos*, 2:1, October 1935: 18ff.). The Anglican Church had still not authorized services for cremation. The rise of cremation forced the Church to tackle this issue both liturgically and theologically. How could the 1902 Act's protection for clergy be maintained, when one funeral in 25 now involved cremation? When the Prayer Book spoke only of the burial of the body and its burial in consecrated ground, was it lawful to scatter ashes, especially when the crematorium had no consecrated ground? Furthermore, the cremation procedures had introduced a double ceremony of disposal, first at the committal of the coffin to the furnace, and second, the interment or scattering of the resulting ashes. At which point should the effective committal prayer be offered, and should the clergyman be expected to attend both the committal and the subsequent scattering? These questions were tackled between 1937 and 1944 in debates enhanced by the context of a nation at war.

The issue was debated in the Convocation of Canterbury. The Lower House (Clergy) was generally in favour of cremation, but only as a preliminary to burial in consecrated ground. Clergy also wished to preserve burial as most fittingly symbolic of the resurrection tradition. The bishops generally felt no incompatibility between the resurrection belief and cremation practice, and they commended cremation on social and hygienic grounds: if people requested cremation, then the Church should accept their wishes. In 1944 the convocation announced, 'there is no objection to cremation . . . we attach no theological significance to the practice'.

Would the Church ever have said the same of burial? Yet the new position was a direct consequence of the 1850 Burial Acts. When the Church had surrendered its responsibility for provision of burial land, it also lost the grounds for its controlling interest in the interpretation of death. Secular, local government was now the custodian of corpses: it would discharge its responsibilities not according to transcendent but to rational criteria, funded by the living as ratepayers.

In October 1944 the Convocation's decision was prematurely put into practice. Archbishop Temple died and, after the funeral service at Canterbury Cathedral, was cremated at Charing. Cremationists needed no more powerful symbol of Anglican approval. Hesitant families needed no better precedent.

POST-WAR: THE TRIUMPH OF THE CREMATION INTEREST

The 1945 Labour Government set out to make the most efficient use of British resources to aid the disadvantaged. Its re-evaluation of traditions and reallocation of resources was an auspicious time for the cremation movement. The cremation rate had doubled during the war (7.8 per cent in 1944).

Inexpensive cremation practice coincided with Labour welfare policy. The Labour Party had signalled its intentions for funeral reform before 1945, when it decided to adopt much of the Beveridge Report with its proposals for a welfare state. Benefits for widows and death grants to help funeral bills were introduced in 1946. The Labour Government was intent on phasing out the system of so-called Industrial Assurance, by which families bought funeral policies from a part-time army of 60 000 salesman door-to-door (Clarke 1944). The new death grant was modest, £20 in 1948, but it articulated government abhorrence of the pauper funeral with its social stigma.

The Cremation Society anticipated the post-war era with confidence. Lord Horder, its President, reminded local government delegates to the 1946 Society conference of their financial obligations to ratepayers, particularly concerning public health and land re-use. Nevertheless, the Society had made a policy decision, later revealed as short-sighted. In 1945, it decided to abandon the joint conferences. 'Nothing could be clearer than that to revert to the oldtime system of joint conferences in conjunction with the burial interests would be folly in the highest degree' (*Pharos*, 12:3, August 1946: 3). The result of this separation meant that the future of cremation provision was thereafter linked with the fortunes of local government. In a long perspective, cremation succeeded because it served local government interests.

The influence of Aneurin Bevan was also critical. His responsibilities as Minister for Health, Housing and Local Government (despite his personal support for cremation), involved his housing department's rejection of every application for crematorium building. Meanwhile, the Cremation Society adopted a new policy. After its 1947 Cardiff conference – inspired by their guest, the surviving daughter of Dr William Price – its Council selected 15 local authorities with the most pressing claim for crematoria. It submitted a memorandum to Bevan, as Minister for both Housing and Health. The request was refused. A revised memorandum of the five most needy cases was submitted. Finally, in December 1948, Bevan gave permission for six authorities to submit crematorium building proposals.

This broke the log-jam and signalled a new direction in government policy. At a time when national government held the spending reins, it chose to encourage local government investment in crematoria. The number of cremations continued to grow. By 1951, when the Government's Inter-Departmental Committee on Cremation (IDC) reported, one in six funerals involved cremation.

In September 1947, the Home Secretary, Chuter Ede, had set up his IDC to examine cremation regulations. Whilst the Committee took four years to report, it framed the regulations for cremation growth. Its debates around one particular issue reveal clear institutional tensions. The second medical certificate had been a considerable obstruction to the cremation procedures. Arguments for its abolition were put by the Association of Municipal Corporations, the Cremation Council, the Proprietary Crematoria Association and the Society of Medical Officers of Health. Arguments for its retention were made by the Director of Public Prosecutions, the Coroners' Society and the British Medical Association. It was the old fear of undetected crime, the detectives and doctors versus the rest. The former won. Despite the specific recommendations of the subsequent Brodrick Committee (1971), the second medical certificate is still demanded. The IDC recommendations became the Cremation Act 1952.

Thus there emerged in Britain, within the space of eight years (1944–1952), a new consensus about the promotion of cremation. In the 1950s, an era of rapid crematoria building gave many more families a new choice in disposal. By 1960, 90 more crematoria had been built in the UK and in England and Wales 35.7 per cent of funerals involved cremation. From 1967 there were more cremations than burials in England and Wales. Today, the cremation rate shows signs of peaking at 70 per cent.

CONCLUSION

Thus Britain emerged as the first Western industrial society to popularize cremation. The factors may be briefly summarized.

First, England had declared itself a Protestant nation at the Reformation, and had discontinued the cult of the dead. As long as the churches retained control over the site, mode and rite of burial, they could control interpretations of mortality and manipulate supernatural sanctions for morality which were inspired by belief in resurrection and judgement. After 1852 churches could no longer compete with the new, vast, well-funded local authority cemeteries.

Secondly, the disposal of the dead became a local authority responsibility and a local authority problem. Local authorities inherited from the Church the latent problems of the custody of the dead, their gravestones, maintenance, landscape and land-availability pollution, in an economic era when other policy issues claimed priority. With the suburban housing boom after 1918, town and county councils all over the land discovered the daunting nature of the task. Cremation offered a cost-effective policy. In the post-1945 era of reconstruction local authority demands for crematoria building were sanctioned by the national Government. Egalitarian modes of funeral were finally encouraged by the Labour Government elected in 1945. Cremation is the democratic way of death.

Thirdly, almost from the outset, local government involvement in cremation, once introduced, took on a public-health frame of reference. The Local Government Act 1888 gave more powers to Medical Officers of Health, who wanted to include the establishment of mortuaries as part of a municipal system for hygiene in death. At first, the forensic associations of mortuaries did not commend them to the public, but the spread of post-1918 home-ownership brought house-owners to the discovery that keeping the dead at home was not consistent with their new-found pride in the ownership of a clean and healthy home. Funeral directors finally persuaded the public to trust their new chapels of rest. Once the corpse no longer lay at home, old duties were laid aside by survivors. With the establishment of the National Health Service in 1948, the expansion of hospitals and the development of medical techniques, especially in pain-control, meant that the number of hospital deaths began steadily to grow, first overtaking home-deaths in England and Wales in 1958. Public health and national health thus combined to effect the distancing of death from the home and from domestic control.

This chapter suggests that the critical moment arrived when local authorities, in the reconstruction following the Second World War, found they could best meet their obligations in the disposal of the dead by encouraging cremation. Forced by budget deficits, they promoted cremation by setting competitively low prices. All this was with the encouragement of a national government for whom the demands for the living far outweighed the traditional demands of the dead.

Within the space of nine years, all the major institutions who had control of or a financial stake in funerals and in the disposal of the dead, recognized and collaborated with the legitimacy of a move from burial to cremation: the established Church, local government, national government, the rationalized funeral directing industry and the medical profession. For decades all these groups had been the target of cremation advocacy by a highly organized but voluntary cremation society, who in the course of its successful promotion, lost its control over the cremation movement to local authorities as the proprietors and bankers of most crematoria and cemeteries.

Families, with less labour power available to sustain traditional mourning and commemorative tasks, were on the whole relieved to reduce the investment of their money and leisure time which an increasingly prosperous and secular society afforded them. The Protestants had suggested for years that the funeral could not serve the dead, only benefit the living. The Catholic decision for cremation in 1964, in removing the final theological objection from cremation, meant that cremation was finally free to offer itself as an entirely legitimate convenience for the deceased.

REFERENCES

Annan, N. (1984) *Leslie Stephen: the Godless Victorian*, London: Random House.

ap Nicholas, I. (1940) *A Welsh Heretic*, Upton Wirral, Merseyside: The Ffynnon Press.

Clarke, J.S. (1944) *Funeral Reform*, London: The Social Security League.

Davey, R. (1889) *A History of Mourning*, London: P. Jay.

Davies, D. and Shaw, A. (1995) *Reusing Old Graves: A report on popular British attitudes*, Crayford: Shaw & Sons.

Fussell, P. (1975) *The Great War and Modern Memory*, Oxford: Oxford University Press.

Gregory, A. (1994) *The Silence of Memory*, Oxford: Berg.

Jupp, P.C. (1993a) 'Cremation or Burial? Contemporary choice in city and village', in D. Clark (ed.) *The Sociology of Death*, Oxford: Blackwell.

Jupp, P.C. (1993b) 'The Development of Cremation in England, 1820–1990: a sociological account', unpublished Ph.D. thesis, University of London.

Leaney, J. (1989) 'Ashes to Ashes: Cremation and the celebration of death in nineteenth-century Britain', in R. Houlbrooke (ed.) *Death, Ritual and Bereavement,* London: Routledge.

Marwick, A. (1965) *The Deluge: British society and the First World War,* Harmondsworth: Pelican.

Pharos (1934–) *The Journal of the Cremation Society of Great Britain,* London: The Cremation Society.

Prior, L. (1996) 'Acturial Visions of Death: life, death and chance in the modern world', in P.C. Jupp and G. Howarth (eds.) *The Changing Face of Death,* Basingstoke: Macmillan.

Thompson, H. (1874) 'The Treatment of the Body after Death', *Contemporary Review,* January.

White, S. (1990) 'A Burning Issue', *New Law Journal,* 10 August.

Wilkinson, A. (1978) *The Church of England and The First World War,* London: SPCK.

Winter, J. (1995) *Sites of Memory, Sites of Mourning: the Great War in European cultural history,* Cambridge: Cambridge University Press.

12 The Public Construction of AIDS Deaths in the United Kingdom

Neil Small

WORLD AIDS DAY

On 1 December 1995, like 1 December for several previous years, I was with a group of people remembering those who have lived with and died from HIV-related illness. In my home city of Leeds we met in the Town Hall. There were more than a hundred people, many familiar faces, but some new. We heard people talking about their own life with the virus or about caring for people now dead. It was moving and tender: at times the spontaneity faltered but the sense of comradeship and of reverence did not. People spoke out loud the name of the one they loved. On display were sections of the Quilt, in which individuals are remembered but which also serves to illustrate how, when the sections are put together, the whole tells a further story than that told in the particular. We then moved outside on to the Town Hall steps. We carried candles, sang songs, 'We are the World, We are the People . . .' and released white balloons, one for each person from our region who had died – more balloons than you expected. The wind carried them towards and over the adjacent hospital and the ward where many of those deaths had occurred. There were a few faces in its windows, some nurses, some not. The ubiquitous candles burned bright as those ill or near death looked down on those, standing in the cold December night, who were remembering and contemplating the future.

World AIDS Day, 1 December, is marked by ceremonies in many parts of the world. It is a manifestation of the internationalism of the virus and of the response to it. The red badges, the candles, the confessional, the juxtaposing of the personal and the political, the aesthetic, the 'style' of these occasions would be similar in the UK, USA and Australia, as indeed in other countries. In this it is different from 'days' for other illness, breast cancer and multiple sclerosis for example, which contain some of the same elements but not this internationalism.

GLOBAL NETWORKS AND LOCAL DIFFERENCES

It is something of a cliché of the HIV pandemic that the virus knows no frontiers. It is of course true that in an era of air travel, migrations and the general globalization of commerce, leisure and culture this virus, like others, will not respect national frontiers. But globalization is a paradoxical phenomenon. The intensity and rapidity of cultural flows have contributed to the sense of the world being a singular place. But these flows have also, in their increasingly frequent contact with established cultures, generated points of conflict. The triumph of the global has been contested. The world remains a place with important local differences and, despite our familiarity with the signs and symbols of the global, local surprises remain. In the UK we may feel, for example, that we 'know' New York, Times Square, skyscrapers, Broadway, a sense of 'edge' in the air as we encounter this city. But the Latin life of the Spanish-speaking takes us by surprise. We may think we know Australian culture and style, but a trip to Sydney's King's Cross during Mardi Gras will shock – or delight.

John O'Neill (1990) has written about AIDS as a globalizing panic. It is a panic that has led to an intensification of the sense that the world is one place which must pull together to fight threats. But, at the same time, there has been 'a de-globalizing reaction' concerned with the possibility of sealing off the nation–state from global viral flows. Restricting immigration is the clearest manifestation of this. This has meant that as well as an international phenomenon of AIDS there have also been national, regional, city, local and subcultural phenomena.

HIV and AIDS are present in very different ways in the

neighouring cities of Glasgow and Edinburgh. The epidemic and reactions to it have taken a different form in New York and San Francisco. Different parts of the same city can be contrasted, the Bronx and Manhattan vividly so by Drucker (1990). Contrasts between different boroughs in London are also considerable (see Pye *et al.* 1989).

But there are communities of interest and of identity as well as communities defined by geography. The disproportionate impact of HIV and AIDS on the metropolitan community of gay men in London and many other Western cities represents a crucial dimension of the epidemic.

Dimensions of oppression structure the HIV epidemic. These include the wealth and power inequalities between the first world and the rest, poverty within countries as well as between, racism, the oppression of women and prejudice against gay men and women. It is an intriguing question to consider if minorities have more in common each with the other than they have with the national context they physically live within. Certainly, in relation to the HIV epidemic, the global network of gay men who have co-operated to provide insight and support are an example of sectoral globalization. In the UK a meeting convened by the London Lesbian and Gay Switchboard and the Health Education Authority in April 1983 was addressed by Mel Rosen from the Gay Men's Health Crisis in New York. Tony Whitehead, subsequently chair of Britain's pioneering Terrence Higgins Trust, reports that

> Within ten minutes of him starting to speak everyone in the room was united in disbelieving shock. HIV and AIDS was a sort of vague, almost political threat until we started to meet people whose lives would never be the same again. It was clear that many were going to die. The press cuttings we'd all seen conveyed nothing of the horrors that were just round the corner, it was of paramount importance that we set something up fast. I don't mind telling you I was very, very scared . . . I still am, but at least there is the Trust to help us. (letter to Trust supporters, 1995)

It was as if, in looking to the USA, one could see the future (see Watney 1994).

We must pause here and ask if it is meaningful to talk of AIDS deaths in the UK as an analytic or descriptive concept. We have seen that contrast between globalization and the establishment of sites of resistance and reaction, we have identified the dimension of the local but also of the community of interest that seems to have little to do with political boundaries. What is left for the level of the national interest?

Certainly the extent and the detail of the epidemiology of the epidemic varies from country to country. Examples of figures from March 1994 on the reported prevalence of cumulative AIDS cases in Europe per million of the population are illustrative of differences in scale. Spain has 619, Switzerland 523.1, Italy 376.6, Belgium 158.7, the UK 155.6, Norway 87.2 and Greece 87.2. Dominant routes of infection also differ: in Spain and Italy injecting drug-users make up the largest group of people with AIDS and HIV infection, in Belgium the largest group contracted the virus through heterosexual sex (European Centre for the Epidemiological Monitoring of AIDS 1994).

There are also considerable differences in prevention and treatment offered by health- and social-care systems. In Holland a needle-exchange scheme had been in operation from 1984, and in 1987 a pilot scheme was established in nine UK cities. One city was Glasgow. In 1985 the incidence of HIV infection among drug injectors was about 1 per cent, two years later it was almost 5 per cent. A study of 1,786 drug injectors from the Greater Glasgow area examined between 1986 and 1989 found a level of 3.7 per cent infection. This was widely accepted as one of the few success stories in the world at this time (Gruer *et al.* 1991).

It would be possible to go on listing specific features of the epidemic that can be understood within the parameters of the national. The UK epidemic has these features in terms of its size, its make-up and the panoply of responses to it from the Government, the voluntary sector and from self-help movements. There is a national experience, then, in terms of a structural context, the trajectory of the epidemic and the interface of epidemic and institutions. But the ontological experience of the epidemic is not determined by such factors. Rather, if the scene is set by the specifically national, and if some of the limits and the possibilities are so defined, the script and the plot come from elsewhere. They come from the juxtaposition of global dimensions of solidarity and oppression and from the nature of the virus itself.

STIGMA AND SECRETS

The history of the epidemic is one of mobilization, commitment and achievement. But it is also one that must be located in the context of neglect, hostility and discrimination (see Garfield 1994). The public presentation of the disease had continually to be tempered with the realization that elaborate stigmatization was attached to those with the virus and, indeed, to those identified with what were considered high-risk life-styles, those of gay men in particular. There are many examples. One gay male person with AIDS sums up the experience of many.

> The nurses are scared of me; the doctors wear masks and sometimes gloves. Even the priest doesn't seem too anxious to shake my hand. What the hell is this? I'm not a leper. Do they want to lock me up and shoot me? I've got no family, no friends. Where do I go? What do I do? God, this is horrible! Is He punishing me? The only thing I have got going for me is that I'm not dying – at least not yet. (quoted in Kleinman 1988: 163)

Kleinman identifies the person with HIV as being a recipient of the sorts of stigmata in the past bestowed on people with syphilis and gonorrhoea. The cultural meaning attached to such illnesses derives from a stark social contradiction which sees a prevalence of commercialized sexual imagery and a hypocritical condemnation of what he identifies as its venereal results.

Further, it could be argued that the trade in illicit drugs is itself a grotesque parody of the dominant motif of modern society, trade and profit. It is of course also a phenomenon that has to be explained materially and so be linked with poverty and disempowerment.

The HIV positive diagnosis 'encases the patient in a visible exoskeleton of powerfully peculiar meanings . . . That exoskeleton is a carapace of culturally marked illness, a dominant societal symbol that, once applied to a person, spoils radically that individual's identity and is not easily removed' (Kleinman 1988: 22). Such a powerful symbolic meaning contains a new, emerging, explanatory model in Western medicine. This model is 'responsibility and blame focused; that is, disease, onset and outcome are directly ascribed to the afflicted themselves. These responsible parties are then subject to censure for personal failures which caused their condition' (Finerman and Bennett 1995). Indulgence, overeating, smoking, unsafe drinking, unsafe sex are all invoked in such a way as to take away the 'benefits' of the sick role and to increase the likelihood that the experts will appropriate more and more of the decision-making as to what happens to that body. After all, if one is sick and seen to be to blame for that sickness then it would follow that one is unlikely to make wise choices about treatment (Kirmayer 1988).

But it is not just during treatment that stigma shapes the experience of the person living with the HIV virus, it is also after death. One manifestation of this is in the certification of death. 'Until the advent of AIDS more liberal attitudes in society had lessened the stigma of most causes of death as an obstacle to their accurate certification' (King 1989: 734). In the past relevant facts relating to an illness and a death have been 'overlooked', deaths which might have been attributed to chronic alcoholism were redefined as being from a more acceptable cause, myocardial ischaemia, for example. Cirrhosis of the liver would be attributed to poor nutrition rather than ethanol. Suicides often appeared as accidents. King reports that, in his experience, doctors who complete a death certificate 'may try to preserve the dignity of relatives by substituting other causes of death or not stating the underlying diagnosis of HIV infection' (p. 735). It may be that the doctor considers that they have fulfilled their public duty in reporting the HIV infection to the Centre for Communicable Diseases and their duty to the patients and family by omitting the diagnosis from the certificate.

Sometimes the family does not exist as a meaningful support

for the person with HIV. A poster advertising the services available at London Lighthouse reads:

'Derek lost his entire family to AIDS. One year later, they are still not talking to him. That's why he called us. We always listen. We never judge. We know that family rejection can sometimes be more distressing than the illness.' An alternative scenario is that the family does not know. Oscar Moore, columnist in the newspaper *Guardian Weekend*, wrote in February 1995 of how 'I still get letters from lonely terrified teenagers, unable to tell their family that they are dying because they have not yet told them that they are gay' (p. 5).

PERSONAL TESTAMENT AND PUBLIC MEMORIAL

Through the history of the epidemic there has been a manifestation of stigma in the concern of the press to link observed illness, HIV and the attribution of homosexuality. There are a number of gross examples, and the response to the illness and death of journalist, commentator and television presenter Russell Harty in 1988 can serve as one. First, a Sunday newspaper broke the 'story' that he was a homosexual. Then, in 1988, when he was admitted to hospital with hepatitis, journalists tried to bribe neighbours and hospital workers for stories and hired a flat outside the hospital with a line of sight to Russell's ward for their telephoto lenses. They wanted to discover that he had AIDS, which he did not. His sexuality, coupled with his ill health, were enough for them to assume the trinity (see Alan Bennett's address at Russell Harty's Memorial Service, reprinted in Bennett 1994).

Others who are sick, in some cases at the end of their lives, have had HIV-related illness and have been harassed by the press. In some cases they have taken the initiative and have jumped before they were pushed, and in others they have made a principled decision to speak out and confront the stigma, indeed to seek to help others living with the virus or at risk of contracting it.

Sports stars Arthur Ashe, Magic Johnson and Greg Louganis have all written books which have included discussions about

HIV illness, so has film-maker Derek Jarman and musician Holly Johnson. The death of actor Denholm Elliott was followed by the establishment of a charity to support services for people with HIV. Disc jockey Kenny Everett made known his HIV-positive status in 1993 and campaigned against cuts to HIV charities, notably the Terrence Higgins Trust. He died in April 1995. Rock Hudson was very important in the rise in public prominence for HIV, as was Freddie Mercury, and particularly important for young black communities of the USA, was the death in March 1995 of rap artist Eazy-E. Three thousand people attended his funeral. Photographer Robert Mapplethorpe contributed to the aesthetic of the epidemic. Others – Bruce Chatwin, Liberace, Rudolf Nureyev – struggled with illness and the fear of its public disclosure. The interface of celebrity and the intimate world of sex and death has never been so scrutinized (Small 1993a).[1]

Celebrity and specific causes of death have been linked before. The association of poets and writers with tuberculosis is an earlier example. What is different, and unique with HIV illness, is the added dimension of stigma and the pervasiveness of media interest. But the role of celebrity goes further and allows a route into one of the paradoxes at the heart of the relationship between the public and the private in this epidemic. As we know, HIV is infectious and the risks of its transmission can be greatly reduced by individuals making simple choices, not to share needles and not to have intercourse without a condom, for example. Celebrity is a crucial dimension of getting such messages across. But once the genie is out of the bottle it's not so easy to get it back in! It is not so easy to say we want publicity for this but privacy for that: it should be, but it isn't.

But it is not just celebrity that has shaped effective responses to the epidemic. It is also solidarity, pride. Simon Watney has spoken of how the major advances in prevention of the spread of the virus amongst gay men are an artefact of the specific historical time when the virus appeared. It is only now, after the advances in gay organization in the 1970s and 1980s, that there is an infrastructure and a confidence to respond to the demands of the epidemic both in terms of prevention and care.

It is the advance in both pride and organization that has also provided the context, Watney argues, for much of the cultural response to the epidemic. This response has been both didactic and poetic, to advise and to remember (on *Consuming Passions*, presented by Jeff Watts, BBC Radio 3, 8 December 1995). It has been impassioned and poignant, the cry of anger in Larry Kramer's play *The Normal Heart* and the commitment each to the other by the group of friends in Craig Lucas's film *Longtime Companions* are examples.

The public presentation of the epidemic via celebrity and via the arts risks obscuring the epistemological truth of the epidemic – that people who die of AIDS are also people who die. Catherine Camus, daughter of Albert Camus, reflecting on his death in a car crash in 1960, spoke of how for others Albert Camus, writer and celebrity, had died. For her it was her dad (*The Observer*, 8 October 1995). Nick Partridge of the Terrence Higgins Trust spoke of 'going through my address list . . . and realising how many names and addresses I have to cross out is one of the hardest things' (BBC Radio 5 Live, 2 December 1995). Derek Jarman, writing shortly before his own death, best captures in the images he chooses and the language he uses both the immensity and the intimacy of the epidemic, both the rage and the tenderness that we see displayed: 'I'm walking along the beach in a howling gale. Another year is passing. In the roaring waters I hear the voices of dead friends. Love and life lasts forever. My heart's memory turns to you; David, Howard, Graham, Terry, Paul. . . .' (Derek Jarman, from the soundtrack of the film *Blue*).

FROM MOURNING TO MEMORIAL

I have sought to explore some of the paradoxical features of the HIV epidemic. The relationship between the public and the private is crucial. It is a relationship evident also in those particular kinds of memorial that have accompanied the epidemic. Here we can see attempts to underline three features; first, that people who die from AIDS-related illness are individuals; second, that these individuals are very different sorts of people and third, that looking at the generality of losses illustrates something of the social significance of the epidemic, the whole more than the sum of the parts. The Quilt and the Red Ribbon are the two features of response to the epidemic that I will consider.

In 1987 Cleve Jones began the 'Names Project' in the USA. Those who had died of an AIDS-related illness were commemorated through an originally designed portion of a quilt, the quilt being fashioned from many such contributions (Ruskin 1988). In the UK the 'Quilts of Love' project was inspired by this approach and a further adaptation is the 'Wall of Love' made of almost 1,000 plaques. Alastair Home, director of the NAMES Project in Edinburgh, has called the Quilt 'a monument built of our love, tears, joy, rage, compassion and hope' (Arnold and James 1995: 57). Simon Watney, speaking of the US Quilt, sees it as offering a

> geographical approximation of the scale of the epidemic as well as an ethnographic equivalent. Walk down avenues of quilts and see gay cops from San Francisco next to black babies from Brooklyn, a schoolteacher next to Michel Foucault. It gives an extraordinary picture of the actual population of the USA, as well as of those with AIDS.

He argues, further, that the response to AIDS has, for the first time since the Second World War, produced an art concerned with how we set up a memorial for these people in a late twentieth-century secular society (on *Consuming Passions,* presented by Jeff Watts, BBC Radio 3, 8 December 1995). In this context it can be noted that one description of the Red Ribbon worn to remember and express solidarity with those who are HIV positive is that it is 'the 1990s equivalent of the poppy' (Arnold and James 1995: 53).

The literature about HIV and AIDS has been infused with the metaphors of war. Pushing the enemy back, coming back from the front line, a positive HIV test as a declaration of war, and so on (Sontag 1988; literature summarized in Small 1993b: 60–1). War is one other cause of death that impacts on cohorts of the population over a limited period of time. Those soldiers who have died in recent wars are, characteristically, publicly remembered in special days and through particular sorts of structures (see Davies 1993). Anderson has argued that there are 'no more arresting emblems of the modern culture of nationalism . . . than cenotaphs and tombs of Unknown Soldiers. The public ceremonial reverence accorded these monuments precisely because they are deliberately empty or no one knows who lies inside them, has no true precedents in earlier times' (Anderson 1991: 9).

The contrast between the the unknown and un-named and the construction of a memorial out of the creative response to the life and death of each individual, as exemplified in the NAMES Project, could hardly be greater. The Quilt is indeed a memorial for a community, but a community without nationalism. There are more similarities between the poppy and the Red Ribbon: perhaps the poppy, as a symbol for each fallen soldier, manages to say something at one and the same time individual and, as they fall from the ceiling at the annual Remembrance Day Commemoration, collective.[2]

Anderson's description of the cenotaphs and tombs not only sees them in relation to nationalism but also to the modern. The HIV epidemic and responses to it might best be addressed using the language of postmodernity. Both in its concern with identity (Weeks 1990) and with the multiple and discontinuous representations of AIDS at every level in the media, in science and in the cultural assumptions brought to bear on it (Patton 1990), we see something that can not be reduced to the single. We see something essentially complex and contested (Small 1993b: 23–5).

CONCLUSION

We are, in this place, far from the certainties of the modern, it is indeed an 'unknown country'. The paradoxes surround us. There is a public-health agenda that benefits from disclosure and there is a private need for secrecy. While this may be true for many conditions it is compounded by the stigma attached to those living with, and dying from, this virus and its effects. The virus does not know international barriers but its impact has distinct local characteristics.

A movement of support exists in the UK, the USA, Australia

and in many other countries that is united by something that transcends the national. But while one can collectivize aspects of the epidemic, its context and responses to it, one still experiences dying as an intimate experience.

New ways of supporting the ill and remembering the dying are developing alongside the HIV epidemic. They tell us about ways of recognizing community as being something to do with pride and with interests and not just with place. They all manifest and illustrate aspects of our changing world. They are not modern, even though the epidemic is manifestly structured around the sort of world we have constructed for ourselves in the late twentieth century.

That people live and die with the epidemic in the context of the national is obvious. Indeed it is important. In the UK the decision to pursue needle-exchange schemes has shaped the epidemic. The continuing presence of a National Health Service has ameliorated some of the distress evident in other countries when one's insurance cover runs out. These are but two examples of how the lived experience is shaped by the national context: they are not small matters. But the epidemic and responses to it give us an insight into that interface of the personal and the political that is shaped by chosen and by attributed identity, by pride and by stigma, not by national frontiers that neither the virus, love or hate respect.

Next year, on my Town Hall steps, the experience will be similar, more balloons of course. The scene is, for me, something of a tableau of the whole epidemic. It represents that juxtaposition of a social movement, albeit a postmodern one, with the intimate world of love, death and loss. It reminds me of the distinction between dying in a movement and dying and a movement. There is the personal and the political. The public construction of AIDS death in the UK is part of the reason for being there each 1 December. But so too is the need to join in this particular way of mourning the individuals, wherever they come from, who have died in this epidemic.

NOTES

1. Books by celebrities which discuss, autobiographically, HIV or AIDS include: Greg Louganis, *Breaking the Surface* (1995) (a wonderful title for a book about 'coming out' as gay and winning Olympic diving medals); Magic Johnson, *What you can do to avoid AIDS* (1992); Arthur Ashe, *Days of Grace* (1994); Derek Jarman, *Chroma: a book of colour* (1993); Holly Johnson, *A bone in my flute* (1994).
2. Although HIV and war may share metaphors, one difference is that the dead in war are not also the stigmatized. It may be, though, that the front-line troops are marginalized, or choose marginalization. The trilogy of novels about the First World War by Pat Barker, *Regeneration* (1991), *The Eye in the Door* (1993) and *The Ghost Road* (1995), explore the way in which such front-line troops see themselves as apart from the rest of society and choose to seek out such postings, with the risk of death they imply, rather than live with those who have not encountered the seductive horror of the comradeship of battle.

REFERENCES

Anderson, B. (1991) *Imagined Communities*, London: Verso.

Arnold, K. and James, F. (1995) *AIDS and Fatal Attractions*, London: Wellcome Institute.

Bennett, A. (1994) 'Russell Harty, 1934–1988', in *Writing Home*, London: Faber & Faber.

Davies, J. (1993) 'War Memorials', in D. Clark (ed.) *The Sociology of Death*, Oxford: Blackwell.

Drucker, E. (1990) 'Epidemic in the War Zone: AIDS and community survival in New York City', *International Journal of Health Services*, 20, 4: 601–15.

European Centre for the Epidemiological Monitoring of AIDS (1994) *AIDS Surveillance in Europe*, Quarterly Report No. 41.

Finerman, R. and Bennett, L.A. (1995) 'Guilt, Blame and Shame: Responsibility in Health and Sickness', *Social Science and Medicine*, 40, 1, January: 1–3.

Garfield, S. (1994) *The End of Innocence*, London: Faber & Faber.

Gruer, L. *et al.* (1991) 'Distribution of HIV and Acute Hepatitis B Infection among Drug Injectors in Glasgow', *International Journal of STD's and AIDS*, 2: 356–8.

King, M.B. (1989) 'AIDS on the Death Certificate: the final stigma', *British Medical Journal*, 28, 18 March: 734–6.

Kirmayer L. (1988) 'Mind and Body as Metaphors: hidden values in biomedicine', in M. Lock and D. Gordon, *Biomedicine Examined*, Boston: Kluwer Academic Publishers.

Kleinman, A. (1988) *The Illness Narratives*, New York: Basic Books.

O'Neill, J. (1990) 'AIDS as a Globalizing Panic', in M. Featherstone (ed.) *Global Culture,* London: Sage.

Patton, C. (1990) *Inventing AIDS,* London: Routledge & Kegan Paul.

Pye, M., Kapila, M., Buckley, G. and Cunningham, D. (1989) *Responding to the AIDS Challenge,* London: Health Education Authority and Longman.

Ruskin, C. (1988) *The Quilt: Stories from the NAMES Project,* New York: Simon & Schuster.

Small, N. (1993a) 'Dying in a Public Place; AIDS deaths', in D. Clark (ed.) *The Sociology of Death,* Oxford: Blackwell.

Small, N. (1993b) *AIDS: The Challenge. Understanding, education and care,* Aldershot: Avebury.

Sontag, S. (1988) *AIDS and its Metaphors,* London: Allen Lane.

Watney, S. (1994) *Practices of Freedom,* London: Rivers Oram Press.

Weeks, J. (1990) 'Post-modern AIDS?', in T. Boffin and S. Gupta (eds.) *Ecstatic Antibodies,* London: Rivers Oram Press.

13 The American Ways of Death[1]

Michael R. Leming and George E. Dickinson

Like people from other cultures, Americans are bombarded with pressing issues of the day which involve death and death-related matters: the AIDS crisis, the prolongation of dying from cancer, the growing incidence of chronic illnesses with uncertain courses, murder, ecological disasters, foetal transplants and abortion. The topic of death is 'alive and well' in contemporary American society. Yet Americans tend to deal with death in the same way that Charlie Brown (the 'hero' from the popular American comic strip 'Peanuts') deals with life's other problems: 'There is no problem so big that you can't run away from it.' Consider the following facts:

1. Seventy per cent of all deaths take place in institutional settings – hospitals and nursing homes. Dying in the United States occurs 'offstage', away from the arena of familiar surroundings of kin and friends.
2. With less than 10 per cent of the United States population living on farms, birth and death scenes have largely been confined to television or to the worlds of health-care professionals and removed from personal observations of most individuals.
3. The average life expectancy has increased more than 20 years since 1920.
4. The average attendance at funerals and wakes has decreased significantly during the past 20 years.

Is it any wonder that Americans find it difficult to cope with death when it is experienced infrequently, is highly impersonal, and viewed as virtually abnormal? However, denial is only one method employed by Americans in coping with death and dying in the United States (see Feifel 1990; Riley 1992).

For most Americans the most frequent experience of death comes from the evening news, as reporters attempt to bring us as close to the scene of death as availability and 'good taste' will allow. However, since viewers are unlikely to know the people who have died, the effect of this 'death news' upon them is minimal. This problem has not changed in nearly 25 years, since Robert Kavanaugh (1972: 13) made the following observation:

> Over a two-week period of nighttime (television) viewing, I counted an average of 34 deaths at close range, countless more at a distance. Not one death raised as much as a slight tremor in me. Television feeds our fantasy of forever being a spectator. Even a bloody nose or a fainting spell by a fellow viewer would have aroused more emotion in me than a hundred deaths on the tube.

Death appears to be more abstract for those growing up today than for previous generations of Americans. By the age of 15, some media experts say, the average American has seen 13,000 murders on television and has been exposed to an endless stream of war, famine and holocaust in the daily news (Bordewich 1988: 34). Since we are unlikely to know the deceased individuals, however, the effect of this 'death news' upon us is minimal. Certainly a need for death education seems apparent in today's society.

EXPLAINING DEATH TO CHILDREN

With a note of irony, Edna St Vincent Millay (1969) calls childhood 'the kingdom where nobody dies', referring to the reluctance of many adults to face the need to be open in talking to children about death. Despite the American tendency to deny death and remove death topics from routine social discourse, American children can and do think and talk about death. Analogous to difficulties with talking about sex with children, many American adults project on to the child their own reluctance to deal openly with death.

Death educators advise contemporary Americans that whenever a child asks a question about death – whether of animals, other people, or self – adults should be ready to respond in a natural and matter-of-fact way to the concern raised (see Dickinson 1992; Essa *et al.* 1995; Schaeffer 1988).

Realizing the tendency of Americans to avoid death, 24 years ago Helene Galen (1972) encouraged her readers to capitalize on 'the teachable moment' whenever it arose with children. She felt that children ought to be encouraged to express fear, doubt and curiosity concerning death. Galen's advice is still appropriate for American parents when dealing with the death concerns of their children.

1. Ask yourself: 'How would I treat this action, comment or question if it were not about death?' The answer would usually be, 'Matter-of-factly.'
2. Ask: 'What is this child really seeking by this action, comment or question?' Recognize that children often act out their feelings rather than verbalizing them clearly.
3. Take care to present only basic truths about what is being asked. Total comprehension will be achieved only gradually. Give the child time to grasp the broader implications of the subject.
4. With children younger than eleven or twelve, use concrete terms such as 'died, death, buried.' Abstract or metaphorical terminology such as 'sleep', 'passed on', or 'God wanted another angel' are simply confusing to the child. Euphemisms may meet the needs of adults, but can cause untold problems for children.

DEATH ATTITUDES AND DEATH FEARS

Death *per se* has no meaning other than that which people give it. If this is true, why is it that most of us believe that death is something which intrinsically engenders fear? Anthropologists would be quick to respond that not all cultures in the world hold that death is necessarily something to be feared. For example, B.F. Skinner, the American psychologist who popularized behaviour modification, approached his death from leukaemia with apparently no regrets. The

86-year-old Skinner, just a few weeks before he died, said with a laugh (1990), 'I will be dead in a few months, but it hasn't given me the slightest anxiety or worry or anything. I always knew I was going to die.'

However, it is typical in American culture to attach fearful meanings to death and death-related situations. Why is it that so many people have less than positive views of death? Death universally calls into question the order upon which most societies are based. As a marginal experience to everyday life, death not only disrupts normal patterns of interaction, but also challenges the meaningfulness of life. With the exception of those societies where death is a routine event in the lives of the people (e.g. Uganda, Sudan, Cambodia and New Guinea), death in most societies is a stressful event because it brings disorder to those whose lives it touches.

Any change in ordinary patterns of social interaction requires the individual to adjust. Most of us prefer the security of situations that are predictable, stable and routine. The disorder created by changes in everyday life can make for a stressful situation as individuals attempt to adjust to these changes (Holmes and Rahe 1967). Since death in the United States is removed from everyday life, it is experienced as more stressful.

Death in the United States is viewed as fearful because Americans have been systematically taught to fear it. Horror films portray death, ghosts, skeletons, goblins and ghoulish morticians as things or people to be feared. *Sesame Street* tries to create for children a more positive view of monsters as children are befriended by Grover, Harry, Oscar and Cookie Monster. With the exception of Casper, 'the friendly ghost', death-related fantasy-figures have not received the same positive images. Instead of providing positive images, American culture has chosen to reinforce fearful meanings of death. American cemeteries are portrayed as eerie, funeral homes are to be avoided, and morgues are scary places where you 'wouldn't be caught dead'.

One of the reasons death-education courses in America incorporate field trips to hospices, funeral homes, crematoria, and cemeteries is to confront negative death meanings and fantasies with first-hand objective observations. The preparation room at the mortuary is a good example. A typical American who has never visited a preparation room has a mental image that the room will be similar to Dr Frankenstein's laboratory (complete with bats, strange lighting, body parts and naked dead bodies), and this image causes them to approach the room with fear and caution. When we give college students a tour of the preparation room we find that many of them are deeply disappointed because they find a room that looks like a physician's examination room. 'Is that all there is?' is the comment often overheard after visiting the preparation room.

When one speaks of death fear or death anxiety, it is assumed that the concept is unidimensional and that consensus exists relative to its meaning. Such is not the case, however, since two persons may say that they fear death and yet the content of their fears may not be shared. Death anxiety (or death fear) is a multidimensional concept and is based upon the following four concerns: (1) the death of self; (2) the deaths of significant others; (3) the process of dying; and (4) the state of being dead. The more elaborated form of this model (Leming 1979–80) shows eight types of death fears that can be applied to the death of self and the death of others:

1. dependency
2. the pain in the dying process
3. the indignity in the dying process
4. the isolation, separation and rejection that can be part of the dying process
5. leaving loved ones
6. afterlife concerns
7. the finality of death
8. the fate of the body.

From Table 13.1 we can see that the content of fear will be influenced by whose death the individual is considering. From a personal death perspective, one may have anxiety over the effect that one's dying (or being dead) will have on others. There might also be private worries about how one might be treated by others. From the perspective of the survivor, the individual may be concerned about the

Table 13.1 The Eight Dimensions of Death Anxiety as they relate to the Deaths of Self and Others

SELF	*OTHERS*
	PROCESS OF DYING
1. Fear of dependency	Fear of financial burdens
2. Fear of pain in dying process	Fear of going through the painful experience of others
3. Fear of the indignity in dying process	Fear of being unable to cope with the physical problems of others
4. Fear of loneliness, rejection, and isolation	Fear of being unable to cope emotionally with problems of others
5. Fear of leaving loved ones	Fear of losing loved ones
	STATE OF BEING DEAD
6. Afterlife concerns	Afterlife concerns
Fear of an unknown situation	Fear of the judgement of others
Fear of divine judgement	Fear of the spirit world –
Fear of ghosts, spirits devils, etc.	'What are they thinking?'
Fear of nothingness	Fear of never seeing the person again
7. Fear of the finality of life	Fear of the end of a relationship
Fear of not being able to achieve one's goals	Guilt related to not having done enough for the deceased
Fear of the possible end of physical and symbolic identity	Fear of not seeing the person again
Fear of the end of all social relationships	Fear of losing the social relationship
8. Fear of the fate of the body	Fear of death objects
Fear of body decomposition	Fear of dead bodies
Fear of being buried	Fear of being in cemeteries
Fear of not being treated with respect	Fear of not knowing how to act in death-related situations

financial, emotional, and social problems related to the death of a significant other.

Since there are many factors related to the experience of death and death-related situations that can engender fear, we would expect to find individual differences in type and intensity of death fear, including social circumstance and past experiences. However, with all of the potential sources for differences, repeated administrations of the Leming Death Fear Scale yield consistently high scores for the fears of dependency and pain related to the process of dying, and relatively low anxiety scores for the fears related to the afterlife and the fate of the body. Approximately 65 per cent of the more than 1 000 individuals surveyed had high anxiety concerning dependency and pain, and only 15 per cent experienced the same level of anxiety relative to concerns about the afterlife and the fate of the body (Leming 1979–80). Thus it is the *process of dying* – not the *event of death* – that causes the most concern.

THE AMERICAN WAY OF DYING

We have seen that most Americans fear the process of dying much more than they do the fact that at some point in time they will be dead. Woody Allen once said, 'I'm not afraid of dying. I just don't want to be there when it happens.' The meaning of our dying will depend to a great extent upon the nature of the cause of the death and the social context in which the dying takes place.

If you were to ask a number of Americans the following question: 'When your time comes, how would you wish to die?', with the exception of the comical reply 'When I am ninety-two, at the hands of a jealous lover', most people will respond, 'At home, unexpectedly, in my own bed, when I am asleep, and when I am very old – but with my full mental and physical capabilities.' Unfortunately for most, they will not die as they would like, and for some this may be a source of apprehension and anxiety.

Most Americans will die in institutionalized settings and not at home as they would like. A small percentage of persons die of acute diseases, while most (76 per cent) will die of one of the following chronic diseases: cardiovascular disease, cancer, AIDS, diabetes, liver, kidney and lung diseases. With these chronic diseases, deaths are usually prolonged and are anything but sudden and unexpected as most people would desire.

Human beings do not respond to all deaths in the same manner – humans ascribe meanings to death and then respond to these meanings. The American way of dying places higher values on some causes of death and ascribes less status to others. Likewise, coping with the death of a loved one will be influenced by the cause of the death.

While there are some special problems associated with the way most Americans die (caused by a chronic disease – e.g. heart disease, cancer and diabetes), there are also some real advantages. The following is a partial list of the opportunities provided by a slow death caused by a chronic disease:

1. The dying person is given an opportunity to attend to unfinished business – make out a will, complete uncompleted projects.
2. The dying person and his or her family can attempt to heal broken family relationships, they can say their final farewells, and they can all participate in constructing a meaningful and dignified death.
3. Funerals and other arrangements can be made with the consent and participation of the person who is dying.
4. Anticipatory grief on the part of the survivors and dying patient can take place.

Deaths due to acute diseases (e.g. pneumonia), accidents and suicide also provide special problems and advantages to survivors. For all quick deaths there is the problem of being unprepared for the death. Some of the grieving preceding the death due to a chronic disease cannot be expressed in deaths of this type. Consequently, grief is usually more intense when the dying takes place in a short period of time. Survivors may also experience more intense guilt – 'If only I had done something, she wouldn't have died.' Suicide creates special problems for survivors because they can become stigmatized by having a relative commit suicide – 'They drove him to it.' Finally, when people die without warning, survivors are often troubled because they did not have a chance to mend a broken relationship or say goodbye.

On the other hand, survivors of deaths due to acute diseases, accidents and suicide are spared the following problems associated with chronic diseases:

1. Dying persons may not be willing to accept death, and when learning of their fates, may act in unacceptable ways.
2. Families may also be unwilling to accept the death of a loved one.
3. The dying process may be a long and painful process, not only for the dying patient, but for the family as well.
4. The cost of dying from a chronic disease can be, and usually is, very expensive. The entire assets of a family can be wiped out by the medical bills of a chronically ill patient.

THE DYING PROCESS

In thinking about the dying process, the first thing that comes to our awareness is the concept of time. We are confronted with the fact that time, for the terminal patient, is running out. Yet when does the dying process begin? Are we not all dying, with some reaching the state of being dead before others? From the moment of our births, we are approaching the end of our lives. We assume that terminal patients will experience death before non-dying individuals, but this is not always the case. Since it is possible to diagnose a disease from which most people die, we can assume that patients with these diseases are 'more terminal' than individuals without them. The terminal patient is very much concerned with the time dimension of his or her physical existence. Many popular and scientific surveys have demonstrated that as many as 80 per cent of American patients want to be told if their illness is terminal. However, doctors are not always prepared to give their patients a terminal diagnosis (see Corr and Doka 1994; Dickinson and Tournier 1994; Fellman 1994; Guillemin 1992; Walker 1982; Webb 1992).

One of the reasons that American doctors are reluctant to tell their patients is that, once defined as having a terminal condition, patients begin to view themselves as being 'as good as dead'. These patients have accepted the terminal label, applied it to their understanding of who they are, and have experienced anticipatory death. Families also come to see their loved ones as being in bereavement. This symbolic definition of the patient is reinforced by the role-disengagement process, the spatial isolation of the dying patient, and the terminal label placed upon the patient by the physician and other medical personnel. The patient seems to take on a status somewhere between the living and the dead.

THE CONTEMPORARY AMERICAN FUNERAL

With over two-thirds of American deaths occurring in hospitals or institutions for the care of the sick and infirm, the contemporary process of body disposition begins at the time of death, when the body is removed from the institutional setting. Most frequently the body is taken to a funeral home. There, the body is bathed, embalmed and dressed. It is then placed in a casket selected by the family. Typically, arrangements are made for the ceremony, assuming a ceremony is to follow. The funeral director, in consultation with the family, will determine the type, time, place and day of the ceremony. In most instances, the public rite or ceremony will have a religious content (Pine 1971). The procedure described above is followed in approximately 75 per cent of funerals.

Following this ceremony, final disposition of the body is made by either earth burial (78 per cent), cremation (17 per cent) or entombment (5 per cent) (NFDA 1991). (These percentages are approximate national averages and will vary by geographical region.) The bereavement process will then be followed by a period of post-funeral adjustment for the family.

The American funeral functions as a one-time 'support group' to undergird and sustain the bereaved, providing them with a conducive social environment for mourning. Prior to the funeral, friends and family either go to the home of the bereaved or attend a wake, shiv'ah, or visitation held at the church, synagogue or funeral home for the purpose of extending sympathy to the primary grievers, or work through their own feelings of grief. Since most Americans find it difficult to discuss the death with a member of the family for the first time, they seek the proper atmosphere, time or place. It is during the funeral, the wake, the shiv'ah or the visitation with the bereaved where we are provided the opportunity to express our condolences and sympathy comfortably.

However, increasingly, Americans are exploring alternatives to the traditional funeral (see Barrett 1993; Dolan 1993; Vernon 1993; Walker 1982; Whalen 1990). Three alternatives exist: immediate disposition of the body of the deceased, the bequest of the deceased to a medical institution for anatomical study and research, and the memorial service. Each of these alternatives to the funeral and wake, shiv'ah or visitation *with the deceased body present* is defined and discussed below.

Immediate disposition occurs when the deceased is removed from the place of death to the place of cremation or earth burial without any ceremony; proper certificates are filed and permits received in the interim. In these instances, the family is not present, usually does not view the deceased after death, and is not concerned with any further type of memorialization. It is immediate in that it is accomplished as quickly after death as is possible. In this situation the body will not likely be embalmed, and the only preparation will consist of bathing and washing the body. According to the National Funeral Directors Association (NFDA 1991), approximately 5 per cent of all deaths involved immediate disposition. The frequency of this procedure differs by region of the country – it is performed most in the South Central part of the United States (approximately 7 per cent of cases) and least in New England and the Mountain States (less than 1 per cent of cases).

Body-bequest programmes have become more well known in the last four decades and permit the deceased (prior to death) or the family (after the death) to donate the body to a medical institution. Some American medical schools will pay the cost of transporting the body to the medical school, while others will not. With regard to expenses, this is the least expensive way of disposition of the body, especially if a memorial service is conducted without the body present. In those instances where the family does not desire to have the body or the cremated remains returned, the donee institution will arrange for cremation and/or earth burial – often with an appropriate ceremony. According to the National Funeral Directors Association anatomical gifts account for less than 1 per cent of all deaths in the United States.

The *memorial service* is a service without the body being

present. It is true that every funeral is a memorial service – inasmuch as it is in memory of someone – but a memorial service, by our definition, is an alternative to the typical funeral. It may be conducted on the day of death, within two or three days of death, or sometimes as much as weeks or months following death. The content of the service places little or no emphasis on the death. Instead, it is often a service of acclamation of philosophical concepts. Religious or non-religious in content, these services can meet the needs of the bereaved.

Organizations exist for consumers called *memorial societies.* Such an example exists in Ithaca, New York. The by-laws of this particular non-profit and non-sectarian organization establish the following as purposes of their society:

1. To promote the dignity, simplicity, and spiritual values of funeral rites and memorial services.
2. To facilitate simple disposal of deceased persons at reasonable costs, but with adequate allowances to funeral directors for high-quality services.
3. To increase the opportunity for each person to determine the type of funeral or memorial service he or she desires.
4. To aid its members and promote their interests in achieving the foregoing.

Thus, such a memorial society would help educate consumers regarding death prior to the actual death of a significant other and present options for final disposition of the body. Likewise, many funeral directors today serve as a valuable resource by sharing information regarding death with various community groups.

The American grieving process, like the dying process, is essentially a series of culturally prescribed behaviours and attitudes related to coping with the stressful situation of changing the status of a relationship. The American funeral and its alternatives are cultural devices created to assist individuals in their coping. Many have attempted to understand coping with dying as a series of universal, mutually exclusive and linear stages. However, since most will acknowledge that not all Americans will progress through the stages in the same manner, we will list a number of coping strategies employed by Americans to resolve the pain caused by the loss of a personally significant relationship. The following seven behaviours and feelings are part of the coping process: shock and denial; disorganization; volatile emotions; guilt; loss and loneliness; relief; and re-establishment. It is not difficult to see similarities between these behaviours and Kübler-Ross's five stages (denial, anger, bargaining, depression and acceptance) of the dying process (1969). According to Kavanaugh (1972: 123), 'these seven stages do not subscribe to the logic of the head as much as to the irrational tugs of the heart – the logic of need and permission'.

In 1982 J. William Worden published *Grief Counseling and Grief Therapy*, which summarized the research conclusions of a National Institute of Health study called the Omega Project (occasionally referred to as the Harvard Bereavement Study). Two of the more significant findings of this research, displaying the active nature of the grieving process, are that mourning is necessary for all those who have experienced a loss through death, and that four tasks of mourning must be accomplished before mourning can be completed and re-establishment can take place.

According to Worden (1991: 10), uncompleted grief tasks can impair further growth and development of the individual. Furthermore, the necessity of these tasks suggests that those in bereavement *must* attend to 'grief work' because successful grief resolution is not automatic, as Kavanaugh's (1972) stages might imply. Each bereaved person must accomplish four necessary tasks: (1) accept the reality of the loss, (2) experience the pain of grief, (3) adjust to an environment in which the deceased is missing, and (4) withdraw emotional energy and reinvest it in another relationship (Worden 1991).

NOTES

1. Some of the material for this chapter is based on work published in Michael R. Leming and George E. Dickinson (1994) *Understanding,*

Dying, Death and Bereavement (3rd edn), Fort Worth: Harcourt Brace College Publishers. Adapted with permission.

REFERENCES

Barrett, R.K. (1993) 'Psychocultural Influences on African-American Attitudes toward Death, Dying and Funeral Rites', in J.D. Morgan (ed.), *Personal Care in an Impersonal World: A Multidimensional Look at Bereavement*, Amityville, NY: Baywood.

Bordewich, F.M. (1988) 'Mortal Fears: courses in "Death Education" get mixed reviews', *Atlantic Monthly*, CCLXI, February: 30–4.

Corr, C.A. and Doka, K.J. (1994) 'Current Models of Death, Dying, and Bereavement', *Critical Care Nursing Clinics of North America*, 6, 3: 545–52.

Dickinson, G.E. (1992) 'First Childhood Death Experiences', *Omega*, XXV, 3; 169–82.

Dickinson, G.E. and Tournier, R.E. (1994) 'A Decade beyond Medical School: A longitudinal study of physicians' attitudes toward death and terminally-ill patients', *Social Science and Medicine*, XXXVII, 10: 1397–400.

Dolan, C. (1993) 'Burying Tradition, More People Opt for "Fun" Funerals', *Wall Street Journal*, 20 May: A1–2.

Essa, E.L., Murray, C.I. and Everts, J. (1995) 'Death of a Friend', *Childhood Education*, Spring: 130–3.

Feifel, H. (1990) 'Psychology and Death: meaningful rediscovery', *American Psychologist*, XCV, 4: 537–43.

Fellman, B. (1994) 'Dimensions of Dying', *Yale Alumni Magazine*, October: 54–7.

Formanek, R. (1974) 'When Children Ask About Death', *Elementary School Journal*, LXXV, 2: 92–7.

Galen, H. (1972) 'A Matter of Life and Death', *Young Children*, XXVII, 6: 351–6.

Guillemin, J. (1992) 'Planning to Die', *Society*, July/August: 29–33.

Holmes, T.H. and Rahe, R.H. (1967) 'The Social Readjustment Rating Scale', *Journal of Psychosomatic Research*, XI, August, Table 3–1: 213.

Kavanaugh, R.E. (1972) *Facing Death*, Baltimore: Penguin Books.

Kübler-Ross, E. (1969) *On Death and Dying*, New York: Macmillan.

Leming, M.R. (1979–80) 'Religion and Death: A test of Homans' Thesis', *Omega*, X, 4: 347–64.

National Funeral Directors Association (NFDA) (1991) *Fact Sheet for 1991*, Milwaukee, WI: NFDA.

Pine, V.R. (1971) *Findings of the Professional Census*, Milwaukee, WI: NFDA.

Rando, T. (1992) 'Increasing Prevalence of Complicated Mourning: The onslaught is just beginning', *Omega*, 26, 1: 43–59.

Riley, J.W. Jr (1992) 'Death and Dying', in *Encyclopedia of Sociology*, Basingstoke: Macmillan.

St Vincent Millay, E. (1969) 'Childhood is the Kingdom Where Nobody Dies', in *Collected Lyrics*, New York: Harper & Row, 203–5.

Schaeffer, D.J. (1988) 'Communication among Children, Parents, and Funeral Directors', in *Loss, Grief, and Care*, Binghamton, NY: Haworth Press.

Skinner, B.F. (1990) 'Skinner to Have Last Word', Harvester Personnel, Associated Press, 7 August.

Vernon, J. (1993) 'It's Your Funeral', *New Statesman and Society*, 16 April: 22–3.

Walker, C. (1982) 'Attitudes to Death and Bereavement Among Cultural Minority Groups', *Nursing Times*, 15 December: 2106–8.

Webb, M. (1992) 'The Art of Dying', *New York*, 23 November: 46–53.

Whalen, W.J. (1990) 'How Different Religions Pay Their Final Respects', *U.S. Catholic*, September: 29–35.

Worden, J.W. (1991) *Grief Counseling and Grief Therapy: A Handbook for the Mental Health Practitioner*, 2nd edn, New York: Springer.

14 You Never Have to Die! On Mormons NDEs, Cryonics, and the American Immortalist Ethos

Michael Kearl

> I have been thinking for some time of a machine or apparatus which could be operated by personalities which have passed onto other existence or sphere. . . . I am inclined to believe that our personality hereafter does affect matter. If we can evolve an instrument so delicate as to be affected by our personality as it survives in the next life, such an instrument ought to record something.
>
> Thomas Edison (Lescarboura 1920: 446)

Consider the power of the idea that one's existence does not conclude with death. Is it possible that the directions in which civilizations evolve are ultimately based on their beliefs in and orientations toward life after death? Such issues underlie the present comparative and case-history analyses of the dominant images and experiences of death American-style.

According to thanatological determinists (e.g. Bauman 1992; Becker 1973; Harrington 1977; Kearl 1995), it is a people's orientation towards death that ultimately dictates how their social institutions, symbolic systems and cognitive schema coalesce into distinctive, meaningful cultural wholes. These cultural systems of meaning and social systems of action constructed against the terror of death strongly condition the behaviours of the living. They affect such wide-ranging phenomena as a people's homicide and suicide rates; their personal degree of risk-taking and the entertainment they receive seeing others' lives intentionally at risk; the refinement of medical and mortuary arts; their preferences for burial, cremation or cryonic preservation; their practices of capital punishment, abortion and euthanasia; and their conceptualizations of 'good deaths'.

The dimension of death systems of interest here concerns the cultural orientations toward members' post-mortem fate: their fears of reincarnation, hopes for resurrection, or expectations towards either some personal or collective afterlife existence. American culture can best be understood in terms of its core salvific goal of death control and its embracing of the hereafter. Consider the following images of death in America:

- Since 1967, over 20 Americans have been cryonically suspended for possible resurrection in the distant future when the cure has been found for their demise. For those who cannot afford full body freezing, discount cryonic centres, like the Alcor Life Extension Foundation, only preserve heads.
- A 1981 Gallup survey of American adults found that 15 per cent reported having had near-death experiences (now scientifically abbreviated as NDEs) featuring reunions with deceased relatives and friends, out-of-body experiences and feelings of peace and painlessness (Gallup 1982). The experience became the subject of a 1992 best-seller: Betty Eadie's *Embraced By the Light.*
- A 1994 *US News and World Report* survey (n = 1,000) found that nearly 6 out of 10 Americans believe the world will end or be destroyed (one-third predicting it will happen within a few years or decades), with 61 per cent believing Jesus Christ will return, and 44 per cent expecting a final battle of Armageddon (Sheler 1994). In the same year, a *USA Today*/CNN/Gallup survey revealed that 90 per cent of Americans believed in heaven, 72 per cent believed in angels and 65 per cent believed in the Devil (Miller 1994).

What lessons are to be drawn from this collage of cultural images? As will be seen, if these images are understood in terms of the American *immortalist ethos* they indeed form a coherent collage that gives an insight into broad trends underlying American life.

To establish the distinctiveness of American immortalism, we begin by comparing Americans' transcendent beliefs with those from 16 other nations. Next we will develop the cultural roots of the American death ethos, considering the bearing of radical individualism, scientism, a legacy of spiritualism, and the role of the frontier upon Americans' outlooks. Finally, we will consider the socio-cultural implications of immortalism, such as the growth of the medical–industrial complex, political demands for a risk-free society, and the cultural obsessions with youth and gerontophobia.

THE AMERICAN DEATH ETHOS IN INTERNATIONAL PERSPECTIVE

To compare the American death ethos with those of other cultures, let us summarize findings from the 1991 international religion survey of 17 national samples, derived from multi-stage stratified random/probability samplings of individuals generally 18 years of age and above (ISSP 1994).[1]

With 55 per cent definitely believing and nearly 80 per cent thinking it at least probable, Americans are the least likely to harbour any doubts about a post-mortem existence, even when compared with several strongly Catholic nations. In Russia, the remnant of the first major society to proclaim death's finality (Kluckhohn 1962: 135), 39 per cent of those interviewed believed that life after death probably or definitely existed. Communism's dampening effect appears greatest among East Germans, only 6 per cent of whom are completely convinced and an additional 8 per cent of whom tend to believe in an afterlife.

Only in the Philippines, Norway and New Zealand are there weaker correlations between education and religiosity than in the United States. In fact, according to 12 General Social Surveys (Davis and Smith 1972–94) conducted by the National Opinion Research Center (hereafter referred to as NORC GSS) between 1978 and 1994 (n = 16 432), belief in life after death actually increases with education, regardless of the level of religiosity, among fundamentalist Protestants (who comprise one-third of American adults), Catholics (one-quarter) and members of moderate Protestant denominations (18 per cent). The same pattern of cross-national relationships generally holds towards beliefs in the existence of heaven and hell. Americans, for instance, are over 25 per cent more likely than the British and New Zealanders to believe in Heaven and more than twice as likely to believe in Hell. The percentage of the national populations definitely believing in the existence of the Devil ranges from a high of 45 per cent in the United States to less than 4 per cent in East Germany, with a total mean percentage for all nations of 16 per cent.

Certainly these findings reflect in part the highly religious character of Americans. Next to Filipinos, Americans are most likely to describe themselves as being either extremely or very religious (26 per cent vs. 12 per cent for the entire sample). In general, this pattern holds regardless of education or age. Nevertheless, even 43 per cent of non-religious Americans believe in an afterlife.

To what extent do outlooks toward the hereafter correlate with the ideas of free will and the meaningfulness of life in the minds of people from different nationalities? Does the belief in free will dissolve post-life expectations or does it lead to severe gradations in its perceived qualities? Is it the expectation of an afterlife that gives a sense of purpose to existence?

Among respondents from all 17 countries to the statement 'We each make our own fate', Americans were at a mid-point among countries in terms of agreement.[2] The United States falls into the top third of countries (following the Philippines, Poland, Northern Ireland and the Republic of Ireland) in the rate of agreement with the statement 'The course of our lives is decided by God.' Americans, with nearly four out of ten so believing, are about twice as likely to see divine interventions in the course of their lives than are British or New Zealanders, and three times as likely as East Germans. Further, Americans are the mostly likely to strongly agree that 'There is a God who concerns Himself with every human being personally.' So while being close to average in believing that one makes one's own fate, Americans also see themselves having a personal relationship with God, who is as likely as not to determine the course of their lives. And whatever Americans believe about their free will, their lives are saturated with meaningfulness: of all nationalities, Americans are the most likely to disagree with the statement 'In my opinion, life does not serve any purpose.'[3]

So how do these outlooks toward fate and divine intervention relate to post-life beliefs in the minds of our different nationalities? In the total sample, those disbelieving in life after death are nearly two-thirds more likely than believers to strongly agree that 'We each make our own fate.' However, unlike those within a religious typology of countries,[4] in the United States the relationship is virtually nonexistent: Americans disagreeing that one makes one's own fate are only 11 per cent more likely to believe in an afterlife than those strongly agreeing with free will. Over 70 per cent of Americans disagreeing that the direction of their lives is decided by God nevertheless still believe in an afterlife.

Among the 17 nations of our sample, Americans are also the most likely to definitely believe in religious miracles and to report having experienced idionecrophany (contact with the dead (see MacDonald 1992, 1994)). In fact, 40 per cent of Americans claimed to have had such an experience at least once, roughly twice the percentage of Germans, Italians, Hungarians and Northern Irish, and nearly three times the percentage of Russians.

CULTURAL ROOTS OF AMERICANS' QUEST FOR EVERLASTING LIFE

For what reasons has the immortalist ethos gone further and become bigger in the United States than in the European cultural systems, from where many of its ideas originated? Ingredients in the cultural crucible include not only religiosity but also the climate of scientific curiosity and creativity (evidenced by the US box-score of Nobel prizes and patents), technological innovation (Edison, Bell and the Wright brothers immediately come to mind), public expectations of breakthroughs, American individualism, and traditions of violence.

An impressive trend is Americans' increasing religiosity,

unlike many of their European counterparts. Stark and Finke (1992) found church participation increasing steadily, with declines in the 'main-line' denominations more than compensated for by the rapid growth of evangelical groups. By the mid-1990s, over 90 per cent of Americans have a religious affiliation and only 16 per cent report never attending a religious service (according to the 1993–94 NORC GSS). According to a 1991 survey ('The Great American TV Poll') conducted by Princeton Survey Research Associates, over four out of ten Americans said they valued their relationship with God above all else – more than good health or happy marriages (cited in AP 1991).

This proneness to spiritualism is evident in the tenets of the Church of Latter-day Saints (Mormons), one of the few home-grown American faiths and one of the most successful, with nine million members in its fold. Immortality is a central theme of Mormon theodicy, which holds that all who have ever lived or who will live reside with God in a premortal existence. Members believe that marriage within one of the Church's 46 temples does not end with death but rather, lasts for eternity. Mormons also believe that the Church must practise baptism for the dead, which is why the Church maintains the world's most extensive genealogical records.

There nevertheless exists a life-extending activist impulse within the faith: the Church is well-known for its prohibitions against alcohol and smoking; Mormons were the inventors of the kidney dialysis machine and the artificial heart (also, the first recipient of an artificial heart was a Mormon). Such activism against death within this group in many ways epitomizes the secular facet of American immortalism.

The Duality of the American Mind on Matters of Science and Religion

How is it that the country wherein half the population does not believe in what is arguably the most verified of all scientific theories, namely the theory of evolution (according to the 1993 NORC GSS), is the same country that produced the inventors of the light bulb and heavier-than-air aircraft, wonder drugs, thermonuclear weapons and space travel? Compared with many of their Western counterparts,

Americans are more pragmatic and down-to-earth than introspective and philosophical in dealing with life. There is, in fact, a duality implicit within the American mind – Americans take their religion straight, without much intellectualization.

According to recent national surveys (NORC 1993–94 GSS combined samples), Americans have an ambivalence towards science and yet high confidence in the leaders of the scientific and medical establishments. They are, in general, more likely than not to agree that people 'believe too often in science and not enough in feelings and faith', and yet to disagree that 'overall, modern science does more harm than good'.

The Role of the Frontier in Shaping Activist Immortalism

Origins of Americans' distinctive obsession with and active involvement towards death control undoubtedly derives from the transplantation of relatively advanced Western civilization on to a primordial and particularly savage frontier, which provides one key for grasping the American character.

The American sector of the New World came to symbolize for generations (first for West Europeans, then East Europeans, and later Asians) the possibility for biographical rebirth and salvation – spiritually, socially and economically. The United States has always nurtured hope for better futures, both earthly and other-worldly.

In a land bereft of reminders of the accomplishments of scores of past generations, the proverbial slate was clean for leaving one's own mark. Like the beginning of a new Olympic sport, one did not have to compete against any standards of the past and could instead define the sport. Not being bogged down meant that individuals' fates were no longer pre-programmed by the legacies of feudalism or aristocracy, nor by ancestral deeds and rivalries. But there was a price on such emancipations. The New World was from the beginning a lethal place. There were the high accidental death-rates associated with natural assaults often unseen or long-forgotten in the Old World, such as wild animal attacks, hurricanes, tornadoes and weather extremes. There were the assaults of the omnipresent aboriginal peoples, described in devilish colour (the 'red men') and of barbarian (and even cannibalistic) inclination. Instead of coping with the lethality of the frontier with mysticism and adaptive fatalism, Americans began their all-out war to kill or control that which killed them with the armament available in enlightened and early industrial times. As Slotkin observed:

> The first colonists saw in America an opportunity to regenerate their fortunes, their spirits, and the power of their church and nation; but the means to that regeneration ultimately became the means of violence, and the myth of regeneration through violence became the structuring metaphor of the American experience. (1973: 5)

In a later work, Slotkin observes that for generations of Americans 'the meaning and direction of American history . . . [was] found in the metaphoric representation of history as an extended Indian War' (1985: 531). Mythical American heroes were to become the killers of Indians, Mexicans, bears, outlaws, gunfighters and gangsters.

Out of this cultural goal of death control has arisen the military–medical–industrial complex, the successes of which produced an increasing invisibility of dying and death. Of the countries considered in our international sample, for instance, the United States and New Zealand (the other 'frontier' nation) are the only two not to have had the great world wars encroach their boundaries to directly affect civilian populations. And as if to hide its failure to control those deaths that do occur, death's casualties are removed from everyday life and the very topic becomes taboo.

The Immortalist Impulse of American Individualism

The third broad cultural force underlying Americans' drive to never have to die is their extreme individualism. The immigrants' emancipations from their homelands' traditional restraints against personal self-seeking, coupled with the self-sufficiencies required on the Western frontier, were to forge a distinctive national character featuring an 'anything is possible', 'can do' mindset. Also forged was an accentuated sense of self that dissolved the traditional consolations of collectivist cultures, where what ultimately mattered was the survival of one's people; nearly two-thirds of Americans agree 'You have to take care of yourself first, and if you have any energy left over, then help other people' (NORC 1993 GSS).

This radical individualism can ultimately lead to an extreme narcissism (Lasch 1977), with its associated self-absorption and need for attention.[5] Such thinking has made Americans particularly vulnerable to death. As Baumeister noted, modern life offers people an abundance of forms of meaning but it fails to offer clear guidance about fundamental values.

> This "value gap" . . . is the single biggest problem for the modern Western individual in making life meaningful. A major part of the modern response to this value gap is to elevate selfhood and the cultivation of identity into basic, compelling values. But if we rely on the quest for identity and self-knowledge to give life meaning, we make ourselves vulnerable to death in an almost unprecedented way. The self comes to an end in death, and it ceases to give value. Thus, death takes away not only our life but also what gave it value. In contrast, our ancestors typically drew comfort from values that would outlive them. (1991: 6)

However, as we have seen, this threat to meaningfulness is countered by continuing beliefs in an afterlife – particularly for the most educated.[6]

SOCIO-CULTURAL FACETS OF THE YOU-NEVER-HAVE-TO-DIE ETHOS

Instead of solely tackling the universal fears of death meditatively, Americans have declared an all-out war against death by politically and scientifically attacking that which kills us. The 'you never have to die' ethos underlies the rise of the American military–industrial and medical–industrial complexes, demands for risk-free life, cultural gerontophobia and immortalist themes in popular culture.

During the Cold War years, an increasing proportion of

American economic activity involved atomic weaponry (between one-quarter and one-third of the entire military budget so spent since 1945) and gave rise to a corresponding cultural order called 'nuclearism' (Boyer 1985; Ungar 1992). Americans accepted the ideology of the military–industrial –political order, mutual assured destruction (or MAD): the only (and most cost-effective) way of preserving world order is to threaten the destruction of not only entire societies but (as revealed by stories of nuclear winters and tens of thousands of years of deadly radiation) the natural order itself. Trillions of dollars were spent on this overriding assumption for collective salvation. And with such power came a sense of collective omnipotence (and personal impotence). If such death can be incurred, could not such force be applied to death's conquest as well?

The second broad front in Americans' war against death is its medical establishment. By the mid-1990s the nation's medical system comprised one-seventh of the economy, the largest percentage of GDP expenditure in the world (13.2 per cent versus 6.6 per cent in the United Kingdom and 6.8 per cent in Japan), employing over 11 million people. Results from the field are frequent and encouraging, with well-publicized 'breakthroughs' against diseases using 'magic bullets'. In a 1992 issue of *Life* magazine a story appeared where one medical researcher claimed that there are individuals currently alive who may well see the year 2392 (Darrach 1992). In the same year, the Time/CNN 'Beyond the Year 2000' poll found that 75 per cent of Americans expected a cure for AIDS and 80 per cent a cure for cancer.

By focusing on death prevention, immortalism has worked its way into being the key political objective. Over half of the American federal budget is devoted to either producing the instruments to either cause or prevent death (the military establishment) or caring for those most likely to die, specifically the elderly (including Social Security, Medicare, Medicaid, etc.), for whom entitlements can be perceived as consolations for death.

Because most premature deaths are nowadays man-made and 'unnatural', there is a shared sense that they are avoidable and therefore controllable. Judging from the spate of federal laws requiring warning labels on everything from

5-gallon buckets (so children will not fall in them and drown) to toy balloons, America is becoming a risk-free culture (Fairlie 1989). This sets up the possibility of assigning blame which, with the rise of the 'no-fault' ethic, has shifted over the past few decades from blaming the victim to blaming the social agencies (like the tobacco, automotive and aircraft industries) that made the death possible. Hence the lung-cancer death of a heavy smoker is not his fault but rather that of the tobacco industry; hence the failed 1982 suicide of a man, who threw himself in front of a New York City subway and lost an arm and a leg, yielding a $650,000 settlement from the city's Transit Authority for comparative negligence. Further, the domain of 'victims' has expanded to include not only the deceased and his or her family but even those who viewed the death: in 1990, the California Supreme Court allowed passengers who had seen a fatal park tramway-ride accident to bring a civil lawsuit because of the emotional trauma they suffered from being witnesses. One wonders at the extent to which immortalism underlies the increasing litigiousness of the United States, where over one-third of the world's lawyers live.

Related to Americans' death denials/defiance is their obsession with youth. With death largely confined to older populations the following logic has arisen: to always be youthful means never having to grow old, and never being old means one never has to die. Such thinking has fuelled the expansion of the multi-billion-dollar cosmetic and surgical rejuvenation industries (e.g. face-lifts, breast-lifts, tummy tucks and hair transplants).

Finally, it should not be surprising that this political economy of immortalism has left its mark on American popular culture. The United States, master disseminator of the world's electronic images and sounds, now brings new performances from deceased individuals, as when Natalie Cole sings a duet with her dead father, Nat 'King' Cole, or when the central actor of the 1994 cinematic blockbuster *Forrest Gump* interacts with long-deceased historical figures. Television advertisements of the early 1990s also employ the dead, as in the 1992 Diet Coke ad with Paula Abdul joking and dancing with Groucho Marx and being poured a drink by Cary Grant, or in its 1995 ad with Shaquille O'Neal running through old television shows and interacting with Jackie Gleason and Lucille Ball.

CONCLUSION

Throughout this book we find considerable variation in the death systems of Western cultures. In this chapter it is argued that immortalism is the defining trait of the American death ethos, featuring dual spiritual and activist fronts in what has become a national crusade against death. This ethos underlies why, in our international sample of countries, belief in an afterlife is greatest in the United States and explains the disproportionate warfare, medical and legal expenditures of this nation–state. As a result, death's often-cited taboo status in the contemporary West has a distinct twist in the United States: here one never has to die – unless one wants to.

But as is typically the case of taboos involving obsessive concerns, they have a way of becoming fetishes and, in the case of death, the outcome has been increased death preoccupations (Gorer 1965). Perhaps in no other country are these preoccupations greater than in the United States, where they range from concerns over environmental degradations, to the divisiveness of debates over abortion and euthanasia, to preoccupations over the demise of dinosaurs.

NOTES

1. This module (total n = 22 767) includes data from the United States (n = 1,359), Great Britain (1,257), the Republic of Ireland (1,005), Northern Ireland (838), Norway (1,506), the Netherlands (1,635), Italy (983), Israel (991), West Germany (1,346), East Germany (1,486), Hungary (1,000), Austria (984), Poland (1,063), Slovenia (2,080), Russia (2,964), the Philippines (1,200) and New Zealand (1,070).
2. Rates of strongly agreeing 'we each make our own fate' ranged from 12 per cent in Northern Ireland and the Philippines to 49 per cent in Hungary and 37 per cent in Russia; disagreement was highest in Italy (29 per cent) and Northern Ireland (28 per cent) and lowest in Hungary and Poland (both 6 per cent).

3. The percentage either agreeing strongly, agreeing, or neither agreeing nor disagreeing that life serves no purpose ranges from 8 per cent in the US to 89 per cent in Russia.
4. The nations of our sample (with the exception of Israel) were recorded in terms of their dominant religious tradition: Catholic (Austria, Ireland, Italy, Philippines, Slovenia), Protestant (Great Britain, Northern Ireland, Norway, New Zealand), Protestant–Catholic (where the percentage difference of population raised as Protestants versus Catholics is 11 per cent or less: West Germany, Netherlands), Catholic–Communist (Hungary, Poland) and Communist (East Germany, Russia).
5. The need for attention of Americans' other-directed (Riesman 1950) individualism extends even to their 'postself' (Schmitt and Leonard 1986). In the land of equal opportunity, every man can leave his pyramid – a name on a building, a scholarship fund, a piece of legislation, an athletic record, a mention in the *Guinness Book of World Records,* or a family photograph – to posterity.
6. In analysing the combined NORC General Social Surveys from 1973 to 1994, the percentage of afterlife believers among those with no religious affiliation consistently increases the younger the cohort, from 21 per cent of those born between 1990 and 1919 to 50 per cent of those born after 1960. Among these non-affiliateds having spent four or more years in college this increase is even more impressive: from 7 per cent of those born during the first two decades of the century to 45 per cent of those born after 1960 believing in life after death.

REFERENCES

Associated Press (AP) (1991) 'Americans Say Faith in God Most Important', *San Antonio Express-News,* 4 April: 2-A.

Bauman, Z. (1992) *Mortality, Immortality and Other Life Strategies,* Stanford, CA: Stanford University Press.

Baumeister, R. (1991) *Meanings of Life,* New York: The Guilford Press.

Becker, E. (1973) *The Denial of Death,* New York: Free Press.

Boyer, P. (1985) *By the Bomb's Early Light: American Thought and Culture at the Dawn of the Atomic Age,* New York: Pantheon.

Darrach, B. (1992) 'Aging', *Life,* 15, 10 October: 32–45.

Davis, J.A. and Smith, T.W. (1972–94) *General Social Surveys* (machine-readable data file). Principal investigators, James A. Davis and Tom W. Smith. Produced by the National Opinion Research Center, Chicago. Tape distributed by the Roper Public Opinion Research Center, Storrs, CT. Micro-diskette and codebook prepared and distributed by MicroCase Corporation, Bellevue, Washington, 1994.

Fairlie, H. (1989) 'Fear of Living', *The New Republic 200,* 4 January, 23: 14–19.

Gallup, G., Jr., (1982) *Adventures in Immortality: A Look Beyond the Threshold of Death,* New York: McGraw-Hill.

Gorer, G. (1965) *Death, Grief and Mourning,* New York: Doubleday Anchor.

Harrington, A. (1977) *The Immortalist,* Millbrae, CA: Celestial Arts.

Illich, I. (1975) 'The Political Uses of Natural Death', in P. Steinfels and R.M. Veatch (eds.), *Death Inside Out: The Hastings Center Report,* New York: Harper & Row.

International Social Survey Program (ISSP) (1994) *International Social Survey Program: Religion,* 1991 computer file, Cologne, Germany; Zentralarchiv für empirische Sozialforschung (producer), 1993, Cologne, Germany; Zentralarchiv für empirische Sozialforschung/Ann Arbor, MI; Inter-university Consortium for Political and Social Research (distributors).

Kearl, M. (1995) 'Death and Politics: A psychosocial perspective', in H. Wass and R. Neimeyer (eds.), *Dying: Facing the Facts,* 3rd edn, New York: Taylor & Francis.

Kluckhohn, C. (1962) *Culture and Behavior,* New York: The Free Press.

Lasch, C. (1977) *The Culture of Narcissism: American Life in an Age of Diminishing Expectations,* New York: W.W. Norton.

Lescarboura, A.C. (1920) 'Edison's Views on Life and Death', *Scientific American,* 123: 446.

MacDonald, W.L. (1992) 'Idionecrophanies: The social construction of perceived contact with the dead', *Journal for the Scientific Study of Religion,* 31: 215–23.

MacDonald, W.L. (1994) 'The Popularity of Paranormal Experiences in the United States', *Journal of American Culture,* 17, 3:35–42.

Miller, L. (1994) 'Faith in God at heavenly heights', *USA Today,* 21 December: D1.

Riesman, D. (1950) *The Lonely Crowd: A Study of the Changing American Character,* New Haven, CT: Yale University Press.

Schmitt, R. and Leonard II, W. (1986) 'Immortalizing the Self through Sport', *American Journal of Sociology,* 91:1088–111.

Sheler, J.L. (1994) 'The Christmas Covenant', *U.S. News & World Report,* 117, 24, 19 December: 62–71.

Slotkin, R. (1973) *Regeneration Through Violence: The Mythology of the American Frontier, 1600–1860,* Middletown, CT: Wesleyan University Press.

Slotkin, R. (1985) *The Fatal Environment: The Myth of the Frontier in the Age of Industrialism,* New York: Atheneum.

Stark, R. and Finke, R. (1992) *The Churching of America, 1776–1990: Winners and Losers in our Religious Economy,* New Brunswick, NJ: Rutgers University Press.

Time/CNN Poll conducted by D. Yankelovich (1992) 'Beyond the Year 2000', Special Issue, *Time,* 140, 27, Fall: 12–13.

Ungar, S. (1992) *The Rise and Fall of Nuclearism: Fear and Faith as Determinants of the Arms Race,* University Park, PA: Pennsylvania State University Press.

15 Death, Dying and Bioethics: Current Issues in the USA

Robert Bendiksen

INTRODUCTION[1]

Interesting ethical quandaries challenge health professionals who staff hospices, nursing homes and hospitals, as well as their patients and family members confronting death and dying (Anspach 1993; Buchanan and Brock 1990; Pike 1991; Reiser 1986). In recent years, physicians responsible for complex cases not limited to strictly medical decisions have consulted with a staff clinical ethicist or Institutional Ethics Committee (Hammes and Bendiksen 1990; Jaffe 1989; Jonsen, Siegler and Winslade 1992). Developments in care for the dying should be understood in the institutional context of health-care practice, bioethic protocols and government policy. Several larger themes or issues shape the decision-making of physicians as they and others provide care for dying patients and their families (Selznick 1992; Veatch 1989; Waitzkin 1991; Weisz 1990).

A major issue in the USA is the economic environment of health-care delivery and the political constraints on public Medicare budgets that impact upon elderly persons who are most in need of medical support. All patients, regardless of age, who need complex medical care require competent personnel and sufficient resources that are unevenly distributed and unequally available. However, ethical issues of 'justice', or 'fairness for all concerned', are not the only challenges facing medical decision-makers and health-care providers at the end of life. Tensions continue as the traditional value of medical paternalism challenges patients who increasingly expect their wishes to be respected. In some cases, patient or family preferences may be pitted against the legal liability of physicians and health-care management. These and other decisions regarding provision of comfort care, e.g. hospices, are difficult for physicians, patients and family members desiring recovery to make (Fulton and Bendiksen 1994; Tronto 1993; Veatch 1996).

MEDICAL ETHICAL DECISION-MAKING AT THE END OF LIFE

Observations in this study took place in referral hospitals in the north central region of the USA. The case examples that follow are based on situations in several teaching hospitals and in a variety of medical services. In the one case, the attending oncologist and residents began with a briefing during nursing rounds to clarify medical treatment decisions by the physicians and to learn about nursing and social-work plans. While most of the discussion during nursing rounds focused on medical plans, some psychosocial information was conveyed to physicians by nurses, social workers, chaplains and others in attendance.

Psychosocial information at staffings is typically minimal until patient care includes discharge or transfer to the hospice programme of the hospital. In this situation, there appeared to be limited communication when an oncologist discovered, during his turn at attending rounds in oncology, that a cancer patient whom he had admitted previously had been medically treated by subsequent oncologists in a way other than that he had recommended. Although he retained his composure, he was extremely upset, claiming that this 'improper' care challenged his authority to care for 'his' patient in the best way. This case differs from those typically found in tertiary-care hospitals in the USA, Britain and Australia in that it demonstrates long-term involvement of physician with patient.

We found a similar pattern of long-term lack of patient involvement in the general medicine rounds, conducted by the attending physician and the current residents, which included no other medical or nursing professionals, except when a consultation, e.g. from psychiatry, was requested. Patients were located throughout the hospital, depending on their medical needs, which meant that patients on each unit had a different set of nurses and support staff. This team of physicians moved from floor to floor throughout morning rounds to visit patients who were located in cardiology, oncology, general medicine and intensive care units. In addition, the team would often go to look at X-ray or MRI films of particular patients before making decisions regarding treatment, a practice often found in the oncology unit as well. Attending physicians in both oncology and general medicine found time for extra didactic topics connected to patient treatments when the daily census was lower than average.

Neonatal intensive care, where the next set of rounds took place, had been added as a speciality in this hospital fifteen years earlier. At that time, the neonatologists decided to include neonatal nurses in direct medical care of premature babies. After overcoming resistance from nurses schooled in traditional methods, the physicians trained volunteer staff nurses in techniques such as intubation which could be carried out, if necessary, when the attending physician was not in the unit. Today, certified neonatal nurse practitioners manage the staff nurses and conduct rounds with the attending physician. Discussions of patient care, in this unit, resembled rounds in oncology and general medicine with, in this instance, the nurse practitioner presenting cases to the attending neonatologist.

The culture of this neonatology unit, while retaining the authority and accountability of physicians in medical decision-making, has changed in recent years to become more collegial among the nurse practitioners and physicians. Respect for physician knowledge, opinions and judgement remains. An open dialogue occurs each day within a setting where professional titles are used primarily when parents or guests are on the unit. Interestingly, collegial interaction patterns among physicians and nurses in neonatology were observed in three urban university hospital neonatology units. The evolution in this neonatology subculture of professional work within tertiary care hospitals is much like that of hospice units. However, the majority of physician–staff role relations retain status-related behaviour based on traditional institutional norms and values.

Decision-making is a daily responsibility of attending and resident physicians, as well as other health-care professionals. Physicians have a set of role expectations of themselves, other physicians and ancillary staff. For the past ten years, hospitals have added more expectations for documentation to physicians' duties because of hospital payments from government Medicare, based on a system of average cost per admission diagnosis, a system called Diagnostic Related Groups (DRG). Lengthy hospitalizations cost hospitals, as well as health-maintenance organizations, more than they receive in reimbursement, so physicians are expected to discharge patients as soon as it is medically reasonable. When nursing-home placement is unavailable or when home care is difficult to manage, ethical questions arise as to patient well-being and autonomy, and the legal liability of physicians.

In one such case, a chemically dependent patient could not be placed in a nursing home because he was not eligible for government medical assistance and several nursing homes were reluctant to take responsibility for a 50-year-old mobile man with a history of alcoholism. The major reason for refusal of admission by the three nursing homes contacted was that this patient received minimal monthly governmental subsistence cheques that disqualified him from receiving medical assistance. A consultation by the on-call clinical ethicist resulted in a recommendation of release with monitoring by a private non-profit social-service agency, scheduled medical appointments and follow-up with family members who resided in his distant home community.

Care for severely disabled patients at home raises ethical concerns about beneficence, where physicians attempt to act in the best interests of patients, and about adequate resources and workable systems of reimbursement. In a visit with a quadriplegic patient in a large urban area, a team of clinical ethicist graduate students observed not only the medical maintenance requirements of full-time nursing care by family or visiting nurses, but also the challenge of communicating and relating to a patient in early middle age who had begun to show frustration over his condition. Primary-care medicine, in this case, was being practised by the internist/ethicist, who did not charge for occasional home visits because he did not want to be bothered to meet the complex requirements of the funding agency.

Another case provided an example of the different expectations and needs of a patient's spouse and the physician, who had experienced liability challenges from other patients or family members. The physician's advice to the resident physicians was to order tests that were necessary for good medical care and to carefully document procedures on the medical chart. A request from the patient's spouse for tape-recorded discussions during rounds, for the sake of adult children who lived elsewhere, was not satisfied. The physician appeared to be uncomfortable with this, as he did not attend a later appointment to talk about taping with the spouse. This resulted in an indirect apology from the physician during the following morning rounds. Later in rounds, away from patients and nurses, the attending physician explained to the residents how careful they ought to be in medical documentation, given his experience with a patient liability suit where a nurse had misinterpreted a note on a patient's chart.

Distinctly ethical issues arose in medical rounds more frequently than was recognized by resident physicians themselves, as ethical decisions were only one of the topics of decisions made. This was clear, one day on rounds, when a highly respected second-year resident wondered aloud about the medical problem of his patient. The attending physician took this opportunity to say that this man was dying and that perhaps the resident should consider which tests and procedures were really necessary to keep him comfortable rather than continue to treat him aggressively. The patient's condition continued to deteriorate as limited medical treatments were administered to keep him comfortable. By this time, the middle-aged children of the patient had arrived and expressed great appreciation to the resident for doing all he could in treating their father. He kept his counsel about his desire to provide more palliative rather than aggressive medical care.

The American emphasis on legal rights is not always well received by physicians. In one event, a cancer patient was unwilling to be transferred to a nursing home even though the attending physician repeatedly and assertively argued with her, to the point of walking out of the patient's room on more than one occasion. This physician was convinced that he knew what was in the best interest of the patient, namely, that she be placed in a safe environment that would prevent her from falling. Physician concern for beneficence was in direct conflict with respect for patient autonomy in decision-making. Current American medical practice requires that this type of situation be resolved in terms of the patient's preference even if, as in this case, risk is increased.

CULTURAL CONFLICTS COMPLICATE ISSUES OF CARE FOR THE DYING

The confusion of what is appropriate treatment for a particular patient is complicated at times by different values concerning appropriate care. Cultural conflict may occur in what has become routine death work for some medical professionals. In one tragic situation, an intensive-care patient who had been shot in the back during a drug deal was being kept alive because of disagreements among family members. He had been put on dialysis during admission to the hospital trauma centre and had received unsuccessful treatment for open wounds on his back. This 30-year-old African–American, who was attended by an all-white staff, had not regained consciousness, but at times seemed to track visitors with his eyes. He was not married and had no advance directive.

There was no disagreement with the patient's mother, as she initially supported the physician's advice to stop dialysis and let her son die. Cultural conflict arose a short time later when a sibling learned that his brother was on morphine for pain control. This concerned brother assertively asked, 'Are you trying to euthanize him?' The resident responded by changing the medication. The attending physician, who was not of the same ethnicity as the patient, claimed that, from his point of view, he did not take appropriate medical action because of the disagreements and the unwillingness of the family to meet with him or an ethnic minority physician to discuss alternatives. This was clearly an example of inadequate physician–family communication.

The issue of race and ethnicity is a major sociological

factor in providing medical care in many American hospitals. This case is but one example of cultural conflict between the medical staff and family members. Another case involved an elderly man from Asia who had been visiting his son when he was admitted to oncology because of an advanced case of cancer. The attending physician was asked by the son to not inform his father about his cancer because of traditional Asian norms of patient care. The physician, in this case, believed it to be his obligation to inform his patient of the diagnosis, prognosis and treatment options, even if a translator were required. An ethical consultation, called by the physician, included Institutional Ethics Committee members, none of whom was Central Asian or Asian–American. A successful resolution was found in the recommendation to the physician to offer, repeatedly during several visits, to answer all of his patient's questions before proceeding with treatment rather than telling the patient the specifics of his condition. The American physician with a deep concern for truth-telling with patients was able to respect the Asian family's values of not harming the patient by having to confront potentially devastating facts.

Yet another ethnic value-conflict arose in a paediatric case of a recently-arrived South-east Asian woman who had delivered a child and who needed surgery soon after the birth. The teenage woman was counselled by her family, including clan elders who were in attendance and who appeared to make decisions for the woman. The father of the child was never identified to the physician, but was believed to be in attendance during discussions. The health customs in the South-east Asian culture of this family appeared to use the appearance of the baby, which was fairly good, as an indicator of health status, rather than the medical diagnosis using medical testing procedures well known in American medicine. Surgery was delayed by several weeks, following the family decision not to treat the baby at the initial diagnosis. Surgery was performed, however, close to two months later and the baby was not expected to survive due to the delay. This delay understandably distressed the paediatric surgeon and other members of the health-care team who, to no practical avail, had sought and received advice from the hospital Institutional Ethics Committee.

AMERICAN MEDICINE AND PALLIATIVE CARE OF THE DYING

In general, physicians practice palliative medicine, e.g. in oncology, when they treat symptoms in addition to prescribing chemotherapy to fight the disease. Palliative-care specialists claim that medical education and training does not offer sufficient understanding of the proper management of pain control. In 1994, new guidelines for the management of cancer pain were published by the US Department of Health and Human Services. Too frequent under-treatment of pain by drugs such as morphine is a claim made not only by American palliative-care physicians, but also by hospice medical directors. Comfort care, to temporarily reduce pain from infections, may include liberal doses of pain medication, 'Do Not Attempt Resuscitation' (DNR) orders and antibiotics. It may well be that some physicians actively participate in the timing of their patient's death as they provide pain medications that increase the likelihood of earlier death. For many this is a morally acceptable practice because the intention is to reduce pain and suffering without causing the patient to die (Cleeland *et al.* 1994; Stanley 1992).

Differences in institutional values and organizational priorities can be found among Medical/Institutional Ethics Committees, advance directive protocols and ethical consultations in specific health-care settings in North America, Australia and Britain. Medical/Institutional Ethics Committees and professional clinical ethicists represent additional organizational innovations in hospitals and some nursing homes that provide continuing education on ethical issues to professional staff, draft ethical policy guidelines and offer case consultations either during medical/ethical decision-making or in a *post-hoc* review, i.e. 'ethical autopsy'. Tertiary-care hospitals are more likely to provide on-call consultations to physicians, whereas nursing homes and other health-care organizations more often have developed policies. Staff education regarding ethical issues and ethical autopsies is common to ethics committees in all health-care organizations (Hammes and Bendiksen 1994; La Puma and Schiedermayer 1994; Minogue 1996).

Ethical consultations increasingly include reference to or

development of written advance directives, such as living wills or durable powers of attorney for health care. Advance directives have become a central feature in medical charts of many hospital and nursing-home patients. The Patient Self-determination Act of 1990 in the USA requires that newly-admitted patients be apprised of the option of completing an advance directive. Currently, only 15 per cent of the general public in the USA Midwest report having completed some type of advance directive. New education programmes are advocating that more people complete advance directives and renew them every three to five years. Those who have experience in this area recommend documentation that expresses a patient's wishes about end-of-life medical care. Advance directive statutes vary from state to state. Even when properly executed, advance directives may not fully anticipate all ethical or legal questions (Hammes and Rooney 1996).

The long-standing institutional respect for individuals is expressed in mores and laws that claim certain rights which are rooted not only in common law, but also in the US Constitution and Bill of Rights. The current health-care debate over universal access and elimination of pre-existing conditions for health insurance is presented as an issue of justice or fairness for all citizens. There continues to be a reluctance on the part of the American public and state legislatures to increase taxes that could fulfil what some believe to be a community obligation to help poor people. Rather, health care has been seen as personal responsibility and individuals are expected to obtain insurance or accumulate savings so as not to burden the commonwealth. The strain on middle-class families who have lost health insurance appears as a major factor in motivating political discussion by all parties to join the public debate over how to divide responsibility in providing access to health care. Poverty is the matter of greatest disagreement, especially when it impacts upon critically ill and dying patients.

Medical/ethical decision-making at the end of life does not typically focus on issues of access to health care. Rather, value issues are primarily those of acting in the best interest of a dying patient by continuing to provide aggressive medical care or by changing the medical model of treatment to palliative care and, possibly, hospice staffing. New institutional stakeholders, such as health-care corporations, seek to use federal regulations, medical legal liability and hospital policy to provide incentives and create opportunities. Many physicians in the USA appear to be less often relying exclusively on their own medical judgement in difficult medical/ethical decisions in favour of greater involvement of patients and family members, as well as clinical ethicists, Institutional Ethics Committees and other health-care professionals. When there are changes, these are due to greater uncertainty about consequences and to patients', families' and colleagues' increased expectations that they will participate in crucial decisions. For some, this means assisted dying, or even euthanasia.

Physicians report that they increasingly explain treatment options to their competent patients. One physician in this study uses the imagery of weighing scales. His judgement prevails when treatment issues involve a prognosis of recovery or remission of disease that requires complex medical decisions. As the prognosis deteriorates, patients and family members are asked to increase their participation in selecting treatment options. This may mean withholding or withdrawing medical treatments, that now include nutrition and hydration, as the patient dies. Although the values of autonomy and beneficence are not always in conflict, when they are, a growing number of patients, and family members who have the support of advance directives, are claiming their right to terminate treatment, other than for comfort care. Some physicians interviewed in this study report a belief that there are numerous physicians in the USA who would agree to help certain patients die by euthanasia or assisted suicide, if it were a legal option (Kohl 1975; Markson 1995; Quill 1991, 1993; Shavelson 1995).

Choice-in-dying advocates now include the right of physician-assisted dying as practised by retired pathologist Dr Jack Kevorkian in Michigan, who provides the medical means for suffering, dying patients to take their own lives while he is in attendance. In other cases, activist groups lobby for new laws to protect the right of patients to obtain physician assistance in dying. Attempts to pass physician aid in dying legislation in several states are growing. It is the job of the courts to test and redefine the meaning of the legislation, including the Constitution, through judicial trials, or 'case law'. The front for legislative change in the USA, at this time, appears to be the right of persons to die by their own hand and with the assistance of physicians, rather than the right to euthanasia as it is currently practised, primarily by family physicians in The Netherlands (Cranford 1994; Crigger 1992; Pijnenborg *et al.* 1993; Thomasma and Graber 1990).

The United States has a history of taking legislative action and of letting courts later determine the constitutionality of laws. There is little evidence of extensive, decade-long, prior public debate, as has been the case elsewhere, where professional input on moral issues allows for gradual public shaping of morality. Americans prefer to debate issues in court, including the Supreme Court, when one challenges constitutional rights, even though legislators presume that new legislation meets the test of constitutionality. Current legal and ethical guidelines in the USA support the right of patients to withhold or withdraw medical treatments, including nutrition and hydration. Medical practice does not support active intervention to end a patient's life in euthanasia. Debate continues, usually in legislatures or courts, on whether physicians should be allowed to assist a patient in dying by medical suicide when the quality of life is not acceptable to the patient. Some physicians acknowledge practising assisted dying on a small number of competent, suffering adult patients. A recent Wisconsin study of physicians indicated that even more would consider this option if it were legal in the USA (Carlson and Anwar 1994; Shapiro *et al.* 1994).

CONCLUSION: MORAL COURAGE AND PUBLIC POLICY

Major changes are taking place in medical/ethical decision-making at the end of life. Hospices, first introduced in the USA in 1974, have become institutionalized as a form of palliative care that is appropriate and accepted when aggressive treatment is no longer effective. Advance directives are used to document patient preferences in terminal care. Physicians, while retaining responsibility for medical care of their patients, increasingly consult clinical ethicists or

Institutional Ethics Committees in medical/ethical decision-making. This is less often the case among physicians in Britain and Australia, where Medical Ethics Committees review research protocols rather than advise physicians in clinical ethical decisions. When Medical Ethics Committees are involved in ethical consultations in the USA and elsewhere, cases are often reviewed at the resolution of a dilemma, i.e. in an 'ethical autopsy'.

In the USA, the current focus of public discussion is on advance directives and physician-assisted suicide. A challenge to the United States debate on euthanasia and physician-assisted suicide is to find ways to acknowledge and to discuss medical and ethical issues in treating patients in end-stage disease. This is not easy when cultural forces, such as the media, tend to overly simplify complex moral distinctions. Similarly, the challenge of medical liability tends to undermine physician confidence in difficult decisions about end-of-life issues. Yet tough end-of-life decisions that involve pain and suffering continue to be faced by some dying patients, who seek relief in more careful scheduling of their own deaths. At the same time, Americans who reflect on possible medical needs for themselves or family members claim that health-care practitioners often do not include their wishes in patient-care decisions. Medical insurance companies do not currently provide affordable policies to non-group subscribers, even as some prevent new policies being written for people with pre-existing medical conditions or cancel the writing of policies when costly procedures, such as heart transplants, are medically indicated. The issue is complicated by continuing reports of inadequate use of pain-control medications at the end of life.

Policy forums about medical/ethical decision-making in end-stage disease should encourage physicians to compare experiences in treating dying patients who might benefit from more adequate medical intervention. For some this would mean policies and practices of more adequate administration of palliative care, while for others it would mean access to ethical consultations by staff clinical ethicists or Institutional Ethics Committees. Policy-makers should openly explore creative problem-solving strategies, such as new funding possibilities for critically ill and dying patients and more effective communication about options and priorities. Public discussion is also needed to find more adequate ways of coping with the increasing requests for physician-assisted suicide or beneficent euthanasia. Professionals have much to learn from each other in dealing with medical/ethical decision-making in end-stage disease. Most of all, we all have much to learn from dying patients, health-care professionals, and family members who care for others at the end of life (Clark *et al.* 1990).

NOTE

1. The data reported in this chapter were gathered during a 1993–94 sabbatical on medical/ethical decision-making at the end of life. Appreciation is extended to colleagues and administrators in the Sociology/Archaeology Department of the University of Wisconsin–La Crosse, College of Liberal Studies, UW–La Crosse Foundation, Lutheran Hospital Law Crosse Foundation, Centre for the Study of Bioethics at the Medical College of Wisconsin and Centre for Biomedical Ethics at the University of Minnesota. The author also thanks members of the University of Wisconsin–La Crosse Working Group in Applied Ethics and Drs Bernard Hammes, Marilyn Mathews Bendiksen, Eric Kraemer, Kathy Charmaz and David Witmer for critiquing the manuscript.

REFERENCES

Anspach, R.R. (1993) *Deciding Who Lives: Fateful Choices in the Intensive-Care Nursery*, Berkeley: University of California Press.

Buchanan, A.E. and Brock, D.W. (1990) *Deciding for Others: The Ethics of Surrogate Decision Making*, New York: Cambridge University Press.

Carlson, R.W. and Anwar, M.S. (1994) 'Wisconsin Physicians and Euthanasia: An editorial', *Archives of Internal Medicine*, 154: 501–02.

Clark, E., Fritz, J., Rieker, P., Kutscher, A. and Bendiksen, R. (eds.) (1990) *Clinical Sociological Perspectives on Illness & Loss: The Linkage of Theory & Practice*, Philadelphia, PA: The Charles Press.

Cleeland, C.S. *et al.* (1994) 'Pain and its Treatment in Outpatients with Metastatic Cancer', *New England Journal of Medicine*, 330: 592–6.

Cranford, R.E. (1994) 'On the Brink of Euthanasia: Are we ready?', *Newsletter of The Centre for Biomedical Ethics-University of Minnesota*, Winter, 1.

Crigger, B.J. (ed.) (1992) *Dying Well? A Colloquy on Euthanasia and Assisted Suicide,* Briarcliff Manor, NY: Hastings Centre.

Fulton, R. and Bendiksen, R. (eds.) (1994) *Death and Identity,* 3rd edn, Philadelphia, PA: The Charles Press.

Hammes, B.J. and Bendiksen, R. (1990) 'From the Ivory Tower to the Hospital Ward: A role analysis of a clinical ethicist', in E. Clark, *et al.* (eds.), *Clinical Sociological Perspectives on Illness & Loss: The Linkage of Theory & Practice,* Philadelphia, PA: The Charles Press.

Hammes, B.J. and Bendiksen, R. (1994) 'Prolonging Life – Choosing Death: A clinical sociological perspective in medical-ethical decision-making', in R. Fulton and R. Bendiksen (eds.) *Death and Identity,* 3rd edn, Philadelphia, PA: The Charles Press.

Hammes, B.J. and Rooney, B. (1996) 'Advanced Medical Planning: A longitudinal community study', paper presented at the Midwest Sociological Society, Session on 'Bioethics and Society', Chicago, IL, 3–6 April.

Jaffe, G.A. (1989) 'Institutional Ethics Committees: legitimate and impartial review of ethical health care decisions', *The Journal of Legal Medicine,* 10, 393–431.

Jonsen, A.R., Siegler, M. and Winslade, W.J. (1992) *Clinical Ethics: A Practical Approach to Ethical Decisions in Clinical Medicine,* 3rd edn, New York: McGraw-Hill.

Kohl, M. (ed.) (1975) *Beneficent Euthanasia,* Buffalo, NY: Prometheus Books.

La Puma, J. and Schiedermayer, D. (1994) *Ethics Consultation: A Practical Guide,* Boston: Jones & Bartlett.

Markson, E.W. (1995) 'To Be Or Not To Be: Assisted suicide revisited', *Omega,* 31: 221–35.

Minogue, B.P. (1996) *Bioethics: A Committee Approach,* Sudbury, MA: Jones & Bartlett.

Pijnenborg, L., van der Maas, P.J., van Delden, J.J.M. and Looman, C.W.N. (1993) 'Life-terminating Acts without Explicit Request of Patient', *The Lancet,* 341: 1196–9.

Pike, A.W. (1991) 'Moral Outrage and Moral Discourse in Nurse–Physician Collaboration', *Journal of Professional Nursing,* 7, 351–63.

Quill, T.E. (1991) 'Death and Dignity: A case of individualized decision making', *New England Journal of Medicine,* 324: 691–4.

Quill, T.E. (1993) *Death and Dignity: Making Choices and Taking Chances,* New York: Norton.

Reiser, S.J. (1986) *Ethics and Medicine: Historical Perspectives & Contemporary Issues,* Cambridge, MA: MIT Press.

Selznick, P. (1992) *The Moral Commonwealth: Social Theory and the Promise of Community,* Berkeley, CA: University of California Press.

Shapiro, R.S., Derse, A.R., Gottlieb, M., Schiedermayer, D. and Olson, M. (1994) 'Willingness to Perform Euthanasia: A survey of physician attitudes', *Archives of Internal Medicine,* 154: 575–84.

Shavelson, L. (1995) *A Chosen Death: The Dying Confront Assisted Suicide,* New York: Simon & Schuster.

Singer, S. (1994) *Rethinking Life & Death: The Collapse of Our Traditional Ethics,* New York: St Martin's Press.

Stanley, J.M. (1992) 'The Appleton International Conference: Developing Guidelines for Decisions to Forgo Life-prolonging Medical Treatment', *Journal of Medical Ethics,* 18:3–22.

Starr, P. (1982) *The Social Transformation of American Medicine,* New York: Basic Books.

Thomasma, D.C. and Graber, G.C. (1990) *Euthanasia: Toward an Ethical Social Theory,* New York: Continuum.

Tronto, J.C. (1993) *Moral Boundaries: A Political Argument for an Ethic of Care,* New York: Routledge.

Veatch, R.M. (ed.) (1989) *Cross Cultural Perspectives in Medical Ethics,* Boston: Jones & Bartlett.

Veatch, R.M. (ed.) (1996) *Medical Ethics,* 2nd edn, Sudbury, MA: Jones & Bartlett Cleeland, C.S. *et al.* (1994) 'Pain and Its Treatment in Outpatients with Metastatic Cancer', *New England Journal of Medicine,* 330: 592–6.

Waitzkin, H. (1991) *The Politics of Medical Encounters: How Patients and Doctors Deal with Social Problems,* New Haven: Yale University Press.

Weisz, G. (ed.) (1990) *Social Science Perspectives on Medical Ethics,* Norwell, MA: Kluwer Academic.

16 Managing the Spectre of Death: the War against Drug Use and AIDS in America

Judith A. Levy and Daniel J. Amick

When compared to death from such common illnesses as cancer or heart disease, the prospect of dying of AIDS appears darker, more stigmatizing and more socially ominous. The odium surrounding the spectre of AIDS-related death stems in part from the close relationship between disease and desire and disease and deviance through which HIV is contracted (Gagnon 1990). AIDS typically has its genesis in private acts involving moral issues (Bayer 1990). Also, dying of AIDS is exacerbated by the often horrendous and highly visible physical consequences associated with HIV infection (Masur *et al.* 1985).

The spectre of a disease that evokes such terrible human suffering has led medical and popular imagery to elevate efforts to stop the AIDS epidemic to an all-out 'war' involving an enemy and a struggle to win (Sontag 1978). The metaphor of waging war against a deadly and widely feared disease speaks to the need to marshal national will and resources for the battle at hand. The use of war as a descriptor prepares professional and lay combatants for casualties and losses in the confrontation. It also warns of possible defeat while heralding hope for success and victory.

> Like that on AIDS, a national war also is being waged in the United States against the spread and influence of illegal drug use. (Inciardi 1992)

Echoing decades of antidrug policy, President Bush called attention to this continued war in a 1989 televised speech. 'Victory, victory over drugs is our cause. A just cause, and

> with your help, we are going to win.' (Abadinsky 1993: 331)

Combating the use of illicit drugs in American communities has grown so challenging that many policy-makers and law-enforcement officials now call for the US war on drugs to be internationalized (Goldberg 1996). Although drug production and trafficking occur world-wide, the casualties of this war are felt strongly in American communities. Success in the fight against drugs, like that against AIDS, must be waged at both the global and community levels.

This analysis examines the intersection of the wars against AIDS and against drug abuse as waged in the American inner cities by community-based intervention programmes. The Neighborhood Outreach Demonstration Project (NODP), upon which the analysis is based, served as an example. A five-year longitudinal study,[1] NODP focuses on drug and AIDS intervention efforts affecting the activities of a sample of 200 injecting drug-users (IDUs) recruited through street outreach. Data for the analysis are drawn from periodic in-depth interviews, ethnographic field notes; and transcripts of taped peer support-group meetings.

We begin by describing NODP's setting and situation, which reflect the community sites where significant portions of the war against drugs and AIDS in America occur. Next we examine how active injecting drug-users approach and make sense of their risk for contracting HIV and consequent death. We then explore the social trajectories of living and dying with AIDS, focusing on the experiences of project staff who are HIV-infected. Finally, we analyse how fears of HIV and AIDS-related death structure staff and subject interactions. We end with an overview of how death through drug-related AIDS is disproportionately experienced by specific segments of American society.

THE SETTING AND SITUATION

The NODP project is located in two field stations converted from store-fronts in two geographically distinct areas in Chicago. Both field stations are situated in low-income, high-crime areas with a large density of heroin users. The HIV seropositivity rate among IDUs in these neighbourhoods has been documented at approximately 30 per cent. The north-side field station adjoins 'blood alley', a semi-hidden causeway between buildings where heroin users congregate to purchase drugs, exchange sex for drugs or money, and inject. The south-side field station is directly situated within a popular 'copping' area for drug deals – teenage runners with cellular phones openly ply their trade in front of the building.

Upon entering either field station, visitors immediately confront AIDS-prevention paraphernalia and HIV educational messages. Baskets of condoms to protect against sexual transmission and small bottles of bleach and purified water for sterilizing used needles are placed strategically to encourage visitors to take them. Colourful posters warn of the dangers of transmitting or contracting HIV. Those posted during the earlier years of the project, when scare-tactics were common in AIDS intervention, bear images of coffins, skulls and other symbols depicting the death-threat of AIDS. More recent placards, reflecting the current educational movement towards messages based on positive reinforcement, promote longer and healthier lives through use of condoms and clean needles. Both sets of messages constitute silent yet constant reminders to staff and project participants of the gravity of their situation. For the uninfected or those unaware of their sero-status, these images visibly communicate the deadly potential of AIDS. For HIV-infected staff and participants, these representations portend a foreshortened and ominous future.

In enrolling in the project, study participants assume the dual role of client and subject. As clients, they can access project services and resources for forging behavioural changes that can lead to longer, healthier lives. As subjects, they contribute to research with the potential to curb AIDS and increase the well-being of drug-dependent individuals in general. Fees paid to subjects for interviews add incentive.

Staff members at each field station perform one of two functions: intervention or research. Intervention staff, consisting of one case manager and one indigenous outreach worker per site, help project participants control their drug use and stop transmission of AIDS. Together, each team provides counselling, advocacy and referral services; linkages to medical and social-service providers; and preventive materials and education for stopping the spread of HIV. Although it is not part of their formal job description, they also help arrange funerals and attend burials when clients die. The team works with project participants to organize and facilitate the latter's participation in peer-support self-help groups, which encourage drug abstinence or control and promote behavioural patterns to reduce HIV transmission. These responsibilities bring the intervention team into close contact with the participants' daily struggles with drug use and HIV.

In contrast, the research staff observe and record the drug-use patterns and HIV-risk behaviours of project particpants. Research staff include interviewers, a biostatistician, and a small team of social scientists. Unlike the intervention staff, whose interaction with IDUs and HIV is direct and service-orientated, the research staff's responsibility for stopping HIV transmission is indirect and scientifically driven.

The role responsibilities that divide intervention staff from research staff manifest themselves in differences in how project-related death is experienced. Over the study's four years in the field, 13 members of the original sample of 200 users have died, along with an unrecorded number of their 'shooting' partners and other acquaintances whom staff know. Working on the front lines of direct service, intervention staff experience these deaths at first hand. In contrast, research staff housed at the university typically experience subjects' deaths at a distance, weeks or months later. Such knowledge typically emerges when the deceased's code number appears as 'missing data' in the longitudinal data record. On rare occasions, however, some event fractures this distance to force recognition of the human being behind the numbers. Such an instance occurred, for example, when the county coroner's office called the project's principal investigator to arrange for the pick-up and burial of the corpse of a subject who recently died of AIDS. Having no friends or next of kin, the person had listed the name printed at the top of the project's Human Subjects consent form to contact for funeral arrangements. Unaccustomed to and uncomfortable with attending directly to the death of a subject, the principal investigator was relieved to delegate responsibility for removal and burial of the body to an intervention staff member, for whom this task was more routine.

DEATH AND HEROIN USE

For the most part, death is no stranger to those who regularly inhabit or actively participate in the social world of heroin injection. Within the personal networks of heroin use in major American cities, virtually everyone has a friend or acquaintance who has died from drug-related causes. Overdosing on drugs is common:

> The first time I overdosed was in the bathroom in my first kid's house. I was shooting heroin at the time. I went in the bathroom and was shooting up and overdosed in the bathroom. The second time was in the summer on some person's back porch. He got off and I got off, and the next thing I know I'm in the hospital.

Fatalities can be traced to the inconsistent quality of street drugs and the difficulties of calculating personal tolerance (Louria *et al.* 1967).

Life on the streets, coupled with the illegal pursuit of money or drugs, brings active addicts into activities and situations that can be violent and deadly. Like all social worlds, the subculture of heroin use prescribes rules and expectations for its denizens to follow. Here, however, norm violations such as cheating one's dealer can be exceedingly dangerous and harshly punished (Goldstein 1985). In maintaining an illegal and inherently dangerous dependency, drug-users operate outside the bounds of safe health practices and medical advice (Faltz 1992). As a result, illnesses associated with the practice and life-styles of drug dependency claim the lives of many users each year. These include needle-borne hepatitis, tuberculosis, liver disease and now AIDS.

People who inject drugs know the deadly realities of their dependency, yet continue to use drugs. A high proportion of NODP participants have used drugs for 20 years or more, despite personal danger and the loss of 'running-mates' and other heroin-using acquaintances to drug-related causes. Their persistence as chronic users attests to their willingness to take personal risks.

Although massive community-based educational programming and prevention efforts in the United States have taught street addicts about the dangers of AIDS, their experiences and responses to the threat differ. Oral histories and ethnographic observations reveal that injectors employ varying 'life scripts' to account for and live with their precarious positions *vis-à-vis* the AIDS epidemic. These heuristics range from simple rationalizations to more complex transcendental arguments. Clients generally can be categorized in one of four ways, depending on how they interpret surviving the dangers of the street, including the possibility of HIV infection and death.

First, gamblers define the challenges of life and the possibility of death as a series of odds. As Bob, who is one such gambler, says, 'There is a risk in everything.' Tina, also a gambler, adds: 'There is a possibility that I can get hit by a car when I cross the street. I'm not going to fight myself about all these things that could happen. There are some things that aren't even good to know. I don't want to know the day of my death.' When it comes to AIDS or other life threats, gamblers hope for favourable odds.

The more proactive of gamblers attempt to improve their odds through personal actions. Typically, they follow self-imposed rules and prescribed behaviours when using or pursuing drugs. Such tactics differ by user according to his or her theory of what will work. Sally, for example, moderates the level of heroin she uses, keeping it within "safe" limits and refusing to share needles. Ron, on the other hand, banks on having cultivated a long-term relationship with a dealer to provide him with unadulterated drugs that are unlikely to produce unwanted side-effects. Outcomes of these strategies also differ. So far, Sally's approach appears to have worked, because she remains HIV-negative. Ed, on the other hand, wagered that he could evade the virus by sharing needles only with 'close friends'. He was wrong.

Gamblers who contract HIV tend to describe their situation as having taken a chance and lost. Upon discovering his positive sero-status, Ed reflected: 'I never bothered nobody. I never snitched on nobody. I played the game the way it was supposed to be played. You make a mistake, you pay for it. I always have been able to handle what comes along and like I say, I'm relatively content.' Like many gamblers who acknowledge the risks but choose to play, Ed assumes a measure of personal responsibility for becoming infected. Perhaps people cope with a serious or fatal illness more easily when they perceive that their personal commitment to a line of action carries irrevocable consequences.

In contrast to gamblers, who believe in self-interventions to increase the odds of certain outcomes, fatalists attribute their life circumstances to forces beyond their control. As Tammy, a mother of two, explains, 'Most things are predestined and I was destined to be a drug user.' When confronting a diagnosis of AIDS, fatalists like Tammy believe in a predetermined life script:

> I don't make any plans. I stopped planning a long time ago, 'cause me and plans never go along too well. Whenever I ended up making a lot of plans, and it didn't go according to the way I planned it, I found myself stretched out of shape . . . mad and bitter because the shit didn't come off as I planned it. Now as I get older, I just take it day by day.

Convinced that personal acts cannot counter the more powerful forces of destiny, fatalists view strategies to avoid HIV as futile (McKeganey and Barnard 1992). Once they are infected, such fatalism may convey self-absolution for engaging in behaviour that produced this outcome.

A third response to the threat of HIV and death through AIDS involves perceiving oneself as *one of life's victims.* Life victims see themselves as repeatedly cheated out of health and a good life by fate or others:

> I got drafted and had to go to Korea. It [becoming addicted to heroin] was while I was in the army in Korea. I lost control. I did seek help, but at that time drug addiction was looked upon as not being a sickness but being

> the scrum of the earth. So that is what has ruined my life and they told me to get the hell out of the army. Just go! I always did hold that against the army.

For life's victims, being diagnosed with HIV represents the ultimate victimization in a life of chronic adversity. Like fatalists, victims tend to reject responsibility for their infection – preferring to attribute this outcome to the actions of others or to a malevolent situation.

Finally, *God's children* believe that a supernatural force monitors their lives and can protect them from harm. Tom, for example, explains how he survived the dangers of overdosing and becoming infected: 'It was God. He helped me and took me through a lot of problems. It wasn't me. It was God. I think someone was praying for me. As a matter of fact, I know a lot of people were praying for me. Without their prayers and God's help, I would not have made it.' As is true for gay men (Weitz 1991), some injectors attribute HIV infection as punishment for personal transgressions or guilty acts. They are not alone in such judgements: a segment of the general population shares this sentiment. In the case of heroin use and AIDS, the assignment of meaning revolves around the ethical dilemmas of drug dependency. Such casual explanations transform an AIDS-related death from a medical to a moral problem that is reinforced by the common perception that drug abuse is both illegal and deviant.

DEATH AND HIV IN THE SOCIAL WORLD OF DRUG INTERVENTION

Death from AIDS involves a known trajectory along an elastic time-path. AIDS has a latency period ranging from months to many years, from first infection with HIV to death from full-blown AIDS (Ron and Rogers 1990). Staff experiences, which partly parallel those of the project's subjects, exemplify differing points on the HIV trajectory.

For many individuals, the first stage in the AIDS trajectory begins with the knowledge of being at risk (Weitz 1991). Ed, an outreach worker, confronted his vulnerability to AIDS when attending his first job-training session. During the break, he anxiously questioned the trainer about his possible sero-status, given his many years of drug dependency. Believing that positive test results would represent a 'death sentence', Ed debated for several months before deciding to undergo testing.

Ed's reluctance to be tested extends beyond the fear of discovering a truncated life expectancy. Testing seropositive irrevocably sets in motion a series of losses associated with diagnosis of a terminal illness – even though death may not occur for years. These include the loss of dreams and hopes for the future (Teguis and Ahmed 1992). Friendships and loving relationships may dwindle or die under the pressures that disease and dying evoke. In the case of AIDS, some HIV-positive women of childbearing age face whether or not to conceive or carry a foetus to full term (McKeganey and Barnard 1992). Those with young children worry over who will care for them when they are gone. In some cases, public knowledge of HIV infection has restricted personal freedoms, employment, schooling and insurance (Bayer 1990).

Avoidance of testing permits the individual not only to elude the spectre of *death from* AIDS, but also to escape the spectre of *life with* AIDS. More than mere failure of the body, succumbing to a severe and life-threatening illness signals a definitive defeat of the self (Herzlich and Pierret 1984). HIV infection may be suspected, but it remains unofficial unless confirmed by a positive test result. Without such proof, social interactions continue unhampered by the awkwardness and emotional stresses of a terminal diagnosis.

Will, a project interviewer, chose to be tested several years before joining the project. Now seropositive but nonsymptomatic, he openly discloses his illness. Sitting through training and later questioning others about AIDS has demanded detachment from his own condition to focus on the plight of others. This emotional separation is reinforced by the staff, who engage in what Goffman (1959: 123) refers to as 'front-stage' versus 'back-stage' behaviour. In performing the front-stage duties of educating project participants, staff could not avoid talking about AIDS or the consequences of HIV in Will's presence. Sensitive to his feelings, they downplayed the seriousness of a positive sero-status in their social discourse and avoided discussing the fatality of AIDS when in his company. Back-stage among themselves or out of his presence, staff admitted to discomfort in talking about AIDS-related death in front of a co-worker who is expected to die.

The awkwardness that non-infected individuals feel around those with a positive sero-status mirrors that of interacting with anyone dying of a terminal disease. Initial shock at the news and concern for one's own mortality are common (Puentes and Anthony 1992). Feelings of guilt may arise from being a survivor despite also having engaged in high-risk behaviour (Siegel and Krauss 1991). Many individuals alter their interactions with those who are dying by watching what they say, not being too demanding, and being especially considerate (Marshall 1980). To work, such management strategies need to mesh with the attitudes and role performance of the person who is ill. Will's appearance as an attractive, robust 60-year-old man who rode his bicycle to the field station belied his HIV infection. His seemingly benign progress along the HIV trajectory elicited more sympathy than fear among staff and project participants.

The visibility of AIDS symptoms draws the border between sick and not sick (Calvez 1989: 63). Although they could ignore Will's situation, staff could not ignore another co-worker whose infection had progressed further and who exhibited early symptoms. Ted's condition had worsened since joining the project. On some days, his health appeared normal; on other days, he suffered a sore throat and visible signs of thrush, a cheesy mucus, in his mouth. Experiencing noticeable weight loss and tiring easily, he often rested on the field-station couch. When such markers of infection were visible, both staff and clients adjusted their interactions with him to accommodate his illness. Staff assumed some of Ted's responsibilities; more empathetic clients reduced their demands for services when he appeared too ill to cope with heavy requests.

José, a staff interviewer, died of AIDS six months after being taken on. As his condition worsened, his effectiveness as a worker diminished. Clients avoided coming for interviews, reporting that they feared infection and felt uncomfortable seeing someone so ravaged by disease. José's condition reminded seropositive clients of how they might die. José was in constant pain, and analgesics often left him drowsy and disorientated. Fearing that his condition would necessitate an unwanted disability leave, field staff colluded to cover for him by completing or hiding his unfinished work.

Because some, although not all, staff and project participants at NODP were HIV-positive, interactions at the field stations differed somewhat from AIDS research and intervention projects in which only subjects or clients are infected. That much of the staff were former users fostered a sense of fellow-feeling while precluding moral condemnation of those who contracted the virus through illegal drug use. Staff sensitivity about the biosocial meaning of an AIDS diagnosis was high, based on close or personal knowledge. Conversations about AIDS were monitored to avoid scaring fellow seropositive employees and participants. Staff also had to confront the social crises and emotional traumas of having an HIV-positive co-worker sicken and die. Moreover, social exchanges between mutually HIV-positive staff and subjects were shaped, in part, by which person's illness outpaced the other's. Regardless of sero-status, role reversals occurred when study participants accorded emotional support or made other concessions to HIV-positive staff with visible health complications. Thus, HIV diagnosis, terminal illness, and, in some cases, the finality of death occurred within the co-empathy and mutual experience of a shared community. Through both giving and receiving social support and care, staff and study participants assumed co-responsibility for enacting the rituals and symbolic expressions of human connectedness.

FEAR OF AIDS AND DEATH

Regardless of their particular role as staff or subjects in the project, participation in NODP brought people of both positive and negative sero-status into close proximity. This nearness was not always comfortable. Because HIV is contagious, people who interact with those who are positive may fear that the virus will spread to them. Despite an intellectual knowledge that transmission through casual contact is impossible, irrational fears based on emotions can develop.

Subjects fear other subjects, as Shana's description of a recent interchange with Tina reveals:

> I handed her the pop and she drank directly out of my bottle and handed it back. I poured it into my cup. Then I realized that is just like drinking behind her. I said, "You should give me the option to choose how I feel about that . . . that's not the decision that you should make about my life. How do I know that you don't have no cuts [in your mouth] nowhere?"

Project participants may worry about seropositive staff. As one informant explains, 'What if somebody is HIV-positive like our old buddy Will? How close do you want to be with that person?' Such concerns may be shared by seronegative staff, for even drug and AIDS professionals are not immune to irrational fears. As one staff member recounts:

> I was talking to Ted (a co-worker) at an office birthday party. Someone had brought a great bean dip and Ted and I were scarfing it down. Suddenly I realized that we were sharing food dipped out of the same bowl. Although I knew I couldn't catch AIDS that way, I suddenly felt queasy and stopped eating.

Another staff member reports avoiding unnecessary physical contact with those whom he believes to be HIV-infected. Subtle covering strategies that include not sharing food, not sharing cigarettes and not even shaking hands are employed.

Fear of transmission among health-care workers and service providers working with HIV-positive individuals is common. To assume that a statistical rationale is sufficient to dispel the fears of these workers is to deny their humanity (Friedland 1990). Although the probability of contracting AIDS through service delivery is low, not all fear of HIV transmission from client to staff is unrealistic. In the course of their duties, field staff encounter situations where they contact possible sources of infection. Occurrences such as nosebleeds, accidents, and, in one case, a knife-fight between project participants meant that staff on occasion had to clean blood from field-station floors and furniture. Also, street addicts sometimes use secret places in the field stations to hide their drug paraphernalia or dispose of used needles. New staff are routinely warned not to compact trash with their hands or reach into deep drawers without first examining them thoroughly. For example, a staff interviewer who had been working for a short time on the project found a small box that an HIV-positive client had left behind at the field station. Curious about what it contained, he reached in and pricked himself with a used syringe. This rash act left him with months of worry about contracting HIV while awaiting test results following the disease's incubation period.

CONCLUSION

In post-industrial societies, people expect to live to old age. AIDS has shattered this expectation by truncating an increasing number of young lives. Most deaths from AIDS occur among young people between the ages of 18 and 34. Unlike older persons, who experience the death of peers and friends, most young adults have little experience with serious disease, illness and death.

Independent of AIDS, injecting drug-users encounter death more often than other members of their age cohort. Life on the streets and the complications of drug use cast a daily spectre of death. AIDS exacerbates this vision. Therefore, intervention strategies that rely on threats of mortality as incentives for safer behaviour have a low impact, because death is already omnipresent in users' lives. Positive messages about prolonging and enriching life motivate safe behaviour better than do apparitions of death.

The psychosocial issues surrounding AIDS in the workplace have received wide attention. Fear of AIDS often stems from deep and often irrational feelings about sexuality and death that can invade and disrupt the orderliness of occupational and professional settings involving infected workers (Rowe *et al.* 1986). The recent case of the American dentist-to-patient transmission has raised significant public concern about the role of infected service providers in dealing with non-infected individuals. Laws requiring all medical and social-service providers to reveal their HIV status have been proposed and widely debated in the media.

Response to AIDS partly determines its meaning (Meisenhelder *et al.* 1989). Among the uninfected, a co-worker with AIDS represents a future to be avoided. For the HIV-infected but asymptomatic worker, contact with someone exhibiting the symptoms of full-blown AIDS presents a frightening glimpse of the future. 'Even more than the physical harm, people fear the cultural rejection, loathing, and reproach that this diagnosis implies' (Meisenhelder *et al.* 1989: 33–4). Negative judgements about AIDS become generalized to judgements about those who are infected.

Our experience with NODP transcends those of community-based drug interventions to include all individuals, both professional and quasi-professional, whose work-role places them in contact with injecting drug-users who may or may not be HIV-positive or who may or may not present symptoms of AIDS. Such workers include police officers who are called upon to arrest and process injecting drug-users; the social worker who must arrange child-care for an injecting drug-user who is ill; and the drug-abuse counsellor who works with users in controlling drug use. The spectre of possible infection and eventual death from AIDS is for these individuals a reality that did not exist in the last decade. Our findings suggest that even workers who receive in-service training worry about casual transmission despite reassurance that they are not at risk. Perhaps emotional response to possible contagion and death outweighs substantive knowledge. Thus, while reminding staff to take safety precautions, one must also not raise their fears unduly. Moreover, addressing worries that are embedded *both* in emotion and cognition is imperative, rather than relying solely on 'facts' to dispel fears.

That the war on AIDS in the United States is fused in part with the war on drugs means that many of the battlefields of the struggle are located in the inner-city communities, where the incidence of injecting drug use is high. These sections of the city tend to be populated by the socially disadvantaged, a high proportion of whom are Hispanic or of African–American descent. Because of this segmentation, death from drug-related AIDS in the United States is stratified increasingly along economic lines. Thus, the spectre of death by AIDS is disproportionately experienced and borne by an economic underclass of Americans with the fewest personal resources to deal with its consequences. Continued community outreach, such as that practised by the NODP project, is critical in fighting the wars against AIDS and the negative consequences of illegal drug use.

NOTE

1. Support for this study was provided by the National Institute on Drug Abuse (DA-06994).

REFERENCES

Abadinsky, H. (1993) *Drug Abuse: An Introduction,* Chicago: Nelson Hall.

Bayer, R. (1990) 'AIDS, Privacy, and Responsibility', in S.R. Graubard (ed.), *Living with AIDS,* Cambridge, MA: MIT Press.

Calvez, M. (1989) *Composer avec un Danger: Approche des responses sociales à l'infection au VIH et au SIDA,* Rennes: Institut Régional du Travail Social de Bretagne.

Faltz, B.G. (1992) 'Coping with AIDS and Substance Abuse', in P.I. Ahmed (ed.), *Living and Dying with AIDS,* New York: Plenum Press.

Friedland, G.H. (1990) 'Clinical Care in the AIDS Epidemic', S.R. Graubard (ed.), *Living with AIDS,* Cambridge, MA: MIT Press.

Gagnon, J.H. (1990) 'Disease and Desire', in S.R. Graubard (ed.), *Living with AIDS,* Cambridge, MA: MIT Press.

Goffman, E. (1959) *The Presentation of Self in Everyday Life,* Garden City, NY: Doubleday Anchor Books.

Goldberg, R. (1996) 'Should the War on Drugs be Waged on an International Level?', in R. Goldberg (ed.), *Taking Sides: Clashing Views on Controversial Issues in Drugs and Society,* 2nd edn, Guilford, CT: Dushkin.

Goldstein, P.J. (1985) 'The Drugs/Violence Nexus: A tripartite conceptual framework', *Journal of Drug Issues,* 15: 493–506.

Herzlich, C. and Pierret, J. (1984) *Illness and Self in Society,* Baltimore: Johns Hopkins University Press.

Inciardi J.A. (1992) *The War on Drugs II,* Mountain View, CA: Mayfield.

Louria, D.B., Hensie, T. and Rose, J. (1976) 'The Major Medical Complications of Heroin Addiction', *Annals of Internal Medicine,* 67: 1–22.

McKeganey, N. and Barnard, M. (1992) *AIDS, Drugs, and Sexual Risk: Lives in the Balance,* Buckingham, UK: Open University Press.

Marshall, V.W. (1980) *Last Chapters: A Sociology of Aging and Dying,* Belmont, CA: Wadsworth.

Masur, H., Kovacs, J.A., Ognibene, F., Shelhamer, J. and Parrillo, J.E.

(1985) 'Infectious Complications of AIDS', in V.T. DeVita, Jr, S. Hellman and S.A. Rosenberg (eds.), *AIDS: Etiology, Diagnosis, Treatment and Prevention*, Philadelphia, PA: J.B. Lippincott.

Meisenhelder, J.B., Bell, J. and LaCharite, C.L. (1989) 'Fear of Contagion: A Stress Response to Acquired Immunodeficiency Syndrome', *Advance Nursing Science*, 11: 29–38.

Puentes, A.J. and Anthony, J. (1992) 'A Personal Perspective on Living and Dying with AIDS', in P.I. Ahmed (ed.), *Living and Dying with AIDS*, New York: Plenum Press.

Ron, A. and Rogers, D.E. (1990) 'AIDS in the United States: Patient care and politics', in S.R. Graubard (ed.), *Living with AIDS*, Cambridge, MA: MIT Press.

Rowe, M.P., Russell-Einhorn, M. and Baker, M.A. (1986) 'The Fear of AIDS', *Harvard Business Review*, July–August: 28.

Siegel, K. and Krauss, B.J. (1991) 'Living with HIV infection: Adaptive tasks of seropositive gay men', *The Journal of Health and Social Behaviour*, 32, 3: 1732.

Sontag, S. (1978) *Illness as a Metaphor*, New York: Farrar, Strauss & Giroux.

Teguis, A. and Ahmed, P.I. (1992) 'Living with AIDS: An overview', in P.I. Ahmed (ed.), *Living and Dying with AIDS*, New York: Plenum Press.

Weitz, R. (1991) *Life with AIDS*, New Brunswick, NJ: Rutgers University Press.

17 Grief and Loss of Self[1]

Kathy Charmaz

Arnold Toynbee (1969: 131) once said, 'Death is un-American.'[2] If death is un-American, grief is disallowed. Death and, by extension, grief, symbolize loss and failure. In the dominant culture of the United States, grief is burdened with the residuals of the Protestant ethic with its beliefs in stoicism, individualism, rationality, privacy and systematic hard work. American beliefs and institutionalized practices towards grief separate it from ordinary life, view it as a private affliction, and expect the bereaved to get over it. This cultural backdrop can conflict with minority groups' views of grief and thus result in harsh judgements and powerful constraints. In keeping with the Protestant ethic, many Americans believe in striving towards future goals, not in dwelling on the past, in utilitarianism, and in individual control and achievement. American beliefs and practices isolate the bereaved in profound grief when a significant person dies, and result in loss of self (Charmaz 1980; Marris 1974).

Endorsing the values of the Protestant ethic leads to assumptions about personal worth and earned failure. Elite positions are presumed to be evidence of worth and diligence. Failure is assumed to result from individual inadequacy – lack of will and effort. Correspondingly, Americans judge the bereaved in similar terms. Not all grief is acceptable. Not everyone's grief is acknowledged. Not every survivor copes with grief successfully. Three types of grief discussed below, entitled grief, underestimated grief and disenfranchised grief, hearken back to Protestant values concerning deservingness, priority and worth.

The rationality born with the Protestant ethic also shapes American notions about what to do about grief. While lay persons may try to deny, diminish or dismiss it, professionals analyse grief and attempt to treat it systematically. The consequent professionalization of emotional response stresses hard work, individual responsibility, personal control and achievement. In this view, grief can be demystified and rationally resolved. Grief is something to be 'managed' rather than merely felt or displayed (Lindemann 1944). The major architect of grief counselling, J. William Worden (1991: 35), writes, 'grief creates tasks that need to be accomplished'. Worden advocates grief counselling for handling those tasks. Consistent with the Protestant ethic, work is the metaphor and guiding logic for resolving grief.

THE DOMINANT MEANING OF GRIEF IN THE UNITED STATES

The language of grief in the United States is the language of irretrievable loss. A severing, departing – ending. Grieving means facing and feeling loss of attachment (Bowlby 1980; Lofland 1982). Ultimately, the meaning of grief lies in the meaning of the attached other. That attachment provides images of self, shared activities, identities and links to others. Yet American beliefs in individualism and autonomy make understanding the depth and extent of attachment elusive, especially because Americans usually limit loss to narrow family roles.

American society creates little public context for grief. No sustained collective mourning smoothes transitions for survivors or teaches people about experiencing grief. Staudacher (1987) aptly describes grief as a stranger with no predecessor. Many of those bereaved have no place to put it and few ways to deal with it. None the less, grief is something to be contained – to keep a lid on, to shy away from. Despite seeming American emotional expressivity, tight limits prevent grief from seeping out into the public arena. Deep grief undermines American beliefs in order, progress and personal control. Hence, we relegate it to private life, view it as a psychological problem, and make resolving it the survivor's responsibility.

Such individualizing of grief may derive from a more general deintensification of emotion in American life. Peter Stearns (1994) argues that twentieth-century America has seen a dampening of passions, including grief, guilt and love. During the Victorian era in the United States, Americans valued grief for sweeping the bereaved out of ordinary reality. In contrast, twentieth-century Americans define grief as menacing. Rather than being ennobled through Victorian suffering, twentieth-century Americans see extended grieving as morbid wallowing. For Stearns, 'grief work' means working against grief and, thus, constitutes 'an implicit attack on Victorian savouring of this emotional state' (159). Popular literature admonished mid-twentieth-century Americans neither to indulge in grief nor to depress others with it (Stearns 1994). Though the popular literature has changed, much popular wisdom has not. Grief is to be borne alone without inconveniencing other people. American business norms, for example, put formal clamps on mourning with prescribed limits for absences and informal constraints on expressing grief (Pratt 1994). Current popular self-help books protest that the bereaved are not alone and should feel and share their grief. However, the authors wrote their books precisely because they had suffered grief alone (e.g. Schiff 1986; Tatlebaum 1980; Wrobleski 1991). Self-help books inform the bereaved 'how to manage grief wisely' (Cornils 1992; Staudacher 1987), to take control and act themselves (Cornils 1992; Staudacher 1987), 'if it's going to be it's up to me' (Cornils 1992) and to allow themselves to feel (O'Connor 1984; Staudacher 1987).

In America, grief comes with goals and responsibilities – shoulds and oughts – expectations and obligations. Survivors 'should' work at resolving their grief. Americans commonly view working through grief in linear, progressive terms. Expected improvement can be marred by waves of sorrow, fear and remorse long after survivors feel they 'should' have improved. '"It's been three months, I should be back to normal." Or, "It's been a year." Or, "It's been *five* years." I still slip into that belief that I couldn't even grieve right' (Alexander 1991: 40). Resolving grief becomes a test of self; one can fail by remaining stuck in it. In turn, American condemnation of failure further individualizes grief and makes it unshareable.

Grief is affected by the type of death. Murder and suicide pose special hardships, as does preventable death, prolonged dying or an untimely death. Preventable death evokes feelings of anger, victimization, injustice and blame. Obsession, rumination and lack of closure follow (Rando 1993). Dying young evokes more sorrow than an elder's death, who may hardly be mourned at all. Some people die psychologically and socially before they die physically. Conceptions of whether the deceased had a 'good' or 'bad' death respectively console or evoke remorse, anger or anguish.

GRIEF AS A CRISIS OF THE SELF

Experiencing profound grief is a crisis of the self. The foundation of the bereaved's self-concept shatters, however temporarily. Death irretrievably alters the person's web of social relationships. Beliefs in individualism can result in failing to recognize that our real selves depend upon relationships. We define and know *ourselves* as well as the other through the relationship. The mother of a 20-year-old son who committed suicide said, 'My kids were my world . . . I had no life beyond that, so having him do this really took a big part of me with him' (Alexander 1991: 69). The death means losing hopes and dreams (Rando 1984). It means losing once certain futures. Thus, grief undermines middle-class American time-perspectives emanating from the Protestant ethic that view the future as achievable.

Experiencing profound grief is a *searing disruption* of one's being and way of life. Numbness, rapid shifts between disbelief and acknowledgment of the death, disconnection from present events, and emotional swings from hurt to anger to guilt all occur. Hurt, because death should't occur. Hurt and anger because the deceased other has abandoned one. Anger when death could have been avoided. Guilt because of previously normalizing symptoms, failing to express love or for quarrelling with the deceased.

Ordinarily, Americans think of attachment as love and intimacy. Yet attachment also includes guilt, dependency, ambivalence and anger. Such feelings make grieving complicated (Rando 1993). Given the current American predilection for declaring families 'dysfunctional', and individuals needing to be 'in recovery' from this or that trauma, many attachments are not so positive. A loss is especially searing if survivors had hopes for improving it in the future. As they cannot 'right' the relationship, they cannot 'right' themselves. Their self-concepts then may remain rooted in the past relationship.

Many Americans disallow, underestimate or suppress grief

until overtaken by an existential crisis. Not experiencing lesser griefs causes difficulties in moving on after a major loss. A reservoir of grief can build. Then someone may feel incomprehensible sorrow about a death of an acquaintance. Radical American individualism can hide or minimize knowledge of ourselves as social beings attached to others. A history of disallowed grief leads to becoming saturated with and overwhelmed by it later. All this amounts to:

- an exaggerated notion of one's separation from other people,
- an overwhelming experience of grief when an exceedingly significant person dies,
- a heightened sense of bewilderment and self-blame for being unable to cope with intense grief or for not being able to move on after the death.

LOST ASPECTS OF SELF

What does loss of self in grief mean? Which aspect of oneself does one lose? As Lofland (1982) finds, the lost part of oneself mirrors the form of attachment to the now deceased other.[3] One cannot be a mother without a child, a wife without a husband, a friend without a friend (Lofland 1982), or even an enemy without an enemy, as Robert J. Lifton (1973) observes.

Certainly a major loss is of an invisible, private self only known to the deceased. If this private self is the most valued part of self, the loss is devastating. For example, a young woman reflects on her lover's death:

'For me, it was though a "part" of me had been discovered or uncovered through him, through our unique relationship, and that was a me that I would never want to be with anyone else, ever again. It was as though I consciously allowed that part of me to die. In fact, in a way, I willed that part of me dead' (Charmaz 1980: 298).

The death of someone with whom one shared trust and affirmation is a decided loss. The survivor also loses the self who gave and received trust and affirmation. Constructing shared realities affirms self and other. Through talking and being together, partners develop shared views of events and definitions of reality (Berger and Kellner 1964). For many

Americans, lack of community results in marriage subsuming its functions – a sense of belonging, a common history, known statuses, mutual purposes and shared values, beliefs and rules. Subsequently, marriage becomes overloaded with multiple roles that community might have provided – friend, business partner, lover, companion, confidant, mentor, judge and therapist (see Nisbet 1966). All those relationships within *the* relationship are lost in death.

Thus, reality literally changes and seems distorted. Reality has become undependable, suspect, shifting. No one is there with whom to clarify perceptions and to decide what is real. Earlier taken-for-granted realities can no longer be assumed. A home that formerly felt safe and secure, for example, now feels disquieting and even dangerous to a new widow.

A once-shared reality can disintegrate. Broader assumptions about the world may be called into question. A violent death can invert the survivor's assumptions about human nature, good and evil and justice. An institutionalized death may revise the survivor's views about medical care. For example, his wife's dying caused an elderly man to distrust doctors. Although entubated, his wife had twice indicated that she did not want to be resuscitated. This man believed that physicians callously disregarded her wishes.

The meaning of familiar words drastically changes, even when they remain appropriate (Lofland 1982). Family now means a daughter 3,000 miles away. Home means an empty house. Old age now portends loneliness and, perhaps, fear.

Death of the other means loss of attachments predicated upon the other's presence and actions. The shared purposes and experiences that gave life meaning have been knocked asunder. No wonder a survivor feels that life is meaningless. The self is now incomplete. A young wife with a baby said of her husband's suicide:

> I feel changed for my whole life. I was a glass that was broken. I had this home and these expectations of life, and I was filling up this glass with food and life and experience. And then it was shattered. Everything that I believe in spilled out and went into the earth, and I lost it. I had nothing left. I was lying in this puddle of water that used to be something. Just broken. (Alexander 1991: 133)

Losing a partner, be it a spouse, colleague, or friend, means losing previously shared activities and structure of daily life (Lofland 1982). Partners and helpers sometimes are more or less replaceable. But often they are not. Finding someone else to collaborate on a project may be difficult. Finding someone who understands one's moods without asking may be impossible.

Attachment includes connections to the past and future. Connections to the past are tenuous in a forward-looking society that does not value the past. The attached other person validates the past and anchors the self in continuing relationships. A backlog of shared experiences provides meaning and the comfort of being special, at least in the other's eyes. Connections to a future may depend entirely upon the other person's continued existence. Death of a child means loss of a future (Lofland 1982; Rando 1993). Death of a mentor may result in loss of career advancement. Death of a husband often means a loss of income and a way of life. Death of a spouse may mean loss of retirement dreams. The medical costs of dying may also cost some survivors their life savings. The threat of destitution can hit them precisely when they must face the reality of death. Hence, a death can result in spiralling losses, intensifying grief and pain.

People may have different patterns of attachments. But as Lofland (1982) states, often most significant attachments are with the same person, the spouse or partner. If so, losses of self multiply and devastate the survivor.

TYPES OF GRIEF

Narrow American definitions of significant and worthy relationships grant certain bereaved *entitled grief* and priority status. Entitled grief is legitimate, deserved, expected and, typically, obligatory sorrow over loss.[4] Entitled grief affords its possessor a priority status – this survivor is seen as the deceased's closest kin. Righteous entitlement to express grief (within limits) accompanies the bereaved's justified priority in the hierarchy of loss. Deaths of spouses, especially young and middle-aged, and children grant greatest entitlement and highest priority status. When told of the death of someone's father two years before, newly-widowed Stephanie Ericsson (1993: 212) recalls thinking:

> [S]chmuck, that's supposed to happen, it's a natural part of becoming adult – children are supposed to outlive their parents. Did you lose the only other person in the world who would love your child the way you do? Did you lose the person you held all night, who slept next to you, warmed your bed so much you didn't need an extra blanket in the winter? . . . Don't reduce this experience to something logical, universal. Even if it is, I walk alone amongst the dead, it's my death, my pain. Don't pretend you know it like you know my batting averages. Don't sacrilege all over my crucifixion.

Assumptions of entitled grief and priority status give rise to moral claims, as Ericsson reveals. Her grief permits claims of injustice, prompts claims of broken conventions of sensitivity, reaffirms the hierarchical ordering of loss, and thus, fosters disattending to the losses of others. Sympathy may righteously be withheld. Here, the meaning of loss is predicated on objective structural relationships, not subjectively experienced ones. Entitled grief allows a dramatizing of one's own loss and a minimizing of the meaning of other people's 'lesser' relationships. Entitled grief then gives licence to focus on self. One turns inwards perhaps even as one lashes outwards.

Entitled grief becomes the sacred possession of the bereaved – the shadow of tragedy that sets the bereaved apart and makes him or her unique. In a mass society such as the United States, claims to uniqueness are often rendered hollow despite the cultural belief in individualism. Instead, massive cultural conformity is enforced. Entitled grief becomes the symbol of an ideal relationship, an unequalled possession, the ultimate human test, a badge of honour. Yet worn too long, entitled grief becomes a stigma. It too, becomes disenfranchised.

Entitlement to grief comes with the prescription to cope with it and to move on. The margin of sympathy only stretches so far (Clark 1987). Stein and Winokuer (1989: 95) describe the case of Bill, who held an enviable performance record at work, when his wife died suddenly:

> Bill's absentee rate increased 300 per cent and his ability to handle his work load became impaired. Over the next six months Bill's performance continued to decline. He had trouble concentrating, making decisions, and managing his time .... Bill became socially withdrawn and depressed, he lost weight, and his appearance suffered. His boss kept asking him, "What's wrong Bill? When are you going to be your old self?" Nine months after the death, Bill's supervisor no longer associated his poor performance with his loss .... Seven months short of early retirement, Bill was let go after twenty-three and a half years of service.

Disenfranchised grief is illegitimate and often, unrecognized and invisible (see Doka 1989). It is grief without honour or privilege. Increasingly, American relationships are multiple and complex, and sometimes remain unknown to relatives of the deceased. These relationships include extra-marital affairs, homosexual partnerships and former marriages. Whether intentionally or unwittingly, the most bereaved survivors may be excluded from mourning rituals and denied sympathy. Thus, cherished lovers in an affair or same-sex partners may find themselves relegated to the back of the church during services, if included at all.

Grief is particularly disenfranchised when death occurs suddenly among adversaries. Earlier struggles for power, status and resources may cause an adversary to wonder about having contributed to the death. Audiences of the conflict may underscore the need for remorse. 'If she hadn't been under so much stress, she wouldn't have had the accident.' 'If his boss hadn't been so hard on him, he wouldn't have had the heart attack.'

Narrowly-defined loss leads to both disenfranchised and underestimated grief, even in smooth relationships. *Underestimated grief* derives from brief relationships, peripheral associations and taken-for-granted bonds. Dennis Raymond Ryan (1989: 127) reflects on the death of his first son, Raymond, two weeks after his birth.

> I did not recognize the intensity of my own grief. Surely, I was saddened by my son's death. But in a sense Raymond

> was a stranger to me. I had not carried him for nine months and had not felt him grow and move inside me. I had not cared for him much at all during those first two weeks of life because there were so many other details to be taken care of. Besides I didn't know how to do baby things. Why then should I have felt much grief?

Underestimated grief remains unresolved. Survivors bury it, sometimes literally, in substance abuse. Underestimated grief over earlier losses – a parent who left, an unhappy love, a friend's death, lost chances – can culminate in intense grief. Underestimated grief can also develop when acknowledgement of the deceased is minimized or negated, such as when a former spouse or lover dies.

Whether grief is entitled, disenfranchised or underestimated, it may also be complicated. Extended dying, abusive relationships, violence, death of children, multiple deaths and stigma all complicate grief. Multiple deaths result in a bereavement overload suffered by elders and AIDS and war survivors. Social pressures to avoid stigma provide incentives to lie about the cause of death. It becomes an accident instead of suicide, cancer instead of AIDS.

Rando (1993) argues that the exclusivity of the American family, increasing victimization, and developmental consequences of absent or neglectful parents all contribute to complicated grief. Worden (1991) outlines three conditions under which complicated grief develops: (1) an unspeakable loss, (2) a socially negated death, (3) an absence of social support. Suicide, AIDS, and murder can complicate grief.

CONCLUSION

Although the Protestant ethic fostered values and practices that make grief particularly problematic, it also fostered a pragmatic American stance towards grief. Americans want to *do* something about it. Professionals plan 'interventions'. Support groups encourage expressivity. Americans who take any organized action about their grief mostly *talk* about it. Louis E. LaGrand (1989: 182) says, 'Time and time again the presence of others who are trying to understand and who are willing to listen endlessly and permissively is a common denominator for progress in one's grief work.' Hearing all this sad talk can quickly exhaust friends and relatives. Hence, self-help groups, funeral directors, therapists and counsellors provide limited arenas for such talk. Worden (1991) explains his approach to grief work: '[T]he tasks approach gives the mourner some sense of leverage and hope that there is something he or she can actively do' (91).

Worden emphasizes doing, taking control and maintaining hope – all consistent with the Protestant ethic. He finds complicated grief predictably in younger widows under 45 with children at home, without close relatives nearby, dependent upon or ambivalent about their husbands and a cultural or familial background that inhibits emotional expression. Counsellors then work to make the loss more real, promote expression of feeling, facilitate the bereaved to live without the deceased, and encourage emotional relocation of the deceased.

Americans want to avoid the suffering of profound grief. Meagher (1989) cautions against escaping it with drugs and alcohol. Escape, avoidance and suppression of feeling are perhaps as equally American responses to grief as facing it and working on it. But the experts insist that survivors must actively involve themselves in grief work. These involvements range from contrived exercises to (re-)creating an independent life. Disenfranchised bereaved who cannot participate in planning the funeral rituals can talk through an 'imagined funeral', write a eulogy, or create a ritual with the counsellor (Meagher 1989: 325). Now if American death rituals are already empty and truncated, at least they are public and collective. A session with a counsellor would pale by contrast, even if the counsellor acts as a surrogate family member.

Creating one's own life translates into avoiding overdependence upon spouse or partner. However, many Americans now work more hours than 20 years ago, and thus curtail other involvements that could offer support. Louis E. LaGrand's (1989) young respondents admonish others to protect themselves from the devastation and disenfranchised grief of losing a lover. As one young woman said, 'It is important to rely on *yourself* first because you are the only person who can ultimately be strong. *Never* place your entire future in another person's hands because if that person is ever taken from you in any way, you will be lost. My loss has helped me grow so much as a person' (176).

And that is the paradox of feeling and facing grief. Out of the resolution of grief can come a tremendous blossoming, of confidence, of competence and of compassion. Through experiencing deep grief, the bereaved may gain amazing strength and wisdom.

NOTES

1. Thanks are due to Julia Allen and Catherine Nelson, members of the Sonoma State University Faculty Writing Group, and to Richard G. Mitchell and Debora Paterniti for their comments on an earlier draft of this chapter.
2. I refer here to North America, specifically to the United States.
3. At this point, I am taking Lyn H. Lofland's (1982) analysis of loss and the threads of connection one step further. She insightfully traces the relational aspects of loss. I tie them directly to losses of self. A searing disruption of deep grief cuts into the self and alters the structure of the self.
4. In murder cases, surviving spouses' failure to display obligatory 'natural' grief arouses suspicion.

REFERENCES

Alexander, V. (1991) *Words I Never Thought to Speak: Stories of Life in the Wake of Suicide*, New York: Lexington Books.

Berger, P. and Kellner, H. (1964) 'Marriage and the Construction of Reality', *Diogenes*, 46: 1–23.

Bowlby, J. (1980) *Attachment and Loss: Vol. 3. Loss: Sadness and Depression*, New York: Basic Books.

Charmaz, K. (1980) *The Social Reality of Death*, Reading, MA: Addison-Wesley.

Clark, C. (1987) 'Sympathy Biography and Sympathy Margin', *American Journal of Sociology*, 93: 290–321.

Cornils, S.P. (1992) *The Mourning After: How to Manage Grief Wisely*, Saratoga, CA: R&E Publishers.

Doka, K.J. (1989) 'Disenfranchised Grief', in K.J. Doka (ed.), *Disenfranchised Grief: Recognizing Hidden Sorrow*, Lexington, MA: Lexington Books.

Ericsson, S. (1993) 'The Agony of Grief', in G.E. Dickinson, M.R. Leming and A.C. Mermann (eds.), *Dying, Death, and Bereavement*, Guilford, CT: Dushkin.

LaGrand, L.E. (1989) 'Youth and the Disenfranchised Breakup', in K.J. Doka (ed.), *Disenfranchised Grief: Recognizing Hidden Sorrow*, Lexington, MA: Lexington Books.

Lifton, R.J. (1973) *Home from the War*, New York: Simon & Schuster.

Lindemann, E. (1944) 'Symptomatology and Management of Acute Grief', *American Journal of Psychiatry*, 101: 141–8.

Lofland, L.H. (1982) 'Loss and Human Connection: An Exploration into the Nature of the Social Bond', in W. Ickes and E.S. Knowles (eds.), *Personality, Roles and Social Behavior*, New York: Springer-Verlag.

Lopata, H.Z. (1973) *Widowhood in an American City*, Cambridge, MA: Schenkman.

Marris, P. (1974) *Loss and Change*, New York: Pantheon.

Meagher, D.K. (1989) 'The Counsellor and the Disenfranchised Griever', in K.J. Doka (ed.), *Disenfranchised Grief: Recognizing Hidden Sorrow*, Lexington, MA: Lexington Books.

Nisbet, R.A. (1966) *The Sociological Tradition*, New York: Basic Books.

O'Connor, N. (1984) *Letting Go With Love: The Grieving Process*, Tucson, AZ: La Mariposa Press.

Pratt, L. (1994) 'Business Temporal Norms and Bereavement Behavior', in R. Fulton and R. Bendiksen (eds.), *Death and Identity*, 3rd edn, Philadelphia: Charles Press.

Rando, T.A. (1984) *Grief, Dying, and Death: Clinical Interventions for Caregivers*, Champaign, IL: Research Press.

Rando, T.A. (1993) *Treatment of Complicated Mourning*, Champaign, IL: Research Press.

Ryan, D.R. (1989) 'Raymond: Underestimated grief', in K.J. Doka (ed.), *Disenfranchised Grief: Recognizing Hidden Sorrow*, Lexington, MA: Lexington Books.

Schiff, H.S. (1986) *Living Through Mourning: Finding comfort and hope when a loved one has died*, New York: Viking.

Staudacher, P. (1987) *Beyond Grief: A Guide for Recovering from the Death of a Loved One*, Oakland, CA: New Harbinger.

Stearns, P. (1994) *American Cool: Constructing a Twentieth Century Emotional Style*, New York: New York University Press.

Stein, A.J. and Winokuer, H.R. (1989) 'Monday Mourning: Managing employee grief', in K.J. Doka (ed.), *Disenfranchised Grief: Recognizing Hidden Sorrow*, Lexington, MA: Lexington Books.

Tatelbaum, J. (1980) *The Courage to Grieve: Creative Living Recovery and Growth Through Grief*, New York: Lippincott & Crowell.

Toynbee, A. (1969) 'Changing Attitudes Toward Death in the Modern Western World', in A. Toynbee, A.K. Mann, N. Smart, J. Hinton, S. Yudkin, E. Rhode, R. Heywood and H.H. Price, *Man's Concern with Death*, New York: McGraw-Hill.

Worden, W.J. (1991) *Grief Counselling and Grief Therapy: A Handbook for the Mental Health Practitioner*, 2nd edn, New York: Springer.

Wrobleski, A. (1991) *Suicide Survivors: A Guide for Those Left Behind*, Minneapolis, MN: Afterwords Publishing.

18 Diversity in Universality: Dying, Death and Grief[1]

Donald P. Irish

INTRODUCTION: E PLURIBUS UNUM?

Nations, as well as individuals, live with distinctive myths and different realities. For many Americans, the myth persists that the nation has been, and should be, a 'melting pot', whereby diverse peoples are blended into a tasty stew, seasoned similarly throughout, many mixed colours stirred together, and with equal portions representative of every citizen. Contrariwise, there is a belief among some Euro-americans that *their* country is to be one pervaded by a White, Anglo-Saxon, Christian and Protestant ethos – the so-called WASP bias. 'Minorities' historically have often suffered from these assumptions. The US is no longer evident as just a Black and White or just a 'Judeo-Christian' society.

The USA is a multi-ethnic society which includes a wide variety of cultural customs, racial mixtures and religious faiths. No one pattern can be generalized to the whole population. Differences also exist *within* each cultural group in their experiences of dying, death, and grief, depending on educational level, economic role, residential locale and geographic origin.

Though some myths may be widely shared, many aspects of reality are not. Long-standing patterns of social inequality persist. As a consequence, there are *many* Americas, not just *one*! Indeed, each ethnic group living in these states may perceive the USA as *another* country.

AMERICAN DIVERSITY – WHO ARE WE?

The US 1990 Census stated that 'White' Americans comprised about four-fifths (80.3 per cent) of its approximately

250 million people. One in four residents were defined as members of 'racial minorities'. African–Americans constituted 12.1 per cent of the nation's population (about 1 in 8 individuals). Hispanics constituted 9.1 per cent (about 1 in 11). Asian Americans composed 2.9 per cent (about 1 in 33). Native Americans represented less than one per cent.

Given these 'racial' categories – ten million Americans (4 per cent) marked an 'other' (mixed) category, most of them Hispanics. Due to non-responses, insufficient counting, and inadequate categories, the Census Bureau estimated that as many as six million residents were omitted, including two million African–Americans.

A 'melting pot' *has* operated considerably within the *Euro-american* population through many inter-faith/interdenominational/different-national-origins marriages. Also, the number of inter-racial couples in the USA doubled between 1980 and 1992, with more than one in every fifty marriages being between persons of different 'races' (Minneapolis *Star Tribune* 1993).

ASPECTS REGARDING DYING, DEATH AND GRIEF

The customary behaviours surrounding death will be presented for four ethnic groups: African–American, Mexican–American, Lakota (Native American) and American Hmong. Five aspects of these patterns will be considered: (1) the experiential quality or 'feel' manifested; (2) theology/philosophy of death; (3) actions, rituals and emotions manifested before and after death; (4) death education of the young; (5) changes due to acculturation.

AFRICAN–AMERICAN FUNERAL CUSTOMS

Background

Considerable cultural diversity existed amongst the African slaves who came to America, and such variety has since been elaborated further, related to African–Americans' current rural–urban origins, social–economic–educational status, and religious orientations. Very considerable physical mixture has occurred through miscegenation with the dominant White (and some Indian) populations. Extensive acculturation has made almost all of them more American than African, yet many Africanisms remain.

By 1990, the distribution of Blacks reflected great variation. In several Deep South states, Blacks constituted a *quarter or more* of their populations. In contrast, Blacks comprised *less than one per cent* in some New England, Northern, and Western states. Northern industrial states had Black proportions in ranges between these extremes.

In African–American culture under slavery, then under legalized segregation, the religious arena was virtually the only sphere in which Blacks could function without control by the dominant group. Their religious arenas still provide them opportunities for leadership, social interaction, and networks for collective action. Their 'religiosity' gives them psychological support to endure their societal subordination and to work for change.

About 90 per cent of the church-related Blacks are Protestants, with only about 5 per cent participating in predominantly White religious groups. Roman Catholic Blacks comprise about 9 per cent of their church population (Lincoln and Mamiya 1990: 407).

Dying, Death, and Grief[2]

The funeral customs of Euroamericans and African–Americans are typically very dissimilar. Stoicism is valued by White mourners and not by Blacks. Funeral music is hushed and very quiet in most White, mainstream churches. This is generally not the case with Black Americans. Their church music is spirited and passionate, and grief is openly expressed by wailing and tears.

The vast majority of African–Americans are members of mainstream religious groups. American churches have had a segregated history, and even today this bifurcation by race still exists. Within the Black churches there are regional and class differences that are marked. African–American funerals range from the traditional practices of these groups – the funeral mass and other rituals for the dead – to amalgams that may include gospel music, New Orleans jazz, and African rituals. Media influences have crept into the grieving process with the popularization of video cameras. Often, one sees a member or friend of the family filming the funeral, wake, or body.

A recent practice that manifests pride in African heritage is the draping of narrow Kinte cloth stoles (a popular West African, brightly woven materials) around the departed person's neck. It is now becoming one metaphor for African–American pride.

Another change in the African–American community's grieving patterns is the increasing use of funeral homes as sites for both viewing the body and the funeral. Typically, following the service there is a 'pot-luck' meal, either at the church or the family home, as an expression of love prepared by extended family members and friends. Mourners have this opportunity to reach out to the family with these gifts of food, which continue during the first week of mourning.

The deceased usually has an informal shrine dedicated to him or her in the family's living room, on the mantel-piece or piano. This shrine may include photographs, athletic trophies or dolls to remind the visitor that this person was loved and valued by the family. If space permits, the loved one's bedroom may become the reliquary.

Historically, funeral homes, cemeteries and churches have been segregated by race in America. White funeral homes hire few African–American morticians; so the majority of the African–American business is left to Black funeral homes. Since there are few such morticians in most urban areas, the task of cosmetic preparation of deceased's skin and hair has also been segregated.

Cremation is rarely observed in the African–American pattern. If the body cannot be viewed, there is a closed casket. It is now illegal to segregate cemeteries racially; but since families want to be buried together, there is *de facto* segregation even now. The only differences one continues to see between wealthy and poor African–Americans are the expense of caskets, the number of floral bouquets, and limousines. Poor families are often encouraged by the commercialization of funerals in America to exceed their financial resources in order to give the deceased a 'good send-off'.

Earlier, as children grew up in both North and South, violent deaths were most often car accidents, an occasional suicide or lynching. The style of funeral depended on one's religious and social affiliations. If the adult was a Freemason or a member of a social fraternity/sorority, there were, and still are, highly-stylized ceremonies at both the church and graveside, with members wearing distinctive attire. Their rituals are varied and include prayers, chants and songs.

Ten years ago, violent deaths were not common. They were dealt with in the usual ways – church rituals, weeks of grieving, and community support. Media attention was limited to the most bizarre deaths or those of socially notable persons.

Currently the African–American community is experiencing an explosion in the number of their youth who are dying violent deaths by actions of other young people. The rising death rate of mostly male teenagers from domestic disputes, drug overdoses, diseases, suicide and gang violence is alarming Black communities.

Although gangs are present in many diverse communities, their funerals used to be under the control of the family and were largely indistinguishable from any others. But now, mimicking some adult social organizations, the youth may wear scarves or bandanas in 'colours' associated with gangs and use ritualized handshakes and greetings. It is common to arrive at the viewing of the body at a funeral home and see these young people in their silk jackets or sweatshirts, wearing the emblems of their group. Sometimes, the name of the deceased is printed on T-shirts with a message. Their young female companions are treated with the respect that, were they older women, a wife would receive. Often teenage males are fathers, and it is not unusual for toddlers or infants to be present at the funerals. With so many violent deaths, African–American grieving customs are appearing on the evening news.

The grieving process itself has become differentiated in the more urban North as compared with the more rural South. Families are still usually extended in the South, but they have become nuclear in the North. This may mean a smaller support system; and the nurture period that was once so helpful is shortened. What formerly took weeks and many visits, now may mean one evening with the mourners.

MEXICAN–AMERICAN PERSPECTIVES REGARDING DEATH

Background

Among US Hispanics, the Mexican–Americans (13.5 million), Puerto Ricans (2.7 million) and Cuban Americans (1.0+ million) had the largest numbers in 1990. Hispanics outnumber African–Americans in four of the nation's ten largest cities; and they may exceed the Black population by 2013. These Hispanics share several cultural aspects: the Spanish language, a Catholicism that often includes elements of earlier indigenous cultures, and patriarchal, extended family structures. The Mexican–Americans reside mainly in the Southwestern states, but they also concentrate in some Northern urban areas.

Many Mexican–Americans attend Catholic mass frequently, and they desire religious auspices for their ceremonies surrounding birth, confirmation, marriage and death. The more committed will have representations of saints and the Virgin in their residences or yard shrines. Holy places, miracles, and open emotional expression are involved in their faith experiences. They manifest a need for penitence and various forms of sacrifices. Those in the orthodox tradition believe and expect that what God wants will be done (*gracias a Dios*) and that they will be subject to 'God's will' in the final reckoning (Vasquez 1993: 204). Such 'fatalism' is a mood present often in their approach to life.

Many Hispanics associate illness with being good or bad. The Devil may be considered a primary cause of death. Souls are viewed as part of God; and so God is within them, perhaps from the moment of conception. Thus, a tiny foetus at miscarriage will still be much grieved; and abortions are not generally sanctioned (Vasquez 1993: 204).

Death, Dying and Grief[3]

Younoszai notes that Mexican culture involves frequent contact with death, partly due to widespread poverty. Death is accepted as a natural process of removal and replenishment. In their religious beliefs, life and death have purpose; and they view life as transient. These features coexist also in Mexican–American life, especially for more recent migrants. They give importance to an afterlife concept which perhaps also engenders an easier acceptance of death.

In pre-Colonial times, the little orange flower – the *zempasuchitl* – not unlike the marigold, was associated with death. These blossoms are still used to decorate graves, to form wreaths on the doors of bereaved families, and to be strewn in the house. The pre-Columbian Day of the Dead (31 October–1 November) celebrates death. Cut-out paper designs reveal Death doing anything that the living do. Skeletons, miniature coffins, masks of death and candy skulls are featured in the shops. These ubiquitous motifs are reminders of death, virtually impossible to avoid.

Much of Mexican literature and film centres on death. Octavio Paz, for example, in *The Labyrinth of Solitude* (Paz 1961: 76), portrays death as an ever-present reality. Paz indicates the need to confront death, not to be afraid, to be always ready to die, never giving in, yet to welcome death when it comes for whatever reason and in whatever form, as Dr Younoszai reports.

Dying, death and grieving among Mexican–Americans, whether in a rural or urban setting, generally follow the orthodox Catholic pattern. Paz indicated that priests come to the dying to administer the 'last rites', and home viewings are customary. Funerals are quickly arranged at a church and prompt burials are desired. Cremation is discouraged by the Church. In rural areas friends and relatives visit the home where the body lies in state. The casket will be found on a stand, under which herbs and candles will burn (Paz 1961: 76).

In urban settings, the body would be viewed in a mortuary, with a church ceremony afterwards, and the usual rituals. Friends, extended family and the wider community share in mourning, and emotional responses are openly manifested. Children learn to accept death and participate in the wake and funeral. They accompany their parents/family to the graveside. Relatives will often throw a bit of earth on top of the casket. People may remain in the cemetery longer, even 'talking to the deceased', walking around, looking at additional graves, and recalling the deaths of others. *Novenas* are said during a nine-day period following the death. Candles are lit on an altar, prayers for the deceased are said, and the grievers are consoled.

As with any ethnic group removed in greater or lesser degree from its origins, traditions will be changed through acculturation over time. Mexican–American death customs increasingly look like the traditional Catholic services as changes come and ties to Mexico and its patterns become attenuated.

NATIVE AMERICANS: LAKOTA CULTURE REGARDING DEATH

Background

There are about two million indigenous Native Americans, Inuit and Aleuts (.08 per cent of the US population in 1990) in the USA. Slightly more than a third live on their tribal lands, while the majority reside outside their extremely reduced 'homeland' areas. Nation-wide, the largest tribal groups, in order of size, are the Cherokee, Navaho, Chippewa and Sioux (Euroamerican terms). Movement to urban areas by 1990 had created indigenous concentrations between 20 000 and 87 000 in at least ten major cities, with Los Angeles having the largest number (Klauda 1991).

Upon first contact with Europeans in 1640, the broader Dakota peoples occupied a large area west of the Great Lakes. The three major divisions – Dakota, Nakota and Lakota – comprised a federation of 'seven council fires'. They constitute the largest division of the many tribes that speak Siouan languages (Carmody and Carmody 1993: 46).

The Dakota once survived by hunting, fishing, and gathering lake and forest products, supplementing these dietary elements by growing corn. They were excellent equestrians in hunting buffalo, but invading European settlers killed thousands of buffalo and fatally undermined the traditional Dakota way of life. Today, half of the 'Sioux' live on reservations in the northern plains.

They traditionally viewed the staples of life as gifts from holy powers. The 'Great Mystery' was their principal deity.

Its spirit was believed to be in ceremonial artefacts, songs, natural phenomena, and also animals. Their religion facilitated communication with, while not controlling, these powers (Carmody and Carmody 1993: 71–3).

The sacred pipe, sweat lodge and traditional Sun Dance served important ritualistic functions. The pipe mediated interaction with the Great Spirit and was used to reconcile enemies, unite tribal members, and express fellowship. The sweat lodge was utilized for spiritual cleansing and renewal. The Sun Dance expressed a willingness to sacrifice for the good of the tribe, by self-mutilation and exhaustion from several days' dancing (Carmody and Carmody 1993: 71–3).

Today, almost all Native Americans face harsh conditions on reservations and in urban life: high unemployment, considerable alcoholism, poor health, high suicide rates, and frequent despair. None of these conditions characterized their traditional vigorous, creative and sustainable lives.

Dying, Death, and Grief[4]

Brokenleg indicates that the Lakota religious-belief system includes little consideration of afterlife specifics. Its philosophy is one of a 'balanced universe'. Death is viewed as a natural feature of life, a counterpart of birth, reinforcing their conception of life's cyclical aspects. Both birth and death are sacred. An afterlife is automatic for every Lakota. They emphasize a spirituality for living well in the 'here and now', not for later rewards. Brokenleg indicates that the Lakota traditionally do not ask 'why?', thus differing from many in Western societies.

Death traditionally is not highly feared. Denial and anger are minimized. Death is also a source of motivation to treat others well.

The soul exists before birth, accompanies each individual during life, and leaves some presence in the world after death. The body is revered, for it is the repository of each individual's essence. Accordingly, cremation is not acceptable. One is to care well for the body in life and be cared for by the community after death.

The children learn about dying, death and grieving from their earliest years by observing and participating directly in almost all aspects of life. Some informal verbal instructions are also provided by elders.

Brokenleg alludes to the belief in physical evidence for spiritual events, relationships generally foreign to Western experiences and belief. Death is often forecast by exceptional signs, which are seen as natural: for example, ghosts of a person who dies soon thereafter.

The Lakota family is 'close'. Relatives make every effort to be present for funeral rites. They are sacred occasions and opportunities for mutual support. No Lakota desires to die alone; and a family will suffer guilt if that happens. Lakota want to be buried in their 'home reservations' even if they have been living in an urban area.

Upon death, the body will be taken to a mortuary; but the bereaved insist upon immediate round-the-clock access. The body lies in state for three days. Clergy and medicine men are invited to be present. Prayers are said, condolences expressed, reminisces shared, admonitions given. A major meal follows.

During the death rituals, elders and those who knew the deceased well will speak about the individual's life. Lakota values and beliefs are reinforced. Life has purpose. Grieving is needed; and open emotional expressions of mourning are appropriate for both men and women. The wake or funeral will be held at a site large enough to accommodate the many guests, and the family of the deceased is expected to feed all who come.

There is no taboo against touching the body. Objects significant to the deceased may be put in, or with, the casket before it is buried. Drums are played; traditional Lakota songs are sung. The relatives typically will assist in filling the grave; and they do not leave until that is completed.

Adaptations are now needed to accommodate traditions. Hospitals should arrange for a larger number of relatives at bedsides. The patient or family may wish to have sage burned in the room. Families may request that a medicine man be present rather than a member of the Christian clergy.

A year of mourning follows an individual's death, with family members endeavouring to live exemplary lives. Family goods are accumulated to give away on the anniversary of the death. A large meal then follows.

AMERICAN HMONG DEATH CUSTOMS

Background

By 1993, the Census estimated that 150 000 Hmong lived in the USA, principally in three states: California, Minnesota and Wisconsin. Almost two-thirds of them were then living at or below the 'poverty level'. The younger generation has pursued education. A large minority of Hmong has graduated from high school, a few have already completed college, and some even have now been elected to public office.

The Hmong constitute a young population, by recency of arrival as immigrants and also by average age. Although they represent a tiny proportion of American residents, they comprise a recent immigrant group that contrasts markedly from 'more Americanized' ones. Their social structures, patriarchal families and clans, religious beliefs and traditional agricultural life in Laos differed greatly from their present life in American cities.

Hmong elders now try to reproduce their traditions within very different and more complex US environments. Their traditional attitudes and customs engender strains with the younger generation. Youth now challenge their elders, who face losing control over children, and men over women. Some youth have rebelled strongly, participating in gangs, to the distress of their elders and other peers. 'Reverse socialization' also occurs, as the children quickly learn English, adopt new ways, and help the older generation better understand and adapt to the 'strange' country.

Hmong New Year celebrations, bilingual Hmong drama groups, news broadcasts in Hmong, sections of periodicals printed in 'Hmong', folk festivals, ceremonies surrounding birth, illness, marriage, and death – all assist in retaining Hmong traditions and in facilitating adjustment to new circumstances.

Dying, Death, and Grief[5]

Bliatout emphasizes that Hmong religion is imbued with beliefs regarding death and afterlife, which combine ancestor-worship and animism. Hmong believe that a spiritual world exists coterminously with the physical one. Spirit forces include those for ancestors, houses, nature and evil. House spirits of several types inhabit the residence of each Hmong. A wide variety of spirits exist in all natural things – for example, mountains, trees, caves, winds. Evil spirits also live in nature; and they may attack humans individually, or entire villages.

Bliatout indicates that each Hmong is presumed to have an allotted time on earth by the Chief of Gods. Many ceremonies determine the will of ancestors so that they will protect the living. Hmong use their domestic animals in ritual sacrifices to please ancestors or for birth, marriage and death ceremonies.

Since a proper burial and worship of ancestors affects the well-being of the family, great care is given to the funeral process. Each clan performs slightly different ceremonies.

Hmong believe that in birth the infant is taken from its spirit parents and brought by ritual into the living community. When an individual dies, he or she must be properly returned to the spirit world of their ancestors, lest they be able to harm the living. Sacrifices at the time of death, at the New Year, and other times guarantee the ancestors' favour.

Each person has several souls: three major ones, each of which has three shadow souls (nine shadow souls), making twelve in all, plus others. Life as a human being is viewed as most desirable, and if one lives a moral life, rebirth as a human being will come sooner. If not, the person will have accumulated karmic debts that will have to be paid. Hmong may return as animals, plants, or, worse, as rocks, which never die. Then, the soul could never return to earth as a person.

Traditionally, Hmong endeavoured to avoid dying in someone else's home especially that of non-relatives. Thus, most Hmong wish to live in their family home or with others of their clan.

In anticipation of death, an appropriate grave-site must be chosen, which may require months. Coffins were made from specific types of wood designated for each clan. Traditionally, special clothes and shoes were prepared for the deceased. Families chose some of the officials for specific roles at the funeral; and most of these were males who had learned the rites from elders or through experience.

After a death, family members will weep and wail for a considerable time. They will bathe the body and dress it, then place it on the floor of the house in a specific ceremonial position.

In traditional Hmong society in Laos, Dr Bliatout reports, many designated 'funeral helpers' were involved, a guide to the spirit world, drummer and reed-pipe player, a descendant counsellor, funeral director, stretcher- and shoe-makers, chefs and food servers, firewood gatherers, rice pounders, water carrier, light suppliers, a coffin maker, and slayers of sacrificial animals.

Hmong funerals may last from three to thirty days, with the body remaining in the house for at least three days before burial. Only an auspicious day for burial must be selected, and it is obligatory that all relatives be informed. So, funeral periods may last more than ten days; and they provide occasions for family reunions for those long apart.

The day before the burial, animal sacrifices are conducted for the deceased to take to the spirit world. Gifts for the deceased and to the family are customary. The funeral director co-ordinates the sacrifice of oxen. The meat is divided among family members and helpers. The financial affairs of the deceased are settled.

On the day of interment, the grave will be dug. Afternoon burials are customary, for Hmong believe that souls leave the body at sunset. A stretcher that symbolizes a horse, to take the first major soul to the spirit world, carries the body in the procession. There is a prescribed order for the participants, and there are several ceremonial stops *en route* to the grave. Helpers cover the coffin with dirt.

Hmong tradition holds that the second soul of the body must remain for at least 13 days before joining the first soul in the ancestor world. Food offerings are prepared daily by the family. The grave is decorated three days after the burial. A 'Thirteenth Day End Ceremony' is performed; and a 'soul releasing ceremony' is held. After that, family members may again return to the fields and housework. Children share in all aspects of the funeral period, in accordance with their age, sex and ability.

Coming to America has required many adaptations. Funeral practices are shortened. Most Hmong now die in hospitals. They resist embalming and autopsies, which alter the body's natural state. Drumming may bother neighbours. Animal sacrifices pose 'civic problems'. Fire codes preclude burning objects in mortuaries. Available coffins are not made from traditional woods; and they generally contain metal, which would have a person be reborn deformed. Optimum burial times are difficult to arrange.

Hmong Christians still keep many of the traditions, but singing songs replaces recitation of traditional texts. Butchering of animals is now carried out for pragmatic reasons – to feed guests – not for sacrificial purposes. Christian Hmong believe in one soul that will go to Heaven to be with God rather than to be reborn.

CONCLUSION

Professional practitioners in health-care and personal counselling occupations need to be sensitive to the cultural diversity of their patients and clients. Ignorance of or an uncaring attitude about such variety within their clientele can result in inappropriate diagnoses, less effectual treatments, and frequent violations of individuals' integrity, value-system and worth. There is an urgent need to enhance the quality of services provided to *all* persons in a population, each one confronted with the universal wonderment, anguish and experiences surrounding dying, death and grief.

NOTES

1. Materials in this chapter relating to Mexican–Americans, Native Americans and Hmong are based on materials that originally appeared in Donald P. Irish, Kathleen F. Lundquist and Vivian Jenkins Nelson (1993) *Ethnic Variations in Dying, Death, and Grief*, Washington DC and London: Taylor & Francis. Adapted by permission.
2. This section constitutes an original contribution by African–American colleague Vivian Nelsen, not previously published (Nelsen 1995: 1–4).

3. The author is indebted to colleague Dr Barbara Younoszai for the substance of the material which he has summarized/paraphrased in this section (Younoszai 1993: 71–7).
4. The author is indebted to colleague Dr Martin Brokenleg, Lakota/Rosebud Sioux, for the substance of the material which he has summarized/paraphrased in this section (Brokenleg 1993: 102–12).
5. The author is indebted to Dr Bruce Bliatout, Hmong colleague, for the substance of the material which he has summarized/paraphrased in this section (Bliatout 1993: 82–100).

REFERENCES

Bliatout, B. (1993) 'Hmong Death Customs: Traditional and acculturated', in D. Irish, K. Lundquist and V. Nelsen (eds.) *Ethnic Variations in Dying, Death, and Grief,* Washington, DC and London: Taylor & Francis.

Brokenleg, M. (1993) 'Native Americans: Adapting yet retaining', in D. Irish, K. Lundquist and V. Nelsen (eds.) *Ethnic Variations in Dying, Death, and Grief,* Washington, DC and London: Taylor & Francis.

Carmody, D. and Carmody, J. (1993) *Native American Religion,* New York: Paulist Press.

Klauda, P. and News Services (1991) 'Drop in percentage of Indians living in tribal lands', Minneapolis *Star Tribune,* 11 July, 1A.

Lincoln, C. and Mamiya, L. (1990) *The Black Church In The African American Experience,* Durham and London: Duke University Press.

Minneapolis *Star Tribune* (no author) (1993) 'Number of interracial couples in US has doubled', 12 February, 7A.

Nelsen, V. (1995) 'African American Ways of Death', unpublished original manuscript, 1–4.

Paz, O. (1961) *The Labyrinth of Solitude: Life and Thought in Mexico,* New York: Grove Press.

Vasquez, M. (1993) 'Personal Reflections on the Hispanic Experience', in D. Irish, K. Lundquist and V. Nelsen (eds.), *Ethnic Variations in Dying, Death, and Grief,* Washington, DC and London: Taylor and Francis.

Younoszai, B. (1993) 'Mexican American Perspectives on Death', in D. Irish, K. Lundquist and V. Nelsen (eds.), *Ethnic Variations in Dying, Death, and Grief,* Washington, DC and London: Taylor and Francis.

Subject Index

Names Index